I. I. (Isaac Israel) Hayes

The Land of Desolation

Being a personal Narrative of Observation and Adventure in Greenland

I. I. (Isaac Israel) Hayes

The Land of Desolation
Being a personal Narrative of Observation and Adventure in Greenland

ISBN/EAN: 9783337177539

Printed in Europe, USA, Canada, Australia, Japan

Cover: Foto ©ninafisch / pixelio.de

More available books at **www.hansebooks.com**

THE LAND OF DESOLATION:

BEING A PERSONAL NARRATIVE OF

OBSERVATION AND ADVENTURE IN

GREENLAND.

By ISAAC I. HAYES, M.D.,

GOLD MEDALIST OF THE ROYAL GEOGRAPHICAL SOCIETY, LONDON, AND OF THE SOCIÉTÉ DE GEOGRAPHIE, PARIS; HONORARY MEMBER OF THE GEOGRAPHICAL SOCIETIES OF BERLIN AND OF ITALY; AUTHOR OF "THE OPEN POLAR SEA," "AN ARCTIC BOAT JOURNEY," "CAST AWAY IN THE COLD," ETC.

ILLUSTRATED.

NEW YORK:
HARPER & BROTHERS, PUBLISHERS,
FRANKLIN SQUARE.
1872.

Persons Represented.

An Artist in search of the picturesque.
An Assistant given to caricature.
A Photographer, called "Colonel."
Another, who was "Major."
A Professor who made collections.
A Prince who enjoyed himself.
A great Hunter.
A roaring, tearing tar of a Captain.
A Mate with an inquiring turn of mind.
A Sagaman who made history.
A Parson.
The Belle of a Ball in seal-skin pantaloons.
Other Ladies in the same condition.
Also a Boat's Crew.
Parliamentarians who smelled fishy.
Others equally agreeable.
The northernmost White Man and his family.
Numerous Governors.
Officers and Sailors unlimited.
A Raven.
An Antiquarian.
A Witch.
A Doctor.
Two Enemies, called "Cook" and "Steward."
A Cabin-boy who woke up once.
Ladies from Denmark.
A great many other People.
Dogs, Polar Bears, and other Animals.
A Devil's Thumb.

PREFACE.

THE following pages are a record of a visit to Greenland, made in the summer of 1869, with a small party of friends, in the steam-yacht of Mr. William Bradford, whose widely-celebrated pictures of Arctic scenery have received such deserved commendation; for, whether we consider the difficulties of the subject which that artist has undertaken, or the unusual exposures and hazards he has encountered, his success has been commensurate with his zeal, talent, and unflagging energy.

Since Mr. Bradford was desirous only of obtaining materials for his easel, the voyage was a leisurely one, being mostly near the coast, where halts were from time to time made at such places as presented special attractions to the painter. The summer was therefore devoted to the study of the picturesque rather than to the scientific; yet numerous opportunities were afforded in the latter direction, especially with respect to observing the formation of Greenland glaciers and icebergs—subjects which have not hitherto received much attention. Facilities never before enjoyed by Americans were also obtained for visiting the site of the colonies of the ancient Northmen, who occupied that country from the tenth to the fifteenth centuries, and whose restless love of adventure led them even so far from their native homes as our own shores, at least five hundred years before the renowned voyage of Columbus.

Our range of the Greenland coast was more than a thousand miles, terminating a good way beyond the last outpost of civilization on the globe, in the midst of the much dreaded " ice-pack " of Melville Bay.

CONTENTS.

PART THE FIRST.
RUINS.

CHAPTER I.
Ice and Breakers.. 17

CHAPTER II.
Free from Danger.. 20

CHAPTER III.
A hopeful Town in a hopeless Place................... 26

CHAPTER IV.
Eric the Red... 39

CHAPTER V.
"The Arctic Six".. 45

CHAPTER VI.
Up the Fiord in an Oomiak................................. 51

CHAPTER VII.
The Ruins of Ericsfiord...................................... 62

CHAPTER VIII.
The Northmen in Greenland.............................. 71

CHAPTER IX.
The Northmen in America.................................. 77

CHAPTER X.
THE LAST MAN.. 82

CHAPTER XI.
A DISCONSOLATE LOVER.. 92

CHAPTER XII.
THE CHURCH AT JULIANASHAAB................................. 98

CHAPTER XIII.
A GREENLAND PARLIAMENT..................................... 101

CHAPTER XIV.
A GREENLAND BALL.. 112

PART THE SECOND.

PALACES OF NATURE.

CHAPTER I.
ICE AND SNOW... 125

CHAPTER II.
GLACIERS AND ICEBERGS.. 129

CHAPTER III.
THE SOLITARY HUT OF PETER MOTZFELDT................... 137

CHAPTER IV.
THE GLACIER... 146

CHAPTER V.
CROSSING THE GLACIER... 153

CHAPTER VI.
SPECULATIONS... 166

CHAPTER VII.
Measurements of Glaciers.. 172

CHAPTER VIII.
The Birth of an Iceberg.. 175

CHAPTER IX.
A Narrow Escape.. 179

CHAPTER X.
Icebergs Critically Examined... 186

CHAPTER XI.
Man *versus* Mosquitoes.. 197

CHAPTER XII.
A Picnic on the Glacier.. 201

CHAPTER XIII.
Bound for the Arctic Circle.. 206

PART THE THIRD.
UNDER THE MIDNIGHT SUN.

CHAPTER I.
Across the Arctic Circle... 215

CHAPTER II.
Beyond Civilization.. 240

CHAPTER III.
Ice-Navigation... 253

CHAPTER IV.
Hunting by Steam... 263

CHAPTER V.
Among the Ice-fields of Melville Bay 284

CHAPTER VI.
The Last White Man 294

CHAPTER VII.
The Fiord of Aukpadlartok 309

CHAPTER VIII.
Upernavik 318

CHAPTER IX.
Disco Island 328

CHAPTER X.
Jacobshavn 339

CHAPTER XI.
A Week at Godhavn 348

ILLUSTRATIONS.

	PAGE
THE "PANTHER" AMONG THE ICEBERGS............*Frontispiece.*	
VIEW OF JULIANASHAAB..	27
THE OOMIAK AND CREW..	46
VIEW OF THE OLD NORSE RUINS..	63
GROUND-PLAN OF RUINS..	67
CONCORDIA AT THE PICNIC..	93
A GREENLAND PARLIAMENT IN SESSION............................	104
CONCORDIA DRESSED FOR THE BALL..................................	119
FRONT VIEW OF THE GLACIER..	147
CROSSING THE CREVASSE ON AN ICE-BRIDGE.....................	160
MAP OF THE GLACIER..	162
THE GLACIER OF SERMITSIALIK..	167
VERTICAL SECTION OF GLACIER..	170
THE KRYOLITE MINE AT ARSUT FIORD...............................	207
THE PEAK OF KRESARSOAK..	221
ENTERING THE FIORD..	224
THE LUMME OF THE ARCTIC SEA......................................	226
SHOOTING LUMME...	228
ESAC...	231
ESAC'S HUT...	233
THE GOVERNOR AND FAMILY..	238
VIEW OF UPERNAVIK AND KRESARSOAK...........................	241
EIDER-DUCKS..	246
THE POLAR BEAR..	254
SEALS...	256
THE DEVIL'S THUMB...	261
THE PANTHER AFTER THE BEARS......................................	268
THE CAPTAIN AFTER THE BEAR..	278
MOORED TO A FLOE IN MELVILLE BAY.............................	287
THE ICEBERG CASTLE...	291

	PAGE
WE STEAM AWAY FROM THE MIDNIGHT SUN	295
THE MOST NORTHERN HOUSE ON THE GLOBE	299
JENSEN AND HIS FAMILY	303
AN ARCTIC WITCH	307
WE GO THROUGH AN ICEBERG TO CALL ON PHILIP	310
PHILIP, THE HUNTER, AND HIS SONS	312
THE RAVEN	317
HANS AND HIS FAMILY	322
THE GREAT AUK	337
ICEBERG IN JACOBSHAVN FIORD	346

"Out upon time! it will leave no more
　Of the things to come than the things before!
　Out upon time! who forever will leave
　But enough of the past for the future to grieve
　O'er that which hath been, and o'er that which must be;
　What we have seen our sons shall see—
　Remnants of things that have passed away,
　Fragments of stone, reared by creatures of clay."
Byron's *Siege of Corinth*.

THE LAND OF DESOLATION.

PART THE FIRST.
RUINS.

CHAPTER I.
ICE AND BREAKERS.

On a gloomy night in the month of July, 1585, the ship *Sunshine*, of fifty tons, "fitted out," as the old chronicles inform us, "by divers opulent merchants of London, for the discovery of a north-west passage, came, in a thick and heavy mist, to a place where there was a mighty roaring as of waves dashing on a rocky shore." The captain of this ship was brave old John Davis, who, when he had discovered his perilous situation, put off in a boat, and thereby discovered that his ship was "embayed in fields and hills of ice, the crashing together of which made the fearful sounds that he had heard." The ship drifted helplessly through the night, and when the morning dawned, "the people saw the tops of mountains white with snow, and of a sugar-loaf shape, standing above the clouds; while at their base the land was deformed and rocky, and the shore was everywhere beset with ice, which made such irksome noise that the land was called 'The Land of Desolation.'"

On a gloomy night in the month of July, 1869, the ship *Panther*, of three hundred and fifty tons, fitted out for a summer voyage by a party in pursuit of pleasure, came in like manner, through a thick and heavy mist, to a place where there was a mighty roaring as of waves dashing on a rocky shore. The captain of this ship was John Bartlett, who, when he had discovered his perilous situation, put off in a boat, and returned with the knowledge that the *Panther*, like the *Sunshine* of old, was embayed in "fields and hills of ice," the crashing together of which made the fearful sounds that he had heard; and then, when the morning dawned, "the people saw the tops of mountains white with snow, and of a sugar-loaf shape, standing above the clouds; while at their base the land was deformed and rocky," and the shore was everywhere beset with ice, which made such "irksome noise," that the people knew their ship had drifted to the self-same spot where the *Sunshine* had drifted nearly three hundred years before, and that the land before them was Davis's "Land of Desolation."

A mysterious land to them, and one around which clung many marvellous associations. Its legends had been the wonder of their boyhood; its grandeur was now their admiration. They had heard of it as a land of fable; tradition had peopled it with dwarfs and giants; history recorded that a race of men once occupied it whose fleets of ships traversed the waters in which their own vessel was now so grievously beset, bearing merchandise to hamlets of peace and plenty. Their eyes naturally sought a spot whereon to locate the home of this ancient people; but nothing could they discover save sterile rocks and desert wastes of ice. They saw dark cliffs which rose threateningly above them abruptly from the sea, and beyond these their eye wandered away into the interior, which the snows of centuries had converted into a vast plain of desolate whiteness. Returning from this limitless perspective, the eye fell upon the troubled waters. There were no signs of life anywhere: desolation frowned on every side. Yet the spectacle was sublime; and, as if to render that sublimity the more complete, there was added soon an aspect of the terrible. This came in the form of a gale of wind, which speedily rose to a tempest. Rain, hail, and snow swept down upon the ship, and every distant object was hidden except when the storm-curtain was occasionally rent asunder, and a mountain peak was exposed, with the clouds breaking against its sides. The creaking and groaning ice was around them everywhere, and an occasional iceberg of enormous magnitude broke through the gloom, and, while moving on through the angry and troubled waters, received with cold indifference the fierce lashings of the sea.

CHAPTER II.

FREE FROM DANGER.

I WAS a passenger on board the *Panther*, and shared with my companions the emotions which the Land of Desolation first inspired.

Under ordinary circumstances, there can be no more comfortable situation on board a ship than that of passenger. You are not expected to know any thing, and, if wise, you will not want to know any thing. You are content to trust to the captain, who is presumed to be quite competent to look to the safety of his ship, and therefore to your own. So far as human ingenuity can possibly be exercised to escape danger, his, you are sure, will be, and you trust to him as to a superior being—at least you know he has all the interest at stake that you have, and something more; for the handling of a ship in a storm is like the manœuvring of troops on the field of battle; success brings glory to the commander, and the acquisition of it is perhaps all the more precious that it is not shared with any body.

In our case there was a still further motive to confidence. Our captain owned one half the ship, which was a Newfoundland screw-steamer, and was built unusually strong. Besides this, we had confidence in his judgment, which was the next best thing to confidence in his caution; and then, to crown all, he was a thoroughly good fellow. To quote the gentleman who devoted himself to the duties of sagaman for the cruise, "A roaring, tearing, jolly tar was he, as ever boxed the compass on the sea." During the eight days occupied in coming over from St. John's, we had all conceived a high opinion of his qualities. He might be sometimes a little rash and venturesome, but rashness, as every body knows, is a safer quality than timidity; and we bore in recollection the old saying, "Nothing venture, nothing have." We might, perhaps, have found a little fault with him at first for having run us in so close to the Land of Desolation without halting for daylight and better weather; but then we all knew that to "heave to" was something which the captain had a great horror of, and he spoke of heaving to with such constant disrespect that the people generally had conceived the idea that it was a peculiarly terrible thing to indulge in. It seemed, therefore, that we were all right, and must necessarily escape shipwreck, even when the peril appeared greatest—when, for instance, we found ourselves threatened with an island rock on the one side and an island of ice on the other, in a sea white with foam, and breaking everywhere so wildly that the captain's trumpet-voice could scarce be heard above the tumult.

The worst of it was, we did not know within fifty miles of where we were. "There," said the captain, triumphantly, with his outspread hand upon the chart of Baffin's Bay, covering at least ten thousand square miles of land and sea, "There's where we are!" It was certain, at all events, that we had drifted within a line of skerries, for the waves broke on all sides, and where the rocks did not keep us from going, the ice did.

We had made the land with the intention of seeking a modern fishing-station of Danes and Esquimaux, which we knew to lie somewhere on that part of the coast; but where we could not even guess. As well seek charity in a bigot as hunt for a harbor in such weather, on a coast where there are neither light-houses nor pilots.

Yet we knew that human beings might be started somewhere if we only *could* free ourselves from our uncomfortable predicament, and the storm only *would* hold up. But it would not and did not until after we had, without exactly knowing how it came about, at length found ourselves in the open sea, and had given the Land of Desolation a wide berth.

The weather clearing finally, the *Panther* was pointed for a promising opening in the belt of ice which beset the shore; and now, without much risk or difficulty, we got behind a cluster of islands not far from the main-land and a good way to the south of where we had been so much troubled.

Here there was no ice at all, and we began to look up the fishing-town. First of all the signal-gun was fired, and the *Panther* whistled her loudest. This woke the echoes, and startled some sea-gulls, but nothing more. Then we crept cautiously along, passing island after island, the *Panther* whistling constantly and the guns firing occasionally.

Presently we saw something dark moving upon the water, which appeared to have the body of a beast, and the head and shoulders of a man. It might be a marine centaur! who could tell? In fact, we rather expected to see some such monsters long before; and if the sea had been alive with them, we would not have been, I think, much surprised.

"Hi! hi!" was the first greeting of this strange-looking creature, with a voice that sounded very human; "Hi! hi!" and afterwards he shouted, "Me Julianashaab pilot!" an announcement which greatly delighted us, even if the pilot did come in such very questionable shape.

He was not long in arriving alongside, and then, after getting the bight of a rope under each end of him, we hauled him in on deck, whereupon the head and shoulders speedily shook themselves out from the body, and our marine centaur stood forth with the proper complement of legs to show his affinity to man.

To see a pilot shed himself thus is not to increase one's confidence in him. And then his looks were by no means prepossessing. A broad face that was all cheeks, except what was mouth, with the least speck of a nose, and nothing to mention in the way of eyes, might be a curious study for a naturalist, but was hardly the sort of thing one seems to stand in need of when he seeks a harbor along a very ugly coast. And then his body was all covered with hair, and was all wet, as if he had just risen from the bottom of the sea. Besides, he smelt fishy. Yet this was clearly the best we could do if we ever meant to get into port, and, disregarding his unprepossessing appearance, the captain called him aft and ordered him to point out Julianashaab.

"Eh, tyma!" he answered; and off he started for the bridge, and off soon started the *Panther* under his direction.

Julianashaab we found to be no easy port to make, even with a marine centaur for a pilot. The *Panther* was twisted and turned about so much among the islands, and our pilot spoke so strangely, and made so many strange gestures, that he fairly turned the captain's head. The captain would indeed hardly believe that we were going anywhere at all, but were, on the contrary, whirling about for the temporary amusement of this creature whom we had fished up out of salt water.

The fact is, Julianashaab is some twenty miles from the sea, on the bank of a very long and tortuous frith or fiord, which is studded with islands. Difficult of access at all times, it is peculiarly so in July, for then the ice from the

Spitzbergen side of Greenland comes drifting down with the great polar current, a branch of which sweeps around Cape Farewell into Davis's Strait and Baffin's Bay, and proceeds north for a while before it is deflected to the westward to join the ice-incumbered stream that chills the region of Labrador, and bathes the coast of America even to the Floridas. Cape Farewell is in latitude 59° 49′, and Julianashaab lies some eighty miles to the north and west of it; that is to say, in latitude 60° 44′, or 5° 48′ south of the Arctic circle. It is not, therefore, much nearer the North Pole than St. Petersburg, Russia, though in a very different climate.

It was fortunate that we secured even this strange pilot when we did, else we should have lain outside all the night; for there was a night, even although it was scarce deserving the name. When one can plainly see to read by the light of the sun as late as ten o'clock P.M., there is not much of a night to boast of. There was a faint twilight even at midnight, and to this was added the light of the moon, which threw its brightness on the summits of the snow-clad mountains, and trailed its silvery splendors away over the rippled waters of the fiord.

The scene as we passed on was most impressive. There is indeed in a still arctic night, whether in the winter or summer, a sublimity which one does not feel in a night elsewhere. We passed through many groups of icebergs, and in the moonlight their shapes, at all times full of strange suggestions, were converted into objects of the most fantastic description. The faces and forms of men and beasts were fashioned there in the light and shadow of the night, occasionally with wonderful distinctness. As we passed on, we were sometimes in the cold shelter of a cliff, while the icebergs before us glittered in a full blaze of light, as if they were mammoth gems; again we would pass so near a berg that it seemed but awaiting an opportunity to topple over upon and overwhelm us; and all the while no sounds disturbed the air but the monotonous pulsations of the steamer and the hollow gurgle of the waves of her making as they broke within the icy caves.

At length our pilot told us we were approaching our destination, and as the light of day began to replace the brightness of the moon, he whirled the *Panther* into a little bight, and a few rude habitations, a flag-staff, and the belfry of a little mission church, appeared before us on a dark rocky hill-side.

"Julianashaab!" said our pilot, pointing to it with as much pride and satisfaction as if he were overlooking the finest city of the world. Poor man, he knew no better! He little dreamed how miserable was his lot to be only a Julianashaaber, and dwell in peace! For this was indeed his home. He had gone down the fiord hunting seals and to gather the eggs of wild fowl upon the islands, and when he saw the *Panther* he had just begun his work.

Down went the anchor with its usual rush and rattle, and immediately the rocks were alive with people, who, aroused from their peaceful slumbers by the strange noise, sallied forth as suddenly as the witches from Kirk Alloway. Looking forward to a closer scrutiny of them when the day had fully come, we sought our bunks, and, exhausted with the excitement of the night and the constant exposure of the past few days, we turned in to sleep the sleep of weariness.

B

CHAPTER III.

A HOPEFUL TOWN IN A HOPELESS PLACE.

This "Land of Desolation," to which we had come, is the Greenland of history and of the present time. All the southern part of it, as far up as the sixty-first degree of latitude, is called the "District of Julianashaab," and the town of Julianashaab is its capital. This town is one of the most flourishing in the whole country. It is, perhaps, the most pleasantly situated of all of them, and, standing in a region full of historic and legendary interest, it presents a good type of Greenland life, past and present, and it is well worth looking at.

Being the residence of the Governor of the "District," something of additional importance is attached to it on that account. Country squires who come up to London; backwoodsmen casting their curious eyes about them in Washington; children on a holiday excursion to a neighboring village, are not seized with greater wonder at what they behold, than is the hunter from some remote station of the Julianashaab District, when, after having braved the dangers of flood and field, he finds himself observing the latest fashions, and learning how the world moves generally in the town of Julianashaab. So much, therefore, for its social and political importance.

They call it a colony, and its governor, or director, is the *colonibestyrere*, which is to say, the steerer of it. There are eleven other colonibestyreres in the country, one for each of the other eleven "Districts," which extend northward one above the other from Julianashaab to the very

VIEW OF JULIANASHAAB.

confines of the habitable globe. The northernmost is Upernavik, beyond which there are no Christian people, or people of any kind living on the earth, except a few skin-clad savages. And, strange enough, this most northern place of Christian occupation bears a name which signifies "the summer place," derived from *Upernak*, or, as it might be better spelt, *Oo*pernak, the native Esquimaux word for summer.

Julianashaab, on the other hand, expresses a compliment to royalty. It was founded nearly a hundred years ago, at which time a king sat on the Danish throne who had a queen named Juliana. So, in honor of her majesty, they called this hopeful place the *haab* of Juliana, which is to say, in English, Julia's Hope. I could but wonder if all the expectations that the name bespeaks were ever realized; for if so, the founders of it must have been extremely modest. I was especially impressed with this feeling when I landed next morning, on a visit to the governor's house, and was greeted there by the principal part of the population.

Not a soul of them had, I believe, ever gone to bed after our arrival; but, on the contrary, had remained as they began — gazing at the *Panther* all the morning. When they first saw signs of activity on board, they expressed their delight in a very hilarious fashion; calling to each other, laughing, and running about from place to place, singly and in flocks, in a manner to indicate a very lively state of feeling. The little huts from which they emerged were scarcely distinguishable from the rocks themselves, and the people appeared to be coming out of the earth, and dropping into it again like prairie-dogs. Great was the rush when I got in my boat and started for the landing-place. Here they formed themselves in two lines, a hundred or more of them — men, women, and children — all talking or laughing, and all much delighted. Some pointed with their fingers; others remarked the singular performances of my tailor; others said, properly enough, what an odd-looking thing a round-topped hat was; and they all stood their ground while I marched between the two files, not one of them willing to forego for a moment the gratification of the passion of curiosity, which it is pleasant to know that arctic frosts can no more destroy than civilization unseat from its prying stool.

To see yourself gazed at by so many persons, even although they may be half-savage, is an embarrassing circumstance; and I should no doubt have felt bashful about running the gauntlet of their eyes had not another sense than that of sight claimed its legitimate right of precedence, and with such remarkable energy, too, that all minor emotions were impossible. Accordingly, I made my way through the crowd without any delay whatever, and, in fact, with a speed not at all calculated to give that opportunity for close examination which is always desirable to a traveller. The fact is, like the pilot we had picked up, they smelt fishy, and, had I not been most positively informed otherwise, I should have written the inhabitants of Julianashaab down as amphibious creatures of a fishy nature. And it would have been no very unnatural mistake either—not so bad, at least, as Sir John Mandeville's imagining boles of cotton to be woolly hens.

To explain all this, it is needful only to observe that, this Hope of Juliana being nothing but a fishing-town, the people are all fishermen, and therefore every thing smells of fish exceedingly. The odor extended everywhere; the wharf and rocks were strewn with fish, and the air seemed charged with fish that had evaporated. I became in a little while saturated thoroughly; so much so, indeed, that I felt myself hardened sufficiently to approach and examine the people more carefully than I had done at first.

They proved to be of many shades of color, from the tawny hue of the native Esquimaux (Greenlanders they call them here), to the almost pure Caucasian complexion, with transparent skin and rosy cheeks. Of this latter class was one girl especially, who stood apart from the rest as if she were superior to them, and yet could not wholly restrain her curiosity. Her hair, which was auburn, was very abundant, and had been arranged with much care. A red silk handkerchief was tied about the forehead, and ribbons without stint fluttered from the knob of hair which stood up on the crown of her head. The labors of her toilet had evidently been performed with the greatest nicety. Her boots were as red as her handkerchief and quite as spotless; her trowsers were of the choicest and most shining seal-skin, neatly ornamented with needle-work and beads. Then her jacket, which was of some bright color to match, looked very jaunty. It met the trowsers at the hips, where it was trimmed with a broad band of eider-down. About the neck there was a collar of the same material, and the beads upon the breast and around the wrists, where there was more eider-down, were quite dazzling.

Altogether she was very pretty. Her complexion was a dark brunette, but very delicate. When I approached to speak to her, she blushed and ran away, which was the only fault I had to find with her. The little, savage, coy coquette would not let me have a word with her, but got behind a house, taking good care, however, to show herself from time to time around the corner, peeping there, after the very simple and artless fashion of coquettes the world over. She was not, however, allowed to remain there undisturbed; for following after me came a young gentleman from the *Panther*, who immediately proceeded to invest the house, stealing around in the rear of it.

When he had fairly cornered her she did not seem at all afraid, but spoke to him civilly enough; and then from that time forward, whatever might be my disposition towards a better acquaintance with this lively maiden of Julianashaab, my chances were clearly gone forever; for afterwards she smiled only on this young gentleman. It is said (such was the influence of his engaging manners and the delicacy of his flattery) that she gave him her red boots at the very first interview.

This young gentleman bore among his shipmates the name of Prince; but whether that name was natural to him, or whether it was, as some asserted, on account of a fancied resemblance to the Prince of Wales, or whether on account of his being the prince of good-fellows (which is more likely than all), is not important. But Prince he was, and like a prince he behaved. Concordia was the name, as afterwards appeared, of the coy damsel. I shall hereafter have occasion to relate how the Prince actually (as was said) proposed to abandon the *Panther* that he might make Concordia as happy a little princess as ever was Cinderella.

Proceeding up the path after leaving the native population, I encountered a man who was a full-blooded Dane in appearance, and I should not have known otherwise had he not told me afterwards that his mother had some native blood in her veins. He had been born here in the infant days of the colony, and when we fell into conversation he expatiated upon its growth, and manifested much pride in its prosperity. For a long while he had been the assistant bestyrere; but now he steers an island of his own, some thirty miles away, and he is at present up on a visit, with his family, to see the metropolitan sights. They had seen the church, the parson, the governor and his wonderful store-rooms, and now, to cap the climax, here had unexpectedly come an *Oomeasoak* (big boat) that could breathe, and had feet to kick through the water with! What a journey up to town this had been, to be sure! How envious this would make their fellow-villagers, when they got home and told of all the wonders they had seen!

The name of this man was Peter Motzfeldt, and a very field of moss he was, if a ripe and fresh old age can be called so. Seventy bleak arctic winters had passed above his head, but not a single one had apparently gone into his heart, or even scattered frost upon his coal-black hair. He was as lively and elastic as if he were but twenty, which was the time when he first took service with the Royal Greenland Fishing Company, in whose employ he has been ever since. He had never been to Denmark, and he did not wish to go. It was all that he could do (naturally enough) to look after his two-and-twenty children, two boat-loads of which he had brought up with him to town.

This was the fiftieth anniversary of his employment by the Company, and the Company, in recognition of his faithfulness, had sent him a present, which was unfortunately, he said, down at Kraksimeut, where he lived. I thought he might have started with some of it on board the boat, and was the further confirmed in that suspicion when I ascertained that the present was an importation from Santa Cruz, and that there was no such token of civilization anywhere in Julianashaab as a public bar-room.

He promised to call upon me in the *Panther*, and devote himself to my service if I needed him. That I should need him was most evident, for he was perfectly charged with local knowledge, and besides that, had been with Captain Graah in the exploration which the Danish Government had ordered of this region in 1828–30. His name was therefore familiar to me already, from Graah's narrative. He went with me to the government-house, and there left me to present myself before Colonibestyrere Kursch, who I was glad to find (as I have usually found elsewhere with educated Danes) spoke English fluently, and, gratified with the welcome, I felt quite at home immediately, and began already to entertain a high opinion of Julianashaab. If my first introduction to the Land of Desolation had been somewhat rough, my first intercourse with its people (barring the fishy odor which they carried about with them) was decidedly pleasant.

Mr. Kursch was kind enough to furnish me with some charts of the coast, all drawn with that care and nicety for which the Danish hydrographers are famous. Afterwards we went together over to the house of the missionary, who lived at the opposite end of the town. In going there, we passed two store-houses, the Parliament-house (even here they can not do without a Parliament), the doctor's house, numerous turf-covered huts of the natives, a few of better construction, where some half-breed families reside (including the catechist, the assistant bestyrere, the blacksmith, and the carpenter); then we crossed a narrow, dashing stream upon a bridge, and were at the church and parsonage.

The church is quite a picturesque little building, constructed of wood (of course brought from Denmark), as are indeed all the buildings put up by the Government. The walls are double, and, the space between being made quite air-tight by calking, the interior is easily warmed. Indeed there is little suffering from cold at any time of year in any of the buildings at Julianashaab. They need no fire during three months of the summer, and for the winter the home government sends them out a liberal supply of coal. As a further protection, the houses (which are but one story high) are all plastered over on the outside with pitch, which closes tightly every crack and cranny, and protects them from the weather.

If the church had not been black, it would have been in all respects neat and tidy. Black though it was, it was a pleasant sight to see this house of God here in the desert, and by its very appearance giving proof unmistakable of good, earnest, Christian work. "Cleanliness before godliness," was meant for men, but it will do for a church as well.

The same neatness was observable at the pastor's house. The little building was surrounded with a yard and garden, which was inclosed with a white fence; and in every window of the house plants were growing in brightly-painted pots, filling the rooms with their delicious perfume.

In the pastor I met with a great surprise. I had seen him before in 1860-61 at Upernavik, away up among the polar frosts, almost a thousand miles beyond his present residence. It seemed as if he could not quit Greenland; as if his heart and soul were in his missionary work, and he would not give it up. He had been compelled to ask for change of residence, for the Upernavik winters had been too much for him. I had scarcely crossed the threshold, when I distinguished a pleasant smile and gentle voice that had welcomed me before. "Can this be Mr. Anthon?" I asked.

"Yes;" and the good pastor opened wide his eyes, greatly astonished to see me there; but, recovering himself presently, he addressed me by name, and then called his wife and sister, and I could almost think myself back again in the same neat parsonage where I had first met this interesting family years before. A lovely girl and a bright-eyed boy had been added to the group since then; but now, as then, there was soon a bottle of wine upon the table, fragrant coffee in the urn, some Danish fare soon followed; and there was plenty of Danish heartiness all round. In the afternoon we strolled up the bank of a little stream that runs beside the church and parsonage, and came upon a broad valley, in the centre of which there is a lake. Around the lake there were extensive pasture-grounds, upon which were browsing a herd of cows and a flock of goats. At this I was not a little surprised, for although I knew that in former times cattle had been reared here in great numbers, I had received the impression that at the present time they would not thrive. Mr. Anthon informed me that there was no difficulty in raising them, except the very important one of forage for the winter, for at Julianashaab the grass never grows high enough for hay. Farther up the fiord, however, it is abundant; but since the hay must all be brought in boats, it was both a tedious and expensive operation to gather it. Yet he managed to keep three cows; the governor had an equal number; the doctor had two; others had each one; and, indeed, all the well-to-do people in the village—Danes, half-breeds, and the better class of Greenlanders—had a daily supply of milk the year round.

The lake abounds in trout, a few of which were caught, and, when we returned for dinner, Mrs. Anthon had them for us on the table. She had, besides, some Greenland beef, and Greenland milk and butter; some smoked Greenland salmon too, and some Greenland venison; also some radishes and lettuce from her garden: and now, when these were, after a while, comfortably settled in their proper places with a glass of good old Santa Cruz punch, and an old Dutch pipe was brought to keep it company, and the governor and his assistant, and the doctor and Motzfeldt had come in to join us, we fell into a lively talk of Greenland and its legends; and it was not until a new day was breaking above the solemn hills around that I found my way back to the *Panther*. For fear, however, the reader should think we "made a night of it" at the parsonage, I will remind him that the "break of day" there, in the early part of July, is about two o'clock.

I have rarely passed a more pleasant evening or one more profitable. Our conversation ran mostly upon events of the past rather than of the present; for Julianashaab, although not without interest in itself, is doubly interesting from its locality. It stands on historic ground. Here was the spot that we were seeking when the *Panther* drove in among the "hills and fields of ice" upon the Land of Desolation; a spot which history had made famous, and legend and tradition had been busy with; where brave old Eric the Red had come nearly nine centuries ago, and, with his followers, founded a sort of independent state.

The fiord on the banks of which stands this modern town of Julianashaab extends some forty miles beyond; but, while the modern town stands alone, in ancient days hamlets were dotted beside it everywhere; thousands of cattle once browsed where there are now but a few cows; and peace and plenty reigned here once among a Christian people, who, after maintaining themselves through nearly five hundred years, undisturbed by the elements of discord that afflicted the world elsewhere, became at length extinct, and, while they passed away, left only a few meagre records of their growth and progress, and ruins of their decay. These ruins, I had learned, were still to be seen at many points of the fiord, the walls of some of the buildings being, even at this late period, in a tolerable state of preservation.

To visit these ruins was, in fact, our principal object in putting into Julianashaab. Around them, indeed, centred the principal interest of the voyage—at least, so far as concerned myself; and I did not quit, therefore, the house of the good pastor until we had planned an expedition to the place where the founder of this ancient people dwelt, and the church wherein he worshipped, in those latter days of his life when he had abandoned his war-god, Odin, for the Prince of Peace.

I had hoped Peter Motzfeldt would offer to accompany us, as he had visited some of the ruins forty years before with Captain Graah; but other engagements preventing him, Mr. Anthon was good enough to undertake to be our guide.

CHAPTER IV.

ERIC THE RED.

THE fiord on the border of which stands the colony of Julianashaab is now known as the fiord of Igalliko, meaning, "the fiord of the deserted homes:" the deserted homes being the desolate and long-abandoned ruins of the Norse buildings which are scattered along its picturesque banks.

Its ancient name was Ericsfiord, so named by Red Eric, in commemoration of his discovery, and for the perpetuation of his fame — a sad commentary, truly, upon the instability of human designs, that a name meant to recall the memory of a great achievement should be replaced by one expressive of decay and ruin.

This fiord is a grand inlet from the sea, and is from two to five miles wide. To all appearances, it is a great river, flowing along majestically between its banks. It does not, however, stand alone, for there are many others in Greenland that much resemble it. It is one of a multitude of similar inlets that give such peculiar character to the Greenland coast. In fact, there is no other coast like it, if we except that of Norway. But, unlike the fiords of Norway, glaciers descend into nearly all of them. These glaciers, by their steady growth, have changed the aspect of the country greatly since the Northmen first went there and gave it the name which it at present bears. That it is a misnomer, need hardly be mentioned, though the application of it came about in a very simple way. Davis's "Land of Desolation" suits the country much better than Eric's "Greenland."

The name Ericsfiord, like that of Magellan's Strait, Hispaniola, etc., commemorates a discovery. Perhaps I should rather say, like that of America, it commemorates a *re*-discovery; for as America was known long before Columbus's time, so also was Greenland before Eric's, if we are to credit (and we have no reason to doubt them) the ancient sagas of Iceland. According to these, one Gunnibiorn landed in Greenland in the year 872.

Eric was a high-spirited son of a jarl of Jadar, in Norway, who, opposing the encroachments of the king upon his feudal rights, in common with his class, was forced to flee the country. Escaping with his son, he established himself in Iceland, which was then being peopled by such refugees from tyranny and wrong, and a society was being formed which, for love of liberty and the actual possession of republican freedom, has never been excelled. These Icelanders were then, and they continued to be for centuries afterwards, the most intellectual and refined people of the north of Europe; and this is not surprising when it is remembered that the best blood of Norway and Denmark went to swell its population. In fact, Iceland gave literature and laws to the whole of Scandinavia. The child was wiser than the parent. Her writers first put in shape the Norse mythology; and many of the most distinguished families of Norway and Denmark are now proud to trace their origin back to the old freedom-loving jarls and seakings who founded a nation upon a rock which had been forced up by terrestrial fires into an atmosphere so cold and forbidding that the snows gathered upon its lofty summits, while volcanic heat wrestled in the bowels of its mountains.

Eric received his surname of Red, or Rothe, from the color of his hair; and his corresponding disposition doubled the significance of the name when it was made to signify "he of the red hand," as well as of the red head. The truth is, he was, according to all accounts, much addicted to the then popular pastime of cutting people's throats; and for his last offense of this description he was banished from Iceland for a space of three years. The immediate offense was for killing a churlish knave who would not return a borrowed door-post, which was always a sacred object, and was preserved with pious care by the Scandinavians. Perhaps if the borrowed article had been a book instead of a door-post, as in the case of fighting St. Colomba, the decree might have been different.

Being banished, where should Eric go? He could not return to Norway, and there was no place where he could set his foot with any safety. So he bethought him of the legendary land of Gunnibiorn, for, according to the Iceland Landnama, or Doomsday-book of Aré the Wise, that was the name of the man who had visited the land to the west of Iceland. This land Eric would go in search of, and risk his life and every thing upon the hazard.

He set sail from Bredifiord, in Iceland, some time during the summer of the year 983, in a small half-decked ship, and in three days he sighted land. Not altogether liking the looks of it, he coasted southward until he came to a turning-place, or *Hvarf*, now called Cape Farewell. Thence he made his way northward to the present site of Julianashaab, where he passed the three years of his forced exile. He liked the country well, as much as he had disliked it before when he saw it from the other side. Upon the meadow-lands beside the fiord immense herds of reindeer were browsing on the luxurious grass; sparrows chirruped among the branches of the little trees. He thought the place would do to settle in, and named it Greenland.

But to be precise, as it is always well to be, I quote from an old Norse saga of the before-mentioned Aré the

Wise—a saga written in Iceland about the year 1100, the original of which was in existence up to 1651, and a copy of which is still preserved in Copenhagen. Thus runs the tale:

"The land which is called Greenland was discovered and settled from Iceland. Eric the Red was the man from Bredifiord who passed thither from hence [Iceland] and took possession of that portion of the country now called *Ericsfiord*. But the name he gave the whole country was *Greenland*. 'For,' quoth he, 'if the land have a good name, it will cause many to come hither.' He first colonized the land fourteen or fifteen winters before Christianity was introduced into Iceland, as was told by Thorkil Gelluson in Greenland, by one who had himself accompanied Eric thither." This Thorkil Gelluson was uncle to Aré the Wise, and the historian was pretty likely, therefore, to be accurate in his information.

Upon returning to Iceland, Eric was graciously received; and what with the fine name he had given to his new country, and the fine promises he held out, he had no trouble in obtaining all he asked for—that is, twenty-five ships loaded with adventurous people, and all the appliances for building up a colony. Thus provided, he set sail in the year 985; but only fourteen of these ships ever reached their destination. Some of the remaining eleven were lost at sea; others were wrecked upon the eastern coast of Greenland; others put back to Iceland in distress.

Eric was resolved to found a nation for himself, and these fourteen cargoes of people gave him a sufficient nucleus. He went far up his fiord and began a settlement. A house was also built nearer to the sea—probably a lookout-house; for Eric expected other ships, and he, like a prudent man that he was, would set a watch for them.

The ruins of this house may still be seen, and are not five minutes' walk from the pastor's house at Julianashaab.

According to his expectations, other ships arrived, bringing cattle, sheep, and horses; likewise his wife, and sons and daughters. The settlement grew and prospered. Norwegians, Danes, Icelanders, people from the Hebrides, from the British Isles, from Ireland, and even from the south of Europe, came there in ships to trade. Emigrants poured in, new towns were built, new farms were cleared, and ambitious and adventurous men searched up and down the coast for other fields whereon to display their enterprise. How far north the most adventurous went we can not certainly know; but Rafn places one of their expeditions in latitude 75°, a point to which the stoutest ships of modern times can not now go without encountering serious risk. And all this was ventured, eight hundred years ago, in half-decked ships and open boats. It is positively known that one of their expeditions reached as far as Upernavik, latitude 72° 50', a stone having been discovered near there, in 1824, by Sir Edward Parry, bearing the following inscription in Runic characters:

"Erling Sighvatson and Biorn Thordarson and
Eindrid Oddson on Saturday before Ascension week raised these marks
and cleared ground. 1135."

Think of "clearing ground" in Greenland up in latitude 72° 50'! What kind of ground would now be found to clear? Naked wastes alone; and the desert sands are not more unproductive. But, as intimated already, the climate has certainly changed during the seven hundred years since this event happened; in evidence of which, it is not unimportant to observe that, in the old chronicles of the voyages of those ancient Northmen, there is very little mention made of ice as a disturbing element in navigation. And this brings us back to where we started—to the growth of glaciers in the Greenland fiords. From these glaciers come the icebergs, and a fiord which receives a glacier is not habitable.

There was no glacier in Ericsfiord when Eric went there, and there are none now, but it is surrounded by them. The mountains are of such peculiar formation that they keep back the frozen flood from Ericsfiord itself; and thus it was that this spot of earth was and still is fit for human life—an oasis in a desert, a patch of green in a wilderness of ice. But to this subject we shall have occasion to refer hereafter more at length.

CHAPTER V.

"THE ARCTIC SIX."

ERIC named his first settlement Brattahlid. The next he called Gardar; another, the Norse name of which has been lost, now bears the Esquimaux name of Krakortok, which means, "the place of the white rocks." The rocks are of the same metamorphic character as elsewhere in that neighborhood, and only differ from them in having, by one of Nature's freaks, been made of lighter hue than those of the region round about.

The fiord forks a short distance above Julianashaab, the southern branch leading to Brattahlid and Gardar, the northern, to Krakortok, which place it was our design to visit first.

Mr. Anthon not only offered to be our pilot, as before stated, but he likewise offered us his Greenland boat. We had boats of our own, and good ones too; but then what so appropriate for a Greenland fiord as a Greenland boat? So, at least, said our pastor-pilot, and so we were all willing to confess. But what was a Greenland boat?

A Greenland boat is a curiosity in marine architecture. Mr. Anthon took us down to look at the one he had offered us. It was turned bottom up on a scaffolding, so that we could stand under it and almost see through it, for it was semi-transparent like a bladder. When I thumped it with a stick, it rattled like a drum.

"There it is," said the pastor; "how do you like the looks of it?"

THE OOMIAK AND CREW.

"What! that thing?" exclaimed the captain, with ill-concealed contempt; "go to sea in a thing like that?"

"Certainly," said the pastor; "why not?"

Then he called three or four people, who had it off the scaffolding in a twinkling and down into the water, where it floated like a balloon that had been set adrift by mistake upon the sea.

"It's a woman's boat," explained the pastor.

"Oh yes, I see," answered the professor; "made by women. Quite an interesting object."

It was certainly made with great cunning. It was about thirty-six feet long, by six feet wide, and two and a half deep. There was not a peg, or nail, or screw in it, so far as we could see; and, judging by the same method of inspection, it was all leather.

The pastor asked again how we liked the looks of it, now that it was in the water.

To confess the truth, it looked a little too balloonish to suit any body's fancy. The captain broke into a laugh.

The professor speculated upon the quantity of stones that would be required to ballast it, measured by the ton; our sagaman began to institute comparisons between it and the ancient Phœnician craft, contending that the latter possessed decided advantages in a sea-way, which nobody doubted for a moment. The photographers came running along after it with their camera; the artists ran after it with their pencils—particularly a young gentleman much given to caricature (who, for short, bore the euphonious name of Blob), and who in a twinkling sketched her launched from an iceberg into an atmosphere of green above a golden sea, sailing away like a kite, with our trader for a bob. The trader was not there at first, but he came up in time to make a liberal offer of pork and beans, or a note of hand, in exchange for it—any thing of that description would be so handy to have on board the *Panther*—a boat thirty-six feet long—handy as the door-plate in the Toodles house.

Some one asked Mr. Anthon if he would not be good enough "to have the thing shoved off, that we might get a touch of its quality."

"Of course—by all means," replied the pastor. Then he called the crew together.

"Now, shades of Harvard and Oxford defend us, *what a crew! and what a rig!*" exclaimed the Prince, breaking into a laugh as the crew appeared.

And he was quite right. It was a strange rig for a boat's crew, without any sort of doubt. Very long boots that reached above the knees, of divers colors and pretty shape, gave a trim and natty look to the pedal extremities. Then they wore seal-skin pantaloons, very short, beginning where the boots left off and ending midway on the hips, where they met a jacket bright of hue, and lined with fawn-skin. This jacket was trimmed around the neck with black fur, beneath which peeped up a white covering to the throat. The hair was drawn out of the way, and tied with red ribbon on the top of the head; and altogether the costume was calculated to show off the respective figures of the crew to the greatest possible advantage.

Then the Prince laughed again when the pastor called their names. "They're a jolly lot," said he.

"Go along," said Mr. Anthon; "go along, Maria, and take the others with you."

Maria proved to be stroke-oar, and she called, "Catherina, Christina, Dorothea, Nicholina, Concordia, here, come along."

And off they all ran, chattering and giggling at an amazing rate; and they tumbled into the boat in a manner that made the captain fairly frown to see such lack of discipline. We were all much amused to see the gay and lively manner in which they skipped over the thwarts to their respective places, brimful of fun and mischief, and altogether making quite a shocking exhibition for a boat's crew, whose duties we are usually in the habit of seeing performed in a very sober manner. But they quieted down a little when a more sedate individual (who proved to be the coxswain)—dressed in short boots and long seal-skin pantaloons, and a cap instead of ribbons on the head—came along, and, taking the steering-oar, gave the order to "shove off."

The order was executed in handsome style, and the boat shot out over the little harbor very swiftly, each of the crew rising with the stroke of the oar; and bending to their work with a will, this singular-looking crew made their boat fairly hum again.

"Fine oarsmen!" exclaimed somebody who had just come up, and had not heard the roster called.

"Oars*men!*" replied the pastor, laughing at somebody's exceeding innocence. "Oarsmen! why, dear me, they are oars*women!*"

"Oars what?"

"Oarswomen, to be sure."

"Oars*women!* Man alive! and do they always pull the boat?"

"Always," replied the pastor; "always. A man will never pull an oar in a woman's boat. He would think it a humiliation and disgrace. The most he will do is to take the steering-oar, which is, indeed, quite legitimate business for him. He has his own small boat, the handling of which requires skill, while the woman's boat requires none. A man steers the boat now; the other six, who pull the oars, are all of the other sex, and I could not wish for a better crew."

Upon being asked what duties as a crew they usually performed, he answered:

"They row me about from place to place, as my pastoral duties call me; they gather hay for the cows, and bring home the fish (principally capelin and cod) that the fishermen catch and dry at distant places. Besides this, they do any thing they are told to do, and do not hesitate to expose themselves in any weather, unless it should blow too hard for the safety of the boat."

"Has such a boat any particular name?" the captain asked.

"We call it an *oomiak*, which signifies, simply, a woman's boat; while the man's boat is called a *kayak*."

Here the Prince, who was growing somewhat impatient over this long catechizing, broke in with a query as to whether they pulled the oomiak to-morrow, in case we should conclude to go in her?

"Certainly," replied the pastor.

"Just that same precious crew?"

"The same crew exactly."

"Including the bow-oar you call Concordia?"

"Including her, of course. She is the life of the crew, and I could never get along without Concordia."

"Nor I," replied the Prince. "The boat will do for me. Sink or swim, survive or perish, I ship in that craft for one. Pipe the dear creatures back."

So the pastor called to them to return, which they did in splendid style; and, every body agreeing with the Prince, it was forthwith arranged that we should go in the oomiak upon the morrow.

As the boat came in, the Prince proffered assistance, in a very gallant manner, to the bow-oar, but the girl hurried from the gunwale and ran, laughing, away. Nothing daunted, however, he gave chase; but, fleet as a young deer, she outstripped him and disappeared in the village, where the Prince was observed afterwards to be wandering around looking for her disconsolately.

CHAPTER VI.

UP THE FIORD IN AN OOMIAK.

THE morning came fresh and sparkling as the eyes of our fair oarswomen, who, singing to the music of their splashing oars, came stealing over the still waters, bearing the good pastor in his arctic gondola, while we were yet at breakfast.

Their arrival alongside made a sensation. Such a boat, propelled in such a fashion, was a sight new to sailors' eyes; and it did not seem easy for our people to reconcile such uses and occupations for womankind with a sailor's ideas of gallantry; for a sailor is always quite willing for a woman to be a princess, and as such he would always like to look upon her, but he would never want her for a cook. He could never be happy unless he could abuse the cook, and he never would abuse a woman. But as for pulling at an oar, why, what in the world should he ever do, if he were not allowed to express his preferences as to what might happen to the eyes of any one who disturbed the stroke? and he never would condemn a woman's eyes. Clearly, a woman would not do to pull an oar. But they were good to have a little pleasantry with, even if they did not understand a word that was said to them.

The people all crowded their heads over the bulwarks when the strange boat came up, and Welch addressed himself thus to the stroke-oar, when he had made out her peculiar style of costume: "Ah! my beauty, from the cut of your rig, it's a blood-relation of Brian O'Lin's that you are;" which created a good laugh at the girl's expense, without her, however, being at all aware of the cause of it. Not getting any response from that quarter, he turned his attention to the bow-oar. "And my bow-oar, honey, with the red topknot: ah! sure and she's a beauty. Say, my darlin, you're the one I'd like to be shipmates with till the boat sinks."

The bow-oar, more compliant than the stroke, nodded, smiled graciously, and said, "Ab!" and a great deal more which Welch did not understand.

"Ab?" he repeated, inquiringly; "and a pity it is that a foreigner you are, for I'd like to have a bit of a chat with you."

Somebody told Welch that *ab* meant yes.

"And you'll be shipmates with me?" inquired the sailor, with eagerness.

The bow-oar said "Ab!" again.

"Ah, then, and it's too willin' ye are, honey, entirely; and I'll not ship with you at all, at all. But you're a well-rigged craft alow and aloft, for all that, and I'd like to have the overhaulin' of you."

"You'll get overhauled yourself, and your hull scuttled, and your top-gallant rigging scattered over the sea, if you tackle that craft again," was the sharp reply which the fireman received to this very lively address. But it did not come from the bow-oar. It was from the Prince, who had just got out of bed, and, without pausing to comb his hair, had rushed to the gangway, to behold in the bow-oar the fair Concordia, and to discover that a sailor was making advances to her. The Prince was quite indignant. He soon, however, had Concordia on deck, when the others followed, and then, conducting them all to the galley, the Prince fed them bountifully. Meanwhile, preparation was being made for the journey. Some of us, however, embraced the opportunity to examine with more care than we had been able to before the strange-looking boat in which it was proposed to perform the journey.

We go down into it before the cargo is stowed, and Mr. Anthon explains to us the method of its construction. It is not at all likely that the reader of this book will ever desire or have occasion to make such a boat for his own use; but it may perhaps not be uninteresting to him to know how he might proceed, if he should so desire. According to the pastor, it would be something after this fashion:

You will first obtain five round sticks of wood thirty-six feet long, more or less, according to the length you desire to make the boat. These must be as light as possible, and not over two inches in diameter. Since the country produces no wood, you will of course have to go to the governor for the materials, which he keeps in his storehouse, replenishing the stock each year by shipments from Denmark. But since you will not find a stick thirty-six feet long, you will have to procure several, which you lash together until you have obtained the requisite length. Having done this, you place three of them on the ground parallel with each other, the outer ones being six feet apart. Then across them, at the middle, you lash, with firm thongs of raw seal-hide, a piece of inch plank three inches wide and six feet long. Then you bring the ends of the three long sticks together, lashing them firmly. Next you lash other pieces of board across at intervals of two feet. Of course these are of different lengths. Thus you have obtained the bottom of your oomiak. This done, you proceed to erect the skeleton, fastening the stem and stern posts firmly with lashings; also the ribs. The ribs in their place, you secure along the inside of them, at about sixteen inches above the floor, a strip of plank. On this you place the thwarts, the middle one being six feet long, the others shorter, as you approach either end. Ten thwarts is the proper number. This completes the skeleton, all but the placing of the rails or gunwales, which are the two remaining thirty-six feet sticks. These being fastened with thongs to the ribs, and to the stem and stern posts, your skeleton is finished, and it is exceedingly light, strong, and elastic. But now, instead of covering this novel sort of boat-skeleton with planking, you stretch over it a coat of seal-hide (it can scarcely be called leather). It has been, however, tanned and dried, and afterwards thoroughly saturated with oil, until it is as impervious to water as a plate of iron. A number of skins are necessarily required, and these the women will sew together for you so firmly with sinew thread that not a drop of water can find its way through the seams. This skin coat, being cut and fashioned to fit the skeleton as neatly as a slipper to the foot, is drawn on and firmly tied. It is very soft when you draw it on, but when it dries it is as tight and hard as a drum-head; and when the skin becomes a little old, the light will come through it as through parchment. When afloat in the oomiak, you can always discover how much water you are drawing by looking through the side of it. This is not a pleasant operation, however, for a novice or a nervous person, since one can hardly resist the impression that he is in a very treacherous sort of craft.

This light and elastic boat is propelled with short oars having broad blades, which are tied to the gunwale, instead of being thrust out through rowlocks. These oars are shod with bone, to protect them from the ice. A single mast is erected in the bow, upon which is run up a square sail when the wind is fair. If the owner of the boat is rich enough, he gets the material for his sail from the governor; but if not, he makes it out of seal-skins.

I have observed that he gets the wood from the governor's stores: not all of it, however, for the obliging sea brings him an occasional tree that has floated with the ocean current from the forests of Siberia; or a plank, perhaps, that has fallen overboard from a passing vessel; or a spar or other portion of a wreck. Thus, before the Danes came here, did the Esquimaux obtain all the wood they used. From this source they also procured their iron, in the shape of spikes, nails, bands, and bars, attached to these waifs of the sea. Thus do the ocean currents, which carry heat and cold to the uttermost parts of the earth, scatter also blessings to mankind.

After some unavoidable delays (always occurring when any body sets out anywhere and some other body is to go with him), we finally got all our traps in the oomiak. The photographers were aboard with their cameras, baths, and plates; the artists with their sketch-books, stools, and pencils; the surveyors with their sextants, barometers, compasses, and tape-lines; the hunters with their weapons, game-bags, and ammunition; the steward with his cooking fixtures, and substantial eatables and drinkables; "the Arctic Six" were at their stations; and "All aboard!" was the signal to shove off. The fair oarswomen dipped their paddles, rising with the act, and coming down with a good solid thud upon the thwart when the paddles took the water. The light boat shot away from the ship over the unruffled waters of the silvery-surfaced fiord; and at last we were off.

The day could not have been better chosen. The sky was cloudless; and the great mountains, by which we were on every side surrounded, climbed up into a pearly atmosphere, and their crests of ice and snow blended softly with the pure and lovely air. Every body was in the best possible spirits; every thing was novel, from the boat and its strange crew to the strange shore past which we were gliding, and which presented sometimes cliffs of immense height, and sometimes slopes of green, above which the atmosphere quivered in the sun's warm rays.

I could but contrast my situation with that of a few days before, when I was sweltering in the summer heat of New York. The atmosphere was soft like that of budding spring, though close to the Arctic Circle, and within the region lighted by the midnight sun.

The scenery was everywhere grand and inspiring. The shores, though destitute of human life, were yet rich in historical association. As we passed along, it was hard to realize that voices were not calling to us from the shore; and where miles of rich meadow-land stretched before us, girdling the cliffs with green, the fancy, now catching the lowing of cattle and the bleating of sheep, would sometimes detect the shouts of herdsmen; while again we seemed to hear,

"By distance mellowed, o'er the water's sweep,"

the "song and oar" of some gay inhabitant of the fiord, descendant of that brave band of men who, under the leadership of sturdy Eric, had on these sloping plains, beneath the ice-crowned hills and within the rampart of the ice-girt isles, sought an asylum from their enemies.

But if the fancy discovered those evidences of life, as it recalled the people who once were happy here in this peaceful, pastoral scene, the eye failed to detect any such tokens whatever. An occasional seal, that put up its half-human head to peer at us, or a sparrow or butterfly, that hovered about us when we neared the shore, or now and then a flock of water-fowl, were the only living things we saw.

The spirit of the scene was contagious. Even our native crew were not wanting in the emotional feelings of the hour. Encouraged by their pastor, they broke forth in concert, and with rich melodious voices, timed to the paddles' stroke, they sang an old Norse hymn:

> "Oh, hear thou me, thou mighty Lord,
> And this my cry, oh, heed;
> Oh, give me faith; I trust thy word;
> Oh, help me in my need;"

and as the refrain was echoed back to us over the waters from hill and dale, it struck the fancy more and more that human voices came to us from the depths of those solitudes.

Five hours of this pleasant experience brought us near the end of the fiord, where the water is narrowed to about two miles; but long before this the solemnity of the day had been at times broken by incidents very different from those above described. In fact, there was a great deal of liveliness mingled with the seriousness which every body felt at times, perhaps in spite of himself. The Prince was, as usual, at the bottom of the most of it. That young gentleman had come out to enjoy himself, and have a good time of it generally, and his disposition was not to be restrained by any of the ghosts of ancient Northmen who might haunt the fiord. He attached himself to Concordia as a matter of course. Speaking metaphorically, there can be no doubt that he had had his eye upon that pantalooned lady (now bow-oar) ever since he first discovered her peeping around the corner of the house in Julianashaab. It was not to be supposed, therefore, that he would on the present occasion relax his visual energies, and his first procedure was to place himself beside her on the thwart, where he carried his admiration so far as to insist upon relieving the fair oarswoman of her oar, which resulted in a great deal of sport between the parties immediately interested, and filled the minds of the other damsels with immense disgust — whether because no one offered them the same gallant attentions, or whether because the bow-oar was constantly interfering with the stroke, was not discovered; but I greatly suspect it was the latter rather than the former.

Thus, with alternate gayety and solemnity, did we speed on through the pleasant sunshine. In a general way we might say that there was universal enjoyment in that oomiak; but outside of it there was not altogether so happy a condition of affairs. The lively proceedings of Concordia and the Prince struck terror into one heart which beat its troubled discord in the confinement of a native kayak. The unhappy possessor of this discordant heart was a half-breed, whose name was Marcus, and who, although a half-savage, was yet wholly a Christian in the matter of name and baptism.

This Marcus was a fine-looking fellow, with brown hair and eyes, a frank open face, the complexion, though not the features, leaning rather to the Esquimaux than the Danish hue. The only trouble with him was — and this appeared to distress him greatly—that he loved Concordia. Judging from that distress, he must have loved her desperately.

Marcus was a great favorite with the pastor, and he always accompanied him everywhere he went. His duty was a simple one enough, but a very necessary one, as boating is performed in the Greenland fiords. It was to paddle along beside the oomiak in the capacity of courier, if occasion made it necessary to use one; or, in case of need, to act as outrider—two functions which at once suggest the dangers of oomiak navigation. Suppose, for instance, Mr. Anthon is caught in a heavy blow, and is broadside to the wind. His boat is liable to be blown over, owing to its lightness. Marcus is near at hand; he pulls up quickly alongside, seizes the gunwale of the boat, bears his weight upon it, and prevents a catastrophe. Again, the oomiak runs against a sharp piece of ice, which the steersman has not seen in time to avoid; a hole is cut in the skin, and in rushes the water. The boat is headed for the land, and the pastor and his ladies get ashore with their lives. But where shall they go, or what shall they do? They are, perhaps, on an island, or, if not, they have to scale a mountain and descend again before they can reach a settlement. Marcus saves them this labor, and very likely their lives, by flying away in his kayak and bringing succor.

Twice during the day it seemed to me that we had met with a fatal accident of this nature. The skin of the boat was cut and the water entered, but the circumstance caused no alarm. The cuts proved to be small, and one woman only left her oar to repair them. This she did, and very speedily, by thrusting into the cut a small piece of blubber, which answered every purpose until we reached a convenient landing-place, when the boat was drawn up on the beach far enough for the woman to get at the hole with the sinew-threaded needle, when a patch was quickly fastened over it, and the skin was as good as ever.

That Marcus was jealous of the Prince, any body could see with half an eye. But a kayak is a most inconvenient place for a jealous lover. It is only a little over a foot wide, and does not weigh half as much as the man himself. If he meditates mischief to his rival, his own situation becomes a very dangerous one, since the least indiscretion in his movements, or the imprudent withdrawal of his eyes from his frail boat, would very likely cause him to find himself suddenly floating head down, with his bladder-like kayak inextricably fastened to his heels—a position that would very speedily cure the most ardent lover in the world of the highly ridiculous passion of jealousy.

Compromising, therefore, between the impulse of jealousy and the restraints of prudence, Marcus paddled close to the forward part of our oomiak, where the Prince and Concordia were seated, as if he would overhear their conversation, and so possess himself of some remark of the fickle lady to treasure up against her, thus the more effectually to insure the destruction of his peace of mind—a pastime, by-the-way, in which lovers are very apt to indulge themselves.

If this was, however, his design, he unfortunately failed in it, since there was no conversation audible. Like Haidee, our heroine had long since discovered that her Don did not understand a word she said. Yet, judging from his liveliness of manner, the Prince must have learned something agreeable to his feelings; and it was clear enough that he was being instructed after a fashion quite equal, if not superior, to the ordinary forms of speech, for this fair lady of the oar

> "Had recourse to nods, and signs,
> And smiles, and sparkles of the speaking eye,
> And read (the only book she could) the lines
> Of his fair face,"

which seemed to be quite enough to satisfy her capricious fancy.

The time passed scarcely less pleasantly to the rest of the party than to the Prince, although in a very different manner. At least there was no lack of lively episodes, and we all found ourselves much surprised when we discovered that we were approaching the end of the fiord, which had now assumed less the appearance of a river and more that of a lake. Before us the water was lost to view by a great curve, from the middle of which there appeared a fine valley stretching away to the base of the Redkammen, one of the noblest mountains to the artist's eye, and one of the boldest landmarks to the mariner in all the country, conspicuous as Greenland is for its lofty and commanding scenery.

And there Redkammen stood in its solitary grandeur, away up in a streak of fleecy summer clouds, its white top now melting with them into space, now standing out against a sky of tenderest blue. Then came a cloak of darker vapor, which, resting on the mountain's summit, trailed away into the heavens, bridging the space which divides the known from the vast unknown.

CHAPTER VII.

THE RUINS OF ERICSFIORD.

WE were not long now in reaching our destination, which was the foot of the extensive green slope on the north side of the fiord. Above this slope, and from a quarter to half a mile from the bank, the cliffs rise perpendicularly to an altitude of fifteen hundred feet. To our right, as we approached, rose a lofty range of hills, which separates the two branches of the fiord. Beyond these once flourished the colonies of Brattahlid and Gardar. Behind and to the left of us lies the island of Aukpeitsavik, which extends almost to Julianashaab.

Our first concern was to discover if the church which we knew to have existed there was still standing. To our great satisfaction, its walls were seen upon the green slope long before we reached the land, although a cliff some thirty feet high, which formed its background, prevented us from observing it clearly until we had come almost to the shore.

Upon landing, there was a great scramble for the honor of first entrance into the ruin. The scramble was over a tangled growth of trailing junipers, crake-berry, whortleberry, and willow bushes, which grew in a rich grassy sod that exhibited many plants in bloom, among which were conspicuous the dandelion, butter-cup, bluebell, crow's-foot, and cochlearia.

Leaving the party to their various occupations—the artists to their several chosen tasks, the crew to get the boat ashore and cook the dinner, the lovers to their jeal-

VIEW OF THE OLD NORSE RUINS.

ousies, and the maids to their coquetry, I set out with two friendly assistants to make a complete survey of the ground.

The hill-side upon which stood the ancient town of Krakortok is much broken, but there are many level patches, rich with vegetation, which seem to have been once cultivated, and even now appear like arable lands. Small streams course through them, giving a fine supply of clear fresh water. Beside these streams the angelica grows to the height of three feet. The stem of this plant furnishes the only native production of the soil that the Esquimaux use for food, if we except the cochlearia or scurvy grass, which is but little valued, and is not nutritious. It is said that the old Northmen cultivated barley here, and no one would doubt that such a thing were possible. Even at the present time, if one might judge by the day of our visit as typical of the season, barley might grow and ripen readily. Yet Mr. Anthon informed me that such days were liable to be followed by severe frosts, and that in any case the season is too short for complete fruition. There is, therefore, no attempt made in any part of Greenland, not even here in Ericsfiord, to raise any thing more than the ordinary garden vegetables—namely, such of the crucifera as lettuce, radishes, and cabbage—all of which flourish admirably as far up as the Arctic Circle. The agricultural products of Greenland are not, therefore, to be regarded as important in a commercial point of view, though, with care, each inhabitant of Ericsfiord might be well provided with every needful garden luxury. Potatoes would grow, I believe, if they would only take the trouble to cultivate them properly. To perfect any of the cereals would, however, be at present a hopeless undertaking.

Yet the whole region about Krakortok bears evidence

of former cultivation. Garden patches were in the neighborhood of all the buildings. The church and two other buildings were inclosed by a wall, the outlines of which I had no difficulty in determining, and which, judging from the mass of stones, must have been about five feet high.

The church interested me most. Its walls are still quite perfect to from ten to eighteen feet altitude, and even the form of the gable is yet preserved. The door-ways, three in number, are not in the least disturbed by time; the windows are mostly entire, except on the north side, and the arched window in the eastern end is nearly perfect. Beneath this window was the chancel, and the church was constructed with singular exactness as to orientation. This could scarcely be by accident, for the same accuracy is to be observed in all the other sacred buildings that have been discovered in the neighborhood—the walls standing within less than one degree of the meridian line, and even this may have been an error of my instrument which I had not the means of correcting, rather than an error of the Northmen. They were evidently close observers of the movements of the heavenly bodies, and must have known the north with great exactness, and they built their church walls accordingly. These walls were four and a half feet thick. The stones were flat, and no cement appears to have been used other than blue clay.

In one angle of the church-yard there had been a building which I supposed to have been the almonry; and in another part was the house of the priest or bishop, the walls of which are still perfect to the top of the door-way, and one of the windows.

Outside the church wall, but not far removed from it, there was a building evidently of much pretension. It was divided into three compartments, and was sixty-four by thirty-two feet. There was another still farther to the

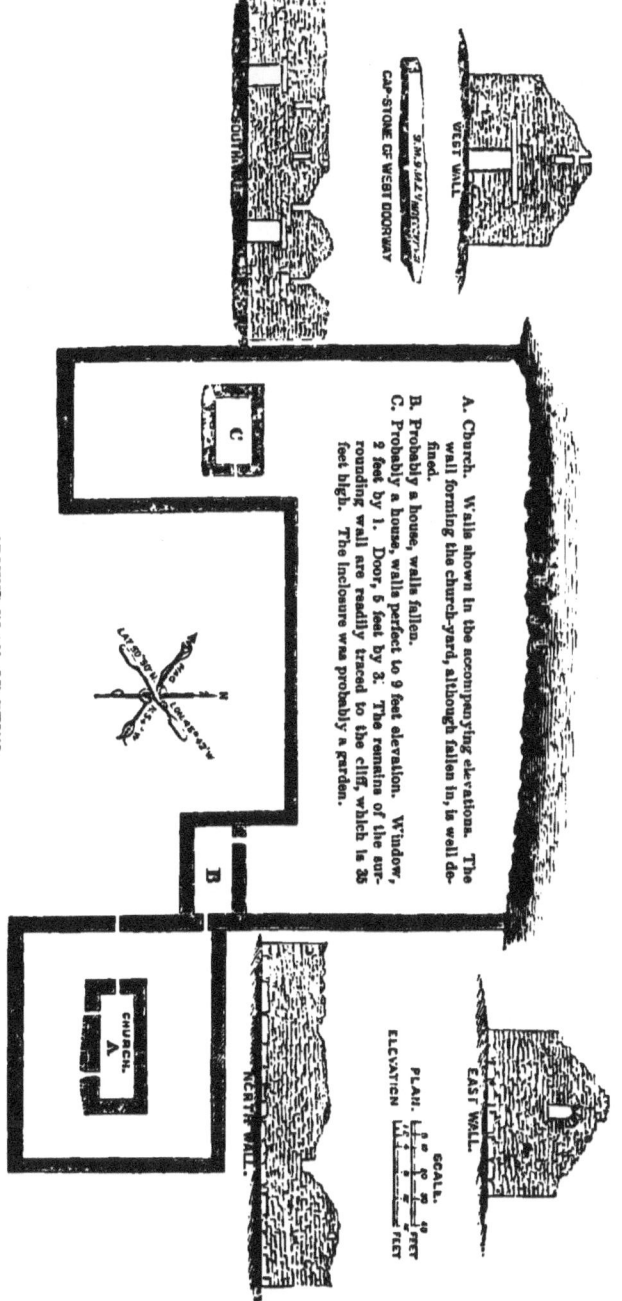

westward, others to the east, and one on the natural terrace above the church. Altogether the cluster of buildings which composed the church estate—where dwelt the officers who governed the country round about, and administered in this distant place, at what was then thought to be "the farthest limit of the habitable globe," the ordinances of the pope at Rome—were nine in number: a church, a tomb, an almonry, five dwellings, and one round structure; the walls of which latter building had, like those of the church-yard, completely fallen, but the outline of the foundation was preserved. The walls had been four feet thick, and the diameter of the building in the clear was forty-eight feet. It had but one door-way, which opened towards the church.

To call this circular building a tower, in the sense of its application to the famous round towers of Ireland, would be a great stretch of the imagination. There is, however, a strange coincidence in the circumstance of proximity to a church. Near all the church edifices that have been discovered in Greenland a structure similar to this one at Krakortok has been found. None of them are, however, so large: its walls could not have been more than seven or eight feet high. Its uses are unknown. Possibly it may have been a work of military defense, perhaps a baptistery; there is nothing, however, except its shape, to indicate that it was not a cow-house.

After completing my survey of this church estate, I visited other parts of the fiord. The buildings have been very numerous hereabout, but all except the church and bishop's house are now levelled with the earth, and so overgrown with willow, juniper, and birch that even their outline is scarcely distinguishable.

What a wonderful change! what a sad wreck of humanity! Here people, weary with war, had come to cultivate the arts of peace; here they had built strong and comfortable dwellings; here they had reared herds of cattle and flocks of sheep upon pastures of limitless extent; here they had worshipped God according to the dictates of their consciences; and now where are they? nothing left but this "ruined trace." A single inscription on a tombstone, carved in Runic characters, is all the record that remains besides the crumbled walls. This inscription reads:

"Vigdis, daughter of M * * *, rests here. May God rejoice her soul."

And may God rejoice the souls of all of those worthies of the olden time!

I could not fail to experience a feeling of sadness as I stood beside the tombs of a people now utterly extinct. It seemed as if voices from the past were speaking to me from out the crumbling church, from the almonry where the priest dispensed his alms, from the holy-water stoup, from the tomb-stones bearing the sacred emblems of our Christian faith; from everywhere, indeed, there was a silent whispering that here a Christian people once dwelt in peace, and from temples dedicated to Almighty God arose their anthems of praise above the glittering crests of snow. That they should ever have come here seems, however, more strange than that they should have perished as they did.

NOTE.—The ruins of Krakortok, shown on page 67, were visited by Captain Graah in 1828, as the cap-stone over the church door-way (west end) will testify for many a day. This cap-stone is 12 feet 7 inches long by 2 feet 2 inches wide, and averages 8 inches thick. It bears this inscription —G. M. G. M. & V. MDCCCXVIII—initial letters, standing for Graah, Mathiesen, Gram, Motzfeldt, and Vahl, the visiting party.—See *Graah's Narrative*, p. 38.

CHAPTER VIII.

THE NORTHMEN IN GREENLAND.

THESE Northmen were certainly a very wonderful people, and they did very wonderful things; but of all their enterprises the most singular would seem to be their coming to Greenland, where they were without the lines of conquest which were so attractive to their brothers and ancestors; for they were kindred of the Northman Rollo, son of Rögnvald, jarl of Maere, and king of the Orkneys, who ravaged the banks of the Seine, and played buffoon with the King of France; the same with those Danes who, in Anglo-Saxon times, conquered the half of England: descendants they were of the same Cimbri who threatened Rome in the days of Marius, and of the Scythian soldiers of conquered Mithridates, who, under Odin, migrated from the borders of the Euxine Sea to the north of Europe, whence their posterity descended within a thousand years by the Mediterranean, and flourished their battle-axes in the streets of Constantinople; fellows they were of all the sea-kings, and vikings, and "barbarians" of the North, whose god of war was their former general, and who, scorning a peaceful death, sought for Odin's "bath of blood" whenever and wherever they could find it. In Greenland they appear like a fragment thrown off from a revolving wheel by centrifugal force. And here they seem to have lost the traditional ferocity of their race, though not its adventurous spirit. Sailing westward, they discovered America, which was the crowning glory of their career. Sailing eastward, they saw the light of

Christianity which was breaking in the North, and its blessings followed them to their distant homes.

These two voyages to the west and east symbolize the character of this wonderful race. Love of change made their conversion to Christianity easy; love of adventure made all enterprises of discovery seem trifling hazards, and gave them the world to roam in. To their achievements in the Western hemisphere the influence of the Christian religion was, no doubt, very powerful. It weaned them from Europe and its perpetual wars, and while it did not destroy, it turned their enterprise into a new channel, and one more consistent with the new faith.

The introduction of Christianity into Greenland was accomplished by Lief, son of Red Eric; and it was the same man who discovered America—two grand achievements which rank Lief Ericson as one of the heroes of history. With respect to the former event, an old Icelandic saga thus briefly records the fact:

"When fourteen winters were passed from the time that Eric the Red set forth to Greenland, his son Lief sailed from thence to Norway, and came thither in the autumn that King Olaf Tryggvason arrived in the North from Helgaland. Lief brought up his ship at Nidaros [Drontheim], and went straightway to the king. Olaf declared unto him the true faith, as was his custom unto all heathens who came before him; and it was not hard for the king to persuade Lief thereto, and he was baptized, and with him all his crew."

Nor was it hard for King Olaf to "persuade" his subjects generally "thereto." His Christianity was very new and rather muscular, and under the persuasive influence of the sword this royal missionary made more proselytes than ever were made before in the same space of time by all the monks and missionaries put together.

When Lief came back to Greenland with a new religion and a priest to boot, his father Eric was much incensed, and declared the act pregnant with mischief; but after a while he was prevailed upon to acknowledge the new religion, and at the same time to give his wife Thjodhilda, who had proved a more ready subject for conversion, leave to build a church. Thus runs the saga:

"Lief straightway began to declare the universal faith throughout the land; and he laid before the people the message of King Olaf, and detailed unto them how much grandeur and great nobleness there was attached to the new belief. Eric was slow to determine to leave his ancient faith, but Thjodhilda, his wife, was quickly persuaded thereto, and she built a kirk, which was called 'Thjodhilda's Kirk.' And from the time she received the faith she separated from her husband, which did sorely grieve him."

And this appears to have been the last, and (as the sequel shows) was the most potent argument for his conversion. To get his wife back, he turned Christian, and ordered the pagan rites to be discontinued, and the pagan images of Thor, and Odin, and the rest of them, to be broken up and burned.

Whether this first Greenland church of Thjodhilda's was built at Brattahlid, or Gardar, or Krakortok, can not now be positively said; but we might, perhaps, find some reason to conclude it was the latter, from the fact that an old man named Grima, as the saga states, who lived then at Brattahlid, made complaint, "I get but seldom to the church to hear the words of learned clerks, for it is a long journey thereto."

This much, however, we do know, that the church — wherever it was situated — was begun in the year 1002, and was known far and wide by the name of its pious lady-founder. Several churches and three monasteries were built afterwards. One of these latter was near a boiling spring, the waters from which, being carried through the building in pipes, gave a pleasant warmth to the good monks who occupied it, and they needed no other heat the year round.

The Christian population of Greenland became, in course of time, so numerous that it was necessary for the Bishop of Iceland to come over there frequently to administer the duties of that part of his see; for the diocese of Gardar, as it was called, was from the first attached to the See of Iceland.

A hundred years thus passed away, and both in spiritual and temporal matters the Northmen in Greenland were getting along finely. Their intercourse with Europe was regular, and their export trade, especially in beef, was considerable. Indeed, Greenland beef was for a long time highly prized in Norway, and there was no greater luxury to "set before the king." The people were almost wholly independent of the Icelandic government. Under a system of their own devising, which appears to have perfectly satisfied their necessities, they lived quite unmolested by the outside world, and, undisturbed by wars and rumors of wars, the descendants of Eric the Red were as happy as any people need wish to be.

They lacked only one thing to complete their scheme of perfect independence: they needed a bishop of their own, which would cut them loose from Iceland altogether; and, in truth, the Icelanders were such a liberty-loving people that they were in no wise disposed to dispute their claims. But a bishop they could not have without the sanction of the powers that ruled in Norway; for the pope would not appoint so high an officer for any of the regions directly or indirectly subject to the control of Norway except upon the nomination of the king, after consultation with his spiritual advisers. Numerous petitions were accordingly sent over to the king, in order to secure his good offices. For a time these efforts were attended with but partial success, since a temporary bishop only was vouchsafed them in the person of Eric (not the Red), who went to Greenland in the year 1120, and, without remaining long, returned home, having, however, visited Vinland in the interval—this Vinland being the America which Columbus thought to be a part of Asia some four centuries later.

Finding they did not get a bishop of their own according to their deserts (as they estimated them), they grew indignant, and one of their chief men, named Sokke, declared that they must and would have one. Their personal honor and the national pride demanded it; and, indeed, the Christian faith itself was not in safety otherwise. Accordingly, under the advice of Sokke, a large present of walrus ivory and valuable furs was voted to the King of Norway; and Einer, son of Sokke, was commissioned to carry the petition and the present.

The result proved that the inhabitants of Ericsfiord were wise in their day and generation; for whether through the earnestness of their appeals, or the value of their gifts, or through the persuasiveness of the ambassador, or through all combined, they obtained, in the year 1126, Bishop Arnold, who forthwith founded his Episcopal See at Gardar, and there erected a cathedral, which was built in the form of a cross.

Arnold seems to have been a most excellent and pious leader of these struggling Christians. Zealous as the famous monk of Iona, without the impulsiveness of that great apostle of Scotland, he bound his charge together in the bonds of Christian love, and gave unity and happiness to a prosperous people. He died in the year 1152, and thenceforth, until 1409, the See of Gardar, which he had founded, was regularly maintained. According to Baron Halberg, in his history of Denmark, seventeen successive bishops administered the ordinances of the Church in Greenland, the list terminating with Andreas, who was consecrated in 1406. The see and Andreas expired together; and the last account we have of either was made in 1409, when it is recorded that he officiated at a marriage, from the issue of which men now living are proud to trace their ancestry. This was his last official act, so far as we have record.

But the people did not then wholly disappear, even if the official see ceased to exist. To the causes which led to their final overthrow we shall have occasion to refer presently.

CHAPTER IX.

THE NORTHMEN IN AMERICA.

To complete the account of the Northmen who dwelt upon the banks of Ericsfiord, it is necessary to trace some of their voyages to the West.

Lief, the son of Eric, was a man of restless disposition. Not content with Greenland, he had visited Europe, and had there studied in the very practical school which the Northmen took good care always to have in operation— the art of war. Dissatisfied with paganism, he accepted the Christian faith, as we have seen, and carried it to his own country. Afterwards, wearied with the enforced monotony of his life at Ericsfiord, he determined to discover new lands for himself, as his father had done before him, and also, like his father, he sought them in the West. He set sail in the year 1001, soon after his return from Norway. Crossing what we now call Davis's Strait, he first sighted Labrador. Not liking the looks of it, any more than his father had liked the first sight he had of the east coast of Greenland, he sailed south until he came to Newfoundland, where he landed. Thence he proceeded on his voyage, discovering Nova Scotia; and finally he arrived at a place which he called Wonderstrand, where he wintered. This was probably the peninsula now called Cape Cod, in Massachusetts. Thence he returned to Brattahlid, in Ericsfiord, and ever afterwards bore the name of Lief the Lucky.

His brother Thorwald followed after him the next year, and the new land was called Vinland (*Vinland hin goda*), from the great quantities of wild grapes they found there, and of which they made wine. Thorwald was set upon and killed by savages, whom they called Skraellings, from their diminutive stature.

A third brother, Thorstein, went in search of Thorwald's body the next year, and died without finding it. Then, after this further disaster, Lief, who had now succeeded Red Eric, his father, in the government of the colonies of Ericsfiord, resolved no longer to pursue the enterprise. No settlement had been made, and no profit had yet accrued to the daring men who had undertaken it. The natives were very numerous and hostile, and the people could only live in a fortified camp.

Nothing more would, in all probability, have been attempted, had not a rich Iceland merchant come to Brattahlid, named Thorfin Karlsefne, and surnamed the Hopeful. This was in 1006. While at Brattahlid, he was the guest of Lief, with whom he spent the winter. There was much feasting, especially at Yule-time, and some love-making besides, for Thorfin married Gudrid, widow of Thorstein, before spring came. They spoke much about Vinland, and finally they resolved on a voyage thither. Accordingly they got together a company of one hundred and sixty, of whom five were women, Gudrid being one. "Then," according to the saga, "they made an agreement with Karlsefne that each should have equal share they made of gain. They had with them all kinds of cattle, intending to settle in Vinland."

They sailed on their voyage in the spring, and came to Wonderstrand, where Lief had erected houses. These they found; but not liking the place, they proceeded to Mount Hope Bay, in Rhode Island. But the natives came out of the woods, and troubled them so much that they had no peace. Finally a great battle was fought, in which many of the natives were killed, as were also several of the whites. Some of the latter fell into the hands of their enemies, and were called before a council of the tribe, as they supposed, to hear the judgment of death pronounced upon them. To their great surprise, they found the council presided over by a man as white as themselves, and who addressed them in their own language. He wore a long beard, which was very gray, but in other respects he was dressed like the others. Through the instrumentality of this man, who appeared to be their chief, the whites were liberated on condition of their leaving the country, which they did, after having lived there three years.

This proved to be a most unfortunate speculation for the rich Iceland merchant. Its only value to him was, that his wife, while there, bore him a son, whom he called Snorre, and from whom was descended a line of men famous in Iceland history.

This strange man whom they found at the head of the Skraellings proved to be Biorn Asbrandson, a native of Bredifiord, in Iceland, and who had once been a famous viking, or sea-rover, and had drifted to America, no one knew how. Doubtless it was even before Lief's time. He had left Iceland, and was never heard of until Karlsefne returned, when, from certain articles which this chief of the savages gave him, with directions how to dispose of them, and from a message which was to be delivered to Biorn's former sweetheart, the identity was established. The man himself would give no explanation of who he was, or how he came there. Biorn was therefore probably the first white man to land on the shores of America, if we may except some Irish monks and others whose adventurous enterprises originated the idea of a "white man's land" far away across the sea.

Humboldt, in his Cosmos, basing his observations on

Rafn's "*Antiquitates Americanæ*," declares that Biorn undertook the voyage to the southward from Greenland in 986, the year following Eric's colonization of Ericsfiord. There is, however, a discrepancy between his statement and those of others concerning the course of Lief, "who," as Humboldt says, "first saw land one degree south of Boston, at the island of Nantucket, then Nova Scotia, and lastly Newfoundland, which was subsequently called Libla Helluland, but never 'Vinland.' The gulf which divides Newfoundland from the mouth of the great river St. Lawrence was called by the Northmen, who had settled in Iceland and Greenland, Markland's Gulf." Nova Scotia was called Markland.

The Eric family did not, however, altogether abandon the idea of reaping some profit from America, even with the death of Thorstein, for a sister named Freydis went to Vinland in 1011, and for some time lived in the same place where her brothers had lived before. More unfortunate than their predecessors, they fell not only to fighting the natives, but each other, being instigated thereto by Freydis, who caused a great number of the party to be treacherously murdered in order that she might get control and reap all the profit; yet no good came of it after all.

Other expeditions followed some years later; but, so far as we know, there were no actual settlements made by these Northmen in America. Yet Bishop Eric went to Vinland in 1121, during his Greenland mission (which would make it appear as if people were there to visit), in his ministerial capacity. Occasional voyages were, however, made to the country, at least as far as Nova Scotia. As late as 1347, we have written accounts of Greenlanders going from Ericsfiord to Markland to cut timber.

It will be seen by the foregoing that history presents quite a number of candidates for being the first discoverers of America. Who knows what influence these adventurous voyages of the Northmen may have had upon the discovery of America by Columbus? That great navigator is stated to have visited Iceland in 1477; and may he not then have heard of this land of the grape and vine to the westward? and may not the tales of the Icelanders have encouraged his western aspirations, which are said to have originated as far back as 1470? This supposition would not, however, detract from the great merit of Columbus; for the idea of crossing the Atlantic, and of reaching Asia by the west, was not original with Columbus, nor even with his generation. The glory was not in the conception, but in the execution. It has been said that the name America is "a monument of man's ingratitude;" but this is hardly true, since the name Columbus gave to his own discoveries was, as we all know, West Indies, in the full belief that he was within reach of the rich treasures of the Orient; and even after Columbus's death, and after the conquests of Cortez, Mexico was marked down upon the maps of the period as a part of China, and, indeed, the capital city of the Montezumas was shown to be only a few days' journey *overland* from the mouths of the Ganges. It was not until Balboa had waded into the waters of the Pacific Ocean, and had thus taken possession of the newly-discovered sea, that the idea of a new world, or new continent, having been discovered began to enter into the minds of men. The belief of Marco Polo, who looked out over the ocean eastward from China, and the belief of the ambitious Genoese navigator, who looked westward from the shores of Spain, was the same, and it was shared by every body: this belief being that the Atlantic Ocean extended from Asia to Europe; and what we now call America was nowhere at all in their imaginations.

CHAPTER X.

THE LAST MAN.

The final destruction of the Northmen in Greenland is a matter of melancholy interest. Exactly when it came about we can not know. We have seen that the bishop's see was abandoned in 1409. Prior to that time, however, we have accounts of the desperate straits to which the people were reduced. In 1383 we find the following curious entry in the Icelandic annals:

"A ship came from Greenland to Norway which had lain in the former country six years, and certain men returned by this vessel who had escaped from the wreck of Thorlast's ship. This ship brought the news of Bishop Alf's death from Greenland, which had taken place there six years before."

Of the causes which led to this state of affairs we are not, however, left wholly to conjecture. First came a royal decree (for by this time Greenland had passed over, along with Iceland, from a state of independence into the possession of the King of Norway) laying a prohibition on the foreign trade, and creating Greenland a monopoly of the crown. This was a dreadful blow, and the shipping was practically at an end. Trade must, indeed, have been sadly languishing when six years were required to obtain a return cargo. But "misfortunes never come singly." In 1418 a hostile fleet made a descent upon the coast, and, after laying waste the buildings, carried off what plunder and as many captives as they could. With respect to this latter event, and the generally poor condition to which the colonies were reduced, we find the following appeal of Pope Nicholas the Fifth, written to the Bishop of Iceland in the year 1448:

"In regard," says the pope's letter, "to my beloved children born in and inhabiting the island of Greenland, which is said to be situated at the farthest limits of the great ocean, north of the kingdom of Norway, and in the Sea of Trondheim—their pitiable complaints have reached our ears, and awakened our compassion; hearing that they have, for a period of near six hundred years, maintained, in firm and inviolate subjection to the authority and ordinances of the apostolic chair, the Christian faith established among them by the preaching of their renowned teacher, King Olaf, and have, actuated by a pious zeal for the interests of religion, erected many churches, and, among others, a cathedral, in that island, where religious service was diligently performed until about thirty years ago, when some heathen foreigners from the neighboring coast came against them with a fleet, fell upon them furiously, laid waste the country and its holy buildings with fire and sword, sparing nothing throughout the whole island of Greenland but the small parishes said to be situated a long way off, and which they were prevented from reaching by the mountains and precipices intervening, and carrying away into captivity the wretched inhabitants of both sexes, particularly such of them as were considered to be strong of body and able to endure the labors of perpetual slavery."

Furthermore, the letter states that some of those who were carried away captive have returned, but that the organization of the colonies is destroyed, and the worship of God is given up because there are no priests or bishops; and finally, the Bishop of Iceland is enjoined to send to Greenland "some fit and proper person for their bishop, if the distance between you and them permit."

But the distance did not permit. At least, there is no evidence of any action having been taken, so that this is the last we know of ancient Greenland, and from that time "the lost colonies" passed into tradition.

Who the raiders were who thus gave rise to the necessity which existed for the pope's earnest interference we are not positively informed, but about this time the savages attacked the colonists, as we know from the sagas of Ivar Bere. Previous to this, however, they had appeared upon the coast. This was about the middle of the fourteenth century.

In a former chapter I have alluded to the progress of the Northmen up the Greenland coast, and have mentioned their occupation of an island near Upernavik. But no important settlements were effected farther in that direction than those which were founded upon the banks of what is now Baal's River, where stands the modern colony of Godthaab—a deep fiord, alike in character with that of Ericsfiord. Here there was a considerable population, the colonies being distinguished by the name of West Buygd; while those about Ericsfiord and to the south, towards Cape Farewell, were called the East Buygd, meaning the western and eastern inhabited places.

In the year 1349 intelligence was brought to Ericsfiord from the West Buygd that a descent had been made upon them by the Skraellings. An expedition was immediately fitted out for their defense and succor, and was placed in charge of Ivar Bere (the same who left a written account of his Greenland experiences), who was secretary to the bishop, and lay superintendent of Gardar. He found, however, on arriving there, not a human being left, but merely a few cattle, which he brought away with him. Nor did he discover any enemies. Having accomplished their murderous and plundering design, the savages had retreated with the fruits of their raid, and for a time were not again heard from. But at length they learned of the still greater wealth of the white men lower down the coast, and there they began to show themselves—at first in small bands, but finally in great numbers, until they overran the habitable parts of the country; and, driving the Northmen from place to place, at length wiped them out as completely here as they had formerly done in the West Buygd. The churches were pillaged and burned, and the monasteries of St. Olaf, St. Michael, and St. Thomas were levelled with the earth.

A peculiar interest attaches to the church at Krakortok from the circumstance that here the Northmen made their last stand, and, under the leadership of a man named Ungitok, for some years maintained an obstinate and successful resistance. At this time great numbers of the savages were collected upon the island of Aukpeitsavik (about midway between Krakortok and Julianashaab), under the lead of their chief, Krassippe.

These savages, or Skraellings, were the Esquimaux of the present time. Originally they appear to have been warlike and aggressive. At present they are an inoffensive, harmless people—a change entirely due to the influence of the Danish missionaries and the Moravian Brethren, who have been among them during the past hundred and fifty years.

Whence they came, we can of course only conjecture, since they had formerly no written language of any kind, and possessed only vague traditions of having come from the West. That they crossed from Asia by Behring's Straits, and then wandered eastward along the coasts of Arctic America, until, in course of time, they reached Greenland, there can be no reasonable doubt. Of the period of their original migration we can not, of course, have ground for even a rational speculation. This is, however, wholly unimportant to our present purpose, which concerns only their appearance in Greenland—an event which, as we have seen, happened in the fourteenth century. Could it be that these same savages were identical with those of similar character which Lief and his successors, three centuries before, had found on the shores of Massachusetts, and who were there in sufficient numbers to prevent the Northmen from occupying the country? I think it very probable; and their appearance in Greenland is, perhaps, due to the fact that the tribes now known as Indians (who first appeared upon the eastern slope of the Alleghanies about that time) drove them from their southern hunting-grounds, and forced them to seek safety in the inhospitable North, compelling them to reside upon the sea-shore, because the land produced but little game, while the sea everywhere abounded in fish. Hence their name, derived from the Indian word *Esquimatlik*, applied to them in derision, and signifying "eaters of fish."

In what manner they crossed Baffin's Bay is left in doubt. It would not have been impossible for them to do so in their skin boats. Possibly, however, they went higher up, and crossed over on the ice of Smith's Sound. Some tribes still exist in that neighborhood; and to show their insatiable love of wandering, I may mention that I have found evidences of their presence upon the shores of Grinnell's Land as far north as latitude 81°. It has been conjectured that they came over in fleets of boats, crossing the narrowest part of Davis's Strait, which is less than two hundred miles wide, from land to land. It may be that they were not less influenced by a motive of revenge for the wrongs of their ancestors than fleeing from the Indians who possessed their lands, for they had been sadly ill-used in Massachusetts by the Northmen when they first came there. These Northmen had killed and tortured a great many of them in very wantonness, before actual hostilities began. There might seem to be, therefore, in the destruction of the Northmen by these Skraellings something of retributive justice.

This destruction went on, as we have seen, until the remnant of the race was brought to bay and driven to defend themselves at Krakortok. But they could neither be dislodged nor completely destroyed until stratagem was brought to bear; and the device to which these savages resorted in order to accomplish their purpose deserves to rank with the famous wooden horse of Troy.

This did not, however, happen until after a most desperate attempt had been made by Ungitok to get free from the clutches of his brutal adversaries. He managed, with a large party of his followers, to get over to the island, and in the dead of night he surprised them in their huts, and, with the loss of only one man, destroyed the entire party, putting men, women, and children to the sword. It was a fearful massacre, and a dreadful revenge; but it only further imbittered the savages against the whites, and caused them to redouble their efforts. One man escaped the general slaughter, and carried with him the memory of their burning huts and bleeding wives and children. Two there were at first, and, unhappily for the whites, one of those men was the chief, Krassippe; while the second was his brother. These Ungitok pursued upon the ice (the attack was made in winter), with several men following after; but Ungitok outstripped them all, and, overtaking the brother, ran him through the body, and then cutting off the right arm of his fallen enemy he brandished it in the air, shouting at the same time to Krassippe (who by this time had reached the shore), intimating to him, in an obliging manner, that if he ever wanted an arm he would know where to come for it. Krassippe was now beyond pursuit, so Ungitok returned, well pleased with the trophy he had cut from his victim.

After this Krassippe neither rested by night nor day until he had compassed the destruction of Ungitok and his band. In a fair fight every Northman was good for at least half a dozen savages, and, notwithstanding the destruction they had spread elsewhere, the people of Krakortok held them personally in the greatest contempt. But Krassippe was nevertheless, by numbers and strategy, to get the best of them at last. He constructed an immense raft of boats, over which he erected a low and irregular scaffolding. This he covered with tanned and bleached seal-skins, so that when afloat the structure looked like an iceberg. This he filled with armed men, and turned it adrift upon the fiord, allowing it to float down with the tide towards Krakortok among some pieces of ice. When it floated too fast, the people threw overboard stones, with lines attached to them. These, by retarding the progress of the raft, enabled them to keep in company with the icebergs. Ungitok and his people saw the raft; but so much did it appear like the ice alongside of it, that they never once suspected its character, and the armed men drifted around into a bight almost at the rear of the town. Running the raft ashore, they then rushed up and made for the church by an unfrequented route, which was left unguarded, except close to the town. The sentinel was killed, and the church was surrounded before a single person escaped from it. Then it was fired, and all who were not burned or smothered with smoke met death, as they rushed out, on the points of their enemies' spears. Not a soul escaped except Ungitok and his son, who was but a small boy. With him Ungitok fled to the mountains, and there hid for a time in a cave, where at length he was discovered through the indefatigable exertions of Krassippe. The hiding chieftain was surrounded, and, discovering that his case was hopeless, he threw his son into the lake to prevent his falling into the hands of the savages, who would be sure to torture him, and then prepared to sell his life as dearly as possible. In the end he was overpowered and borne down. While yet sensible, Krassippe completed his revenge by cutting off his right arm, and, flourishing it before the expiring chieftain, he exclaimed, "Thou didst tell me where to come for an arm if I should want one. I have come for it."

Thus perished the last man of his race; and since that day the Esquimaux, whom their defeated rivals had so contemptuously called Skraellings, have held possession of the country undisturbed. They have, however, very evidently decreased in numbers, and where there were once tens of thousands, there are only thousands now. For a long period of time they remained the sole occupants of the country, and nothing was known of them save vague and exaggerated accounts brought by occasional ships—such as those of Davis, Baffin, and Frobisher, who touched at Greenland on their way to the discovery of a north-west passage. In later times, however, the Danish Government (to which Greenland as well as Iceland had become subject) made numerous efforts to recover the "lost colonies," with the hope of sustaining the trade and fisheries. Admiral Lindenau reached the coast in 1605, and carried off some of the savages. Afterwards Captain Hall, an Englishman in the employ of Denmark, took away four others, and shot what more he could, as if by way of amusement. Another, who was not versed in ocean currents, did not get near the land at all; but, becoming frightened at being able to make no progress, he declared that there was a huge magnet in the sea holding his ship, which so alarmed him that he returned home. About half a dozen enterprises followed, the last in 1670, without any further result than the killing of a few more of the savages. Then the "lost colonies" were given up altogether, until that excellent missionary, Hans Egede, went there in 1721, and established himself in Baal's River, near where the West Buygd had flourished. Here he founded the colony of Godthaab. Then came the Moravians; and from that time to the present the re-establishment of colonies, and the civilizing and Christianizing of the natives, has gone steadily on. But nowhere did Egede or his followers find any traces of the race that had dwelt there in ancient times, save those evidences of their decay which I have described. Egede travelled very extensively; and others coming after him have described all we shall probably ever know of this Land of Desolation as it was in the days of Red Eric. Among the most important discoveries were those of Captain Graah, of the Danish navy, who visited both coasts in oomiaks during the years between 1828 and 1832; and after him Dr. Henry Rink.

I will close this historical account of Greenland with a paragraph from the *Dublin Review* of twenty years ago, which has not less interest at the present time than then. "Few people," observes the *Review*, "imagine the extent of these ancient Greenland colonies. At best, it seems to most persons some sort of Arctic fable, and they are hardly prepared to learn that of this Greenland nation contemporary records, histories, papal briefs, and grants of land yet exist. So complete was the destruction of the colonies, and so absolutely were they lost to the rest of the world, that for centuries Europe was in doubt respecting their fate, and, up to a very recent period, was ignorant of their geographical position. To the Catholic they must be doubly interesting when he learns that here, as in his own land, the traces of his faith—of that faith which is everywhere the same—are yet distinctly to be found; that the sacred temples of his worship may still be identified; nay, that in at least one instance the church itself, with its burial-ground, its aumbries, its holy-water stoup, and its tomb-stones, bearing the sacred emblems of the Catholic belief, and the pious petitions for the prayers of the surviving faithful, still remain to attest that here once dwelt a people who were our brethren in the Church of God. It was not, as in our own land, that these churches, these fair establishments of the true faith, were ruined by the lust and avarice of a tyrant. No change of religion marked the history of the Church of Greenland; the colonies had been lost before the fearful religious calamities of the sixteenth century. How or when they were swept away we scarcely know, save from a few scattered notices, and from the traditions of wandering Esquimaux—a heathen people that burst in upon the old colonists of Greenland, and laid desolate their sanctuaries and their homes, 'till not one man was left alive.'"

CHAPTER XI.

A DISCONSOLATE LOVER.

To resume the thread of our narrative. Taking it up where it was dropped some chapters back, I must first recall the day and the situation.

Our lunch was spread under the ample shelter of a tent, which screened us from the rays of the sun, and formed a no bad substitute for the protecting trees under which our picnics are enjoyed in other lands. There seemed to be but one drawback to complete enjoyment. The noonday heat rose above 70°, and started great quantities of small flies and musquitoes. From these pestiferous insects we thought we surely had escaped when we came to Greenland. But no! this was not to be. They attacked us in perfect clouds during the afternoon, and before I had quite completed my survey most of the party had betaken themselves to the oomiak, and hauled out into the middle of the fiord to escape their assaults. But the day was then well spent, and the pleasure-seekers had by this time enough of sport to satisfy them. All had enjoyed the day, Marcus alone excepted. That youth could never restrain his mortification at the havoc he at heart believed the Prince was making with his matrimonial prospects. For that young gentleman persistently devoted himself to the lively Concordia, despite the heat and musquitoes, while she, in grateful appreciation of his attentions, wove wreaths of wild flowers for his cap, sung for him in irreproachable Esquimaux, and performed other coquettish acts of that kind with which recognized lovers are not unfrequently tantalized in other places than Greenland.

Whether Marcus would sensibly have staid at home, had he not been ordered to go by the pastor, I can not pretend to say; but having gone, he was certainly deserv-

CONCORDIA AT THE PICNIC.

ing (or at least he evidently thought so, like any other lover would have done) of better treatment from his inamorata; and, to look at him, you would have thought so too, for he was really a fine-looking fellow—at least for a half-breed. The stolid mask of the Esquimaux did not suit his frank, open face at all, and it was quite impossible for him to show himself at ease when he was not. Whether the Prince discovered the disturbed state of his feelings is not certain, but it is certain that he did not treat the matter with much attention. He never allowed Marcus to approach the object of his devotion to speak with her except once, and then Marcus was overheard to reproach her with flirting with the American—an opinion which was very generally entertained. The lively young lady of the seal-skin pantaloons grew indignant, declaring very pointedly that it was none of his business what she did with the American. Quite taken aback, the young man began to remonstrate with her, evidently under the impression that the Prince had already installed himself deep in the affections which, until this most unhappy day, he thought he had possessed all to himself. Then he began to institute comparisons between himself and the Prince. "Look at him," exclaimed the much-injured lover, "with his pockets full of beads and jewelry! Look at him there, with his pop-gun of a rifle! Do you imagine he could shoot a seal? No, never! And if he did, could he get it home? No! Can he go in the fleet kayak? Can he climb the cliffs of the kittiwake, or gather the eggs of the lumme? Can he dart the spear at the eider-duck? Can he scale the mountain-sides in pursuit of the reindeer? Look at his pale face, and answer me!" and by this time fairly boiling over with rage and vexation as he recounted the Prince's negative qualifications, he exclaimed, "No! he can do none of these things. He is good for nothing!" Then he straightened himself and said, with great self-complacency, "Look at me!"

"I don't want to," said the girl; "I won't!" which terminated the colloquy, for the Prince himself came up at that very moment, and, addressing himself to the indignant lover, desired to know if his mother was intimately acquainted with his whereabouts—an inquiry which might have resulted in serious consequences had the lover understood even so much as a word of it. Without wasting much time, however, upon the injured youth, the Prince called for the music (the boy who steered our oomiak had brought up a cracked fiddle), and then, seizing Concordia by the waist, he whirled her through the old Norseman's grave-yard in a fantastic waltz that must have made the very bones of the dead heroes fairly rattle again. Could those ancient priests, with the bishops at their head, have arisen then and there, they would doubtless have anathematized the whole party on the spot; for others were not slow to follow, and the dance did not wind up until they had gone through with several hornpipes and Greenland reels of a kind, I dare avow, never dreamed of by Terpsichore. Meanwhile Marcus, leaning against the old church wall, looked on in a most disconsolate and defiant manner, with his fists thrust far down into his pockets, as if that were the only safe place for them.

Whatever may have been Marcus's recollections of the day, certainly all the rest of the party had a thoroughly good time of it. The day, however, lost something of its romantic character when the shades of evening began to trail over us, and the sun going down behind the distant glacier-crowned hills left the chilliness of evening to succeed the warmth of noon, as fatigue succeeded to the freshness of the morning.

When, therefore, we had completed our survey of the spot, we were a much more orderly party than we had been previously; and, when once more afloat in our oomiak, we went about from place to place in the fiord, visiting other ruins, with a solemnity more befitting explorers. The jealous Marcus had not now so much cause of complaint against the Prince, yet he did not recover his liveliness of disposition. He paddled along at his post of duty, looking neither to the right nor to the left, saying never a word, but evidently thinking very hard.

As he appeared to be of a very simple and gentle nature, I could but sympathize with him in his present trouble. There could be no doubt that he looked upon his hopes of happiness as forever gone. He had discovered his lady-love to be mercenary—her mind carried away by the Prince's lavish expenditure of beads, ribbons, and jewelry; and all this for a young foreigner with a fair face, who could neither shoot a seal, nor go in a kayak, nor cast a spear! It was altogether most unaccountable. He seemed to be all the time, and naturally enough, comparing himself with his rival, to the great disparagement, of course, of the said rival, else he would not have been a lover, and with great wonderment as to what she possibly could see to admire in the other man. That Concordia meant to run off to America, Marcus evidently did not have a doubt, and his face seemed to indicate at times that he was capable of any deed of desperation in order to prevent so dire a catastrophe. Should he spear him, or put a bullet through him, or any thing of that sort? Especially did his countenance assume a malignant expression when, upon the homeward journey, the coquette would break out with her favorite song, the chorus of which was, "Tesseinowah, tesseinowah," repeated over and over again. At this the Prince always manifested great delight, while Marcus grew correspondingly gloomy.

When we had at length reached Julianashaab, and had thanked the good pastor, to whom we were so much indebted, and had said "good-night" to our oarswomen, I took the unhappy Marcus aside to condole with him. "Are you not," said I, "son of the head man of Bungetak?"

"Ab," said Marcus, and I thought a glow of satisfaction overspread his features at being reminded of his superior parentage.

"Concordia is very pretty," I continued.

"Ab!" said Marcus again, his countenance falling at the recollection of his previous hopes and present discomfiture.

I asked him, "Do you know what pretty girls do in my country?"

"Na-mik" (no), he answered, his countenance falling still more at the further mention of the pretty girl that he had lost.

"When the pretty girl has the chance, she always marries the son of the head man," said I.

Then his countenance assumed a joyous expression, and he went his way with a smile, which said plainly that, if he thought it was not much to be Marcus, it was good to be the son of the head man of Bungetak.

E

CHAPTER XII.

THE CHURCH AT JULIANASHAAB.

The day following our return from Krakortok being Sunday, I gladly availed myself of Mr. Anthon's invitation to attend service at his little church.

Julianashaab is not at any time a particularly lively place, but there is sufficient activity during six days of the week to make the silence of the seventh very marked. Solemnly silent it was to me, as I landed on the beach, and then, beside the stream which flows through the town, made my way towards the temple dedicated to God among the majestic hills. The people, savage and civilized alike, had rested from their labors—the fishermen from their lines and nets; the hunters from their search after game in the valleys; the sound of the cooper's hammer, and the ring of the blacksmith's anvil were no longer heard; even the voices of the inhabitants seemed to be hushed, as if awed by the presence of that divinely ordained day which, it is commanded, shall be remembered and kept holy.

It was delightfully calm; the sun gave a pleasant autumnal warmth to the atmosphere; and altogether it was one of those peaceful Sunday mornings which one enjoys so much at home in the country, when the mind instinctively dwells upon the wonders of nature, and the very soul goes out to the great universal Father whose dwelling-place is everywhere, and whose presence is nowhere felt more strongly than amidst the solemn grandeur of the cloud-piercing hills.

As I approached the church, the only sounds that greeted me were those made by the tumbling waters of the brook until I came very near, when the sweet music of an organ rose above the voice of the glad stream. It was a most agreeable surprise; for I had hardly expected to find here in Greenland any such artificial means of inspiring religious feeling. How far this circumstance may have had an influence with me I can not say; but certain it is, I would not exchange the memory of the notes of that little organ of the small Julianashaab church, as I first caught them there on that peaceful Sunday morning in that Greenland dell, for those of any other church-organ that I ever heard. Afterwards, when I had taken my seat among the congregation, the effect was not the less pleasing as I listened to the voices of the choir, and reflected that they were the voices of God's children, who, through the instrumentality of Christian love, had been reclaimed from barbarism.

As sometimes happens elsewhere, a large majority of the worshippers were women. They generally appeared to be inspired with a devout feeling, which even the presence of strangers could not disturb, and they sang the hymns in a manner peculiarly agreeable.

The Esquimaux language is by no means lacking in euphonious sounds, and, as pronounced by a native, is often music itself. Mr. Anthon had caught the accent and pronunciation perfectly, and the entire service, sermon included, was in the common tongue—a language peculiar to the Esquimaux, and the same with all the tribes.

The organ of the little church is of the quaint device of a hundred years ago, having been presented to the mission by Queen Juliana, in recognition of the compliment paid her by the naming of the town. A native played it with reasonable skill, and the catechist led the singing, in which the entire congregation joined with a good voice.

I have never seen a congregation pay closer attention to their pastor than these rude people paid to Mr. Anthon. They seemed eager for instruction, and drank in his every word. The sermon was well adapted to the minds of a people exposed to the dangers of the sea, as they are continually. As I sat looking at their upturned faces, I could not but reflect upon the great change that had come over the people who subdued the Northmen. Then they were steeped in the worst form of barbarous superstition. Earth, sea, and air were peopled with horrid spirits; now the love of Christ rules in every heart, and they are all, without exception, converts to the Christian faith.

As a specimen of their language, I quote a stanza from one of the hymns sung (with a literal translation appended), which no doubt my readers will find no difficulty in singing for themselves.

Aut nellekangitsok,	That blood, that inestimable,
Pirsaunekangarpok,	Hath a very great power;
Kuttingub attausingut,	A single drop,
Innuit nunametut,	The men that are upon earth,
Annau-sinna-kullugit	That it has power to redeem them
Kringarsairsub karnanit.	From the cruel hater's jaws.

Another, which was an exhortation to all men to come to Jesus, began thus:

"Krikiektorsimarsok
Jesuse innulerkipok."

The services ended, I went with Mr. Anthon to the parsonage, and passed the greater part of the day with his agreeable family. The pastor himself has devoted much attention to gathering the traditions and legends of the people, and in his recital of them I found much entertainment.

CHAPTER XIII.
A GREENLAND PARLIAMENT.

THE condition of the Esquimaux has not only improved spiritually since they arrived in Greenland, but they have improved in their temporal affairs as well. Formerly they led a purely nomadic life, and dressed solely in the skins of wild beasts; now they live in permanent communities, and have adopted the habits and, in some measure, the costume of civilized men. Unlike many savage peoples, the introduction of the forms of civilization among them has not been attended with any corresponding mischief; a circumstance due, in a great measure, if not wholly, to the paternal care of the Danish Government, aided by the missionaries. That care, beginning with the missionary, Hans Egede, has been continued with much skill by his successors, and by none more conspicuously than Dr. H. J. Rink, who has passed a considerable portion of his life in the country, and was, until lately, Royal Inspector for the Southern Districts.

The principal feature of Dr. Rink's administration is the Parliament of natives; and in the establishment of this arrangement Dr. Rink has earned as much credit for skilled benevolence as he had before acquired for scientific explorations; and his efforts are entitled to the highest encomiums.

The civil organization of Greenland is very simple. The six northern districts constitute the Northern Inspectorate, the inspector's residence being at Godhavn; the six southern constitute the Southern Inspectorate, with the inspector's residence at Godthaab. Each inspector's authority is absolute throughout his jurisdiction, and there is no appeal, except to the home government, against his decisions and decrees; but each district within the Inspectorate has certain privileges of its own, granted by the royal will. These privileges are exercised by the Parliament, which is based upon the principle that every native is a subject of Denmark, and amenable to Danish law. Happily, in the administration of that law the people themselves are not denied a voice.

The idea of a Greenland Parliament struck me as something ludicrous when I first heard of it ; but upon gaining an intimate acquaintance with its workings, I changed my mind, and became convinced that if all Parliaments did their work only half as well, the world would be better governed.

The population of Greenland at the present time equals about 7000 souls—an average to each of the twelve districts of near 600. In the district of Julianashaab there are about 800 people, distributed, along the line of its extended coast of a hundred and fifty miles, in a number of small settlements, all pitched either upon the shore of the main-land or some outlying island (it must be borne in mind that the interior is nowhere inhabitable), at some point where there is a convenient harbor. These are all outposts of the capital town of Julianashaab, and their affairs are regulated according to orders received from the governor, or bestyrere, of Julianashaab. Each one is presided over by a Dane or half-breed, whose principal business is to keep the Company's accounts, dispose of the Company's stores, and to gather products for the Company's profit. The stores are brought annually by ship to Julianashaab, and thence they are distributed to the various outposts, and, in like manner, the products are gathered at Julianashaab by the time the ship arrives.

These products consist of stock fish (the cod, dried without salt), eider-down, furs, seal-skins, and blubber, of which the latter furnishes the chief profit.

The Greenlanders, and not the Danes, do the principal hunting and fishing. The store-house of the station is the place of trade, and at certain hours of the day the bestyrere is obliged to have his place of business open.

Now these Greenlanders, or Esquimaux, are not prone to be governed; yet the Danish rule is satisfactory to them, and they submit to it without a murmur, and none the less readily that they have a voice in their own affairs. Each little town or hunting-station is at liberty to send up a representative to sit in the Parliament of Julianashaab. The number of representatives is twelve. The names of the most important towns besides the capital are Nenortalik, Fredericksdal, Lichtenau (these two latter are missions of the Moravian Brethren), Igalliko, and Kraksimeut.

The Parliament-house is not an imposing edifice. I should say its dimensions are about sixteen by twenty feet. It is one story high, is built of boards, lined on the inside, and painted blue, and on the outside is plastered over with pitch. It has no lobby for the accommodation of people who come to the capital with axes for the public grindstone, nor committee-rooms for the better confusion of the public business.

In the centre of the one room there stands a long table of plain pine boards, and along either side there is one long bench of the same material; and on each bench sit six Parliamentarians, dressed in seal-skin pantaloons and boots, and Guernsey frocks, with broad suspenders across their shoulders. The faces of these Parliamentarians are all of a very dusky hue, the color of their hair is very black, and it does not seem to have any greater familiarity with combs and brushes than their faces with soap and towels. However, they are an amiable-looking party—at least they grin and show their fine white teeth when I enter, and are altogether, perhaps, quite clean enough for ordinary Parliamentary work. Every man of them has a pencil in his hand and a piece of paper on the table before him, and each one is as busy taking notes thereon as some of our own honorable members are said to be in taking "notes" of another description.

A GREENLAND PARLIAMENT IN SESSION.

But I must not neglect to mention one article of the Parliamentary costume, for it shines out so conspicuously that it *must* be noticed—I mean the official cap (always worn when the House is in session), which is supplied to each member by royal bounty. This cap is of the brightest kind of scarlet cloth, with a broad gilt band around it; the royal emblems are emblazoned in front, and above these there is a golden polar bear, with a crown on his head, standing uncomfortably on his hind legs, to typify

Greenland. There is a thirteenth cap at the head of the table, and this thirteenth cap covers the head of the genial Mr. Anthon, pastor of Julianashaab, and president of the Julianashaab Parliament, *ex officio*.

The aggregate amount of dignity possessed by this Parliament was quite wonderful, and was, in truth, as overwhelming as the fishy odor with which it was impregnated. But neither the fishy odor nor the dignity appeared to interfere with the transaction of business; on the contrary, they seemed to be working away like beavers, and, indeed, they disposed of matters with such an amazing degree of promptness, that I fell instantly to wondering whether dignity would not be a good thing to introduce into Parliaments, Congresses, Assemblies, and such like things generally; and as to the fishy atmosphere, I have no doubt that it was quite as wholesome as the atmosphere of some of our own legislative halls, where lobbyists are so thick about the doors and avenues, that all the purity which ever does go in is soon done for. Of the kind of business brought before this dignified tribunal, I will give a few samples.

The first was a petition for relief. The petitioner himself stood there in person, looking the very picture of forlorn destitution. He stated that he had lost his canoe (*kayak*), and he produced evidence enough to show, without any swearing, false or otherwise, that it had been crushed and lost in the ice. The man, who had hardly clothes on his back to cover his nakedness, showed further that he had a wife and family, who had no friends to assist them, and were entirely dependent upon himself for support. I thought it a doubtful support at best, and so appeared to think the Parliament, since they voted an order for a small stipend of food and clothing, as per schedule, to be drawn by the wife from the public store-house, and paid for out of the Parliamentary funds. The man was sent to work in the Government blubber-house, at twenty-two skillings (eleven cents) a day.

The next case was similar in character, only the petitioner was a well-known young hunter who had lost his kayak by a fearful accident, which had nearly cost him his life as well as boat, and from the effects of which he had barely now recovered. All that I could comprehend was that some of his ribs had been stove in. The case being proven, the question before Parliament was whether they should grant him relief, which was unanimously voted in the affirmative. How much? was the next question. After thirteen pencils had ciphered for a minute or so, they made it out fourteen dollars (seven American) for material for the kayak, four dollars for harpoon, spear, etc., and six to pay debts contracted at the Government store-house for necessary comforts during his sickness.

A third case was that of an old man who received one dollar to buy a spear with; another was from a man who had a family of girls, and no oomiak. He received twenty-four dollars, one-half of which he was to refund within two years. One hunter got a rifle on the same terms. A sick woman obtained some flannel for a shirt; some orphan children, an order for bread; a widow, the means to bury her dead husband.

These, and a number more of similar character, were soon disposed of. Some of the cases were represented by proxy, the applicant residing at Nenortalik or other distant outpost, whence to come would be difficult; others presented their petitions in person. Some appeals were thrown out in part, or altogether; but these were very few, for public opinion is strong in Greenland, and a lofty sense of pride prevents begging, except in the last extremity. In the case, however, of the kayak and the oomiak there was presented a prospect of future public advantage; for, in encouraging these people by providing them with boats, the public revenues are increased by their adding to the public industry. Thus do we see that as "village Hampdens" and "mute, inglorious Miltons" may sometimes lie in the village church-yard, so savage legislators and lawgivers may be Solons and Adam Smiths all in one, and they not know any thing about it, and the world be none the wiser.

And thus we see these Greenland Parliaments serve an excellent purpose. They take care of the poor; they render assistance to the unfortunate; they provide certain means of punishing the indolent and guilty; they reward the industrious; and when they have finished with their business, they adjourn, and go home to do their talking; and what more do you want with a Parliament? Nobody, certainly, would desire them to vote away millions of acres of the public lands; for, although they might very well do so without injury to any body, there are no dangerous corporations to be benefited thereby, and no public interests to be sacrificed by such procedure, and therefore no motive.

I was much interested in their manner of encouraging industry. The system is regulated on an increased valuation of all products of the hunt and fishery brought to the public store-house after a certain figure has been reached. Then follows a sliding scale of prices, which at the maximum is double the ordinary standard.

The punishments are confined to fines, to be deducted at a certain percentage, until paid, from every thing the hunter sells to the Government; and the means of collection are quite effectual; for, unless the criminal comes into the arrangements of his plan as decreed by Parliament, he is wholly excluded from any participation in the benefits of the colony; that is to say, he is not allowed to buy or trade for any thing—neither a rifle, ammunition, bread, coffee, sugar, nor tobacco — a penalty against which no one was ever known to hold out long. Cases of actual crime are rare. If the offense should be a capital one, or one involving the sentence of a court of justice, the offender, or supposed offender, is sent home for trial to Denmark. But one case falling under this head came to my knowledge. This was a young mother suspected of infanticide. The child that would have dishonored her was found upon a rock whence the tide would soon have carried it off, had not some prying individual there discovered it and taken it to the village, where it was interred. The young woman was charged with having destroyed it. She confessed that it was hers, but that it was dead when born; and since she could not bury it, and could not bear to throw it into the sea herself, she placed it on the rock and hid herself away, that she might not see it disappear. Her story was accepted on the simple ground of the unnaturalness of the crime charged; for the love of the mother for her offspring among these Greenlanders is wonderfully strong. What would our ancesters of a few hundred years back have said to being hauled up for an act like this, when they had not only natural law, as they thought, but human law as well, to support them in "exposure of infants," when they were either too poor or too lazy to provide for all the little ones that were brought into the world?

The funds for the disbursements above mentioned are provided liberally by the Danish Government—not directly, but indirectly—so that the system works to mutual advantage. For instance, the price paid, according to Government, at the public store-room for a seal-skin is, say ten cents, and for the fox-skin fifty cents; which amounts are paid, either in money or in kind, to the hunter, who goes away well satisfied. To this payment the Government then adds a further payment of twenty per cent.—that is, two cents on the seal-skin and ten cents on the fox-skin, which is credited to the Parliamentary account; and so on for every barrel of blubber or other article. Thus, if the cost price of the products of the district of Julianashaab should reach fifteen thousand dollars, the Parliament would have a fund of three thousand to dispense in charities and benefits. This sum bears no relation, however, to the commercial value of the several articles in the Copenhagen market. For there a fox-skin, which is worth in Greenland one Danish dollar (nearly equalling our half-dollar), is worth in Copenhagen from ten to thirty; and most of the other products swell in the same proportion during the voyage across the Atlantic. So in like manner, though not in the same degree, the value of a pound of bread increases on the voyage from Copenhagen to Greenland. Yet such are the expenses attendant upon the transportation, the keeping up of special Greenland bureaus at home, the wear and tear of the sixteen ships of their fleet, and the cost of the Mission, that, notwithstanding this arrangement of values, the Royal Greenland Fishing and Trading Company turns in a very small sum annually to the royal treasury. Some years they actually run behind. And so it comes about that, since there is not much in the best of times to be squeezed out of this Land of Desolation, the Company simply suffers its business to go on in the old even tenor of its ways—every thing systematic and orderly, its ships neat and well disciplined, its officers honest and capable, its sailors well drilled for any emergency that may call them into the naval service, the mission schools and the churches well kept up. If by this means a few officers are provided with small but sufficient salaries, and a number of people are supplied with comfortable livings (and are sure of a pension if disabled, and their families provided for when they die), surely no great harm is done to any body if the Danish Government is not greatly enriched; while, on the other hand, seven thousand human beings, but for this admirable system, instead of living in the light of Christian civilization, and in the enjoyment of its benefits, would still be steeped in that same condition of barbarism that their forefathers were when they overran the fair villages of the ancient Northmen. To-day the two races live in perfect harmony, and in mutual dependence on each other. A single Dane may be surrounded by a hundred descendants of the murdering and revengeful Krassippe, and is encouraged by them in every thing he may attempt to do.

These all seem like homely practices; but then it must be borne in mind that Greenland is a long way off, and the Danes are a gallant people. I do not believe there is any other country in the world that would maintain colonies and support missions without some prospective advantage to themselves. There is one prohibitory act, which the Company exercises in all these colonies, which I can not refrain from mentioning before I quit this interesting subject. It is the commendable policy which they pursue in absolutely excluding that villainous "fire-water," that has played such a conspicuous part in the demoralization and destruction of our own Indians. Once a year only are the people allowed to smile at the bottom of an empty glass. This is on the king's birthday, when every ablebodied man in Greenland is allowed to march up to the Government store-room, there to receive, each in his turn, a glass of "schnapps," which he drains to the health and happiness of the mighty *Nalegaksoak* who occupies the Danish throne. The women are excluded; but a man may kiss his wife just when he pleases, without offense to any body; and, while in the act, he may drop from his own capacious maw (like the cooing dove that feeds its mate within the cot) whatever portion of the king's bounty he may feel inclined to spare, and nobody be any the wiser for it; nor can any body be much hurt, as the schnapps glass is none of the largest, and the wife's portion is not likely to be more than the half.

A system which is thus kept so well under control, with the niceties of administration so carefully preserved, could hardly be otherwise than successful. In fact, I do not see that any thing of human devising could better suit the purpose of its founding than this Greenland Company, which transacts business and does good works under the name and title of "Kongelige Grönlandske Handel, i Kiöbenhavn."

It was founded in the year 1781, much upon the same plan as that of the Hudson Bay Company. The whole trade of Greenland is, through this Company, an absolute monopoly of the Crown, and a foreigner is not allowed to trade to the value of a skilling with Dane or Esquimaux— a system which all the better enables the benevolent intentions of the Government to be carried out, as spirits and other hurtful articles can be excluded from the country. The Company is controlled by a Directory in Copenhagen (Kiöbenhavn properly); and to its present presiding officer, Herr Justitsraad C. S. M. Olrik, knight of Dannebrog, and formerly the enlightened and genial Inspector of North Greenland, the Company's increasing prosperity and usefulness are largely due.

CHAPTER XIV.

A GREENLAND BALL.

Monday was occupied by our party in a very agreeable and profitable manner—by the photographers especially, who, early in the day, took possession of one of the governor's rooms, and photographed the whole town and nearly every body in it. The following day was fixed upon for our departure; but the only pilot in the place was otherwise employed, and we were forced to wait until he was ready for us. In short, he was bringing in another vessel, and one of infinitely more importance to Julianashaab than any number of *Panthers*. It was the one ship of the year, a ship bringing to the colonists their supplies for the next twelve months, and was to return home laden with the wealth which they had gathered.

I do not remember any thing in all my experience in Greenland that has left a stronger impression upon my mind than the arrival of this ship, nor any thing which made the isolation of the Danes who dwelt there so apparent. In these days of telegraphs, and steamships, and quick transit everywhere, it is rather painful to contemplate civilized, refined, and Christian families being a whole year without once hearing from the world. To be sure, it has its advantages, for they are saved many annoyances, and are spared the everlasting bore of writing letters for the mail. But then, what hopes and fears the mail must come charged with when it comes but once a year! with what almost terrible anxiety they must look for news from home! what changes may have taken place in the year gone by! what may Death not have done with the loved ones in that long interval! Fathers and mothers, brothers, sisters, and friends, are sending tokens by that winged messenger across the sea; but what if they should be sad ones, and not those they hoped for?

When the announcement was made that the ship was in the offing, the excitement was at first intense, and the hours of the day while the ship was coming up the fiord, with baffling winds, were most anxious ones. Of course, there were many exceptions. Indeed, the people generally could have no other possible interest in the arrival of the ship than the mere selfish one of what they would gain thereby. I speak only of those Danish residents who were bred in Denmark, and whose friends dwell there now. To these, the arrival had something in it of a painful character, mingled with anticipated pleasure. Hope and fear seemed alternately to prevail in the breasts of the families of the governor, the pastor, and the doctor.

Meanwhile, every boat in the settlement had gone down to assist in towing up the ship; and at length the sound of splashing oars was heard upon the still night air; then voices were distinguished calling to each other or issuing the word of command. Soon, above the rocky point of the harbor, we saw the tops of two masts, with their black yards, creeping nearer and nearer; then a vessel burst in view, through the brilliant moonlight. The ship was now pointed for the harbor, and was coming slowly up beside us, towed by half a dozen boats, and surrounded by a swarm of men in their little kayaks, shouting, talking, and gesticulating, in their exuberant happiness.

I stood upon the *Panther's* deck watching this scene of animation, until the anchor had gone into the phosphorescent sea with its unearthly "cr-r-r-r-r-r-up." The mooring-lines were soon all out and made fast. The crowd of people then left the sea, and no sounds were heard but the orders on board the newly-arrived vessel for stowing the sails and making every thing snug on board. Then I heard people getting down into a boat; the oars were splashing again, and, as I traced the streak of phosphorescent light that trailed away and lengthened as the boat receded, I knew that it was carrying ashore the mail, with all its freight of words.

The vessel proved to be the *Tjalfe*, one of the best of the Company's vessels—a brig of three hundred tons, and as taut and tidy as a man-of-war. I had a visit from her master in the morning, and was rejoiced to find in him an old friend, to whom, in 1855, when I had escaped with Dr. Kane from the abandoned brig *Advance*, I was indebted for many serviceable attentions—Captain Ammondsen, one of the most tried and trusty servants of the Royal Company.

Upon going ashore in the morning with Captain Ammondsen, I was pleased to learn that every body's letters brought good news. We found them in a wilderness of papers, and books, and packages, containing every conceivable thing that thoughtful friends would think of sending to cheer and gladden lives that must be at times overwhelmed with loneliness. It was very touching to see these evidences of remembrance scattered about, and very gratifying to be a partaker of the general joy. Photographs were there by the dozen; one of a little stranger that had come into the world within the twelvemonth, and sent his compliments and his picture; another, of a newly-married couple, who looked peculiarly happy for people who had been married nearly six months, and sent their picture in proof of it; another was from an aged mother; another, from a brother who had gone into the army; another, from a boy at school. I went from house to house, and everywhere it was the same. Happiness was universal; and it really seemed as if solitude might be " sweet society," if retirement brought such occasional bliss: only, the retirement of a year for the sake of the emotion is a little too much for ordinary mortals.

As for the people in general, they were delighted beyond expression. Nothing but the presence of actual starvation could possibly have induced any hunter to go out at such a time. Shouting and singing were the order of the day. The harbor was alive with their cunning little kayaks, shooting hither and thither, the boatmen indulging themselves in the most ludicrous speech and gesture, by way of exhibiting their satisfaction, not only at the arrival of the Danish ship, but that two vessels were in the harbor at one time—a sight which they had never seen before. Then, to cap the climax, when the evening came they would have a dance. Every body was invited, and, of course, none of the sailors of the two ships made any objection to a frolic of that nature. They had not shared the people's satisfaction in the least; they would be glad enough, on the other hand, to be anywhere else almost; but a dance! what sailor could resist that? And as for our officers and passengers, all were alike ready for a little fun, to break the monotony of life, either as actors or spectators, and willing to take a hand in any thing that might be turning up.

I asked the governor if there was nothing to be feared from letting two ships' companies loose among the peaceful villagers, where there were no police to take rude fellows into custody? "Oh no," he answered, "not in the least; let them come. If the men are rude, the women will take care of themselves, I promise you; and if not, they have big brothers plenty. Have no fear; there are no more modest women in the world than these Greenland girls, and sailors are notoriously quick to detect honesty, and, when found, to respect it."

So a dance was arranged for, or a "ball," as our people facetiously called it. The carpenter-shop was secured for the occasion, and a neighboring shed for a supper-room; and the preparations went on all the afternoon. The orchestra of Julianashaab (consisting of a dilapidated keg with heads of tanned seal-hide, and the cracked fiddle already mentioned) was secured, and all was ready by eight o'clock, when I went ashore to see the opening.

The decorations of the ball-room in the way of flags, and Danish and American bunting generally, were astonishing to the natives. Candles were stuck around the room in reckless profusion. Maria had about a bushel of coffee, which she was roasting and boiling in the shed. The whole village was in commotion. Women in red boots, women in white boots, women in blue, and green, and yellow boots, were hurrying to the ball-room from every quarter. They had all turned out in their very best, and some of the toilets were, to say the least, stunning. Boots, beads, pantaloons, and ribbons were all of the gayest and the finest. The maidens and matrons of Julianashaab sustained the credit of their sex; and they showed, too, that they were conscious of appearing to better advantage than usual; for they looked about with less timidity than on ordinary occasions, as if to say, "Look at me *now*, and see what I *can* do when a great occasion makes it worth my while." Several of them were pretty, and quite stylish, and certainly this is saying much, for their peculiar style of costume is rather trying to the ordinary female figure. As for dancing, no costume could possibly be more suitable, and, when on the floor, its advantages were quite apparent, for I have rarely seen dancers that were more light and graceful in their movements.

I would not, however, be understood to recommend the dress for general adoption by dancing girls.

The confidence with which the ladies approached the ball-room seemed to forsake them when they had got inside and there awaited the men; for the moment they had passed the door they darted to the remotest corner, where they all huddled together as close as they could pack themselves, like a flock of frightened sheep run one by one into a pen. The men did not keep them long in this state of timid embarrassment; but they seemed, however, to be in no very particular hurry, sauntering along quite leisurely, with their hands in their pockets, and short clay pipes in their mouths. Most of them were capless, and none of them seemed to have thought of "dressing" for the occasion, except the Parliamentarians, who, out of respect for their own dignity (as I suppose), wore the official scarlet on their heads, royal emblems, gold lace, and all—a top-covering which, taken in connection with their Guernsey frocks, broad suspenders, and huge seal-skin pantaloons, coming up under the arm-pits, made a style of official get-up not, I fancy, to be seen in any other country. Yet the lord chancellor wears his frizzled wig, and why not they their scarlet caps?

The sailors came ashore from the two ships, jabbering away at each other quite frantically, in Danish and English; and the officers and passengers came likewise.

But where was Concordia the while, and where was the Prince? for they were to open the ball. The question was asked repeatedly, and as often remained unanswered. Whispers began to pass around the room. Had there been an elopement? Marcus was there, trying hard to look unconcerned by smoking a short clay pipe, and keeping his hands in their usual place of safety. Every body seemed to look to him for explanation.

At length the mystery was cleared up, and very suddenly, for the Prince came bouncing into the room holding Concordia by the hand. The arrival created a sensation. Concordia was literally dazzling. The Prince had clearly been assisting at her toilet. She was covered with beads and jewelry. A magnificent plaid shawl which the Prince had sported through the voyage, and which had two days before suddenly disappeared, now reappeared in the shape of a jaunty jacket, trimmed with eider-down, on Concordia's graceful shoulders. And then, what shining pantaloons of the softest silver seal-skin! what spotless, snow-white boots inclosed her dainty little feet! But the Prince — ah! what a stunning get-up, to be sure! Sea-boots matching Concordia's for length, if not in purity of color; a bright scarf across his shoulders and around his waist; a Scotch cap, with a dissipated feather in it — what a picture for a ball-room! No wonder that Marcus grew several shades lighter in color; no wonder that his pipe fell out of his mouth and broke in pieces on the floor; no wonder that he stole out of the room as if the place were too hot for him, and should show himself no more in the ball-room that night!

"Strike up!" shouted the Prince, bringing down a sea-boot on the floor. "Rat-tat-a-tat" went the keg, "cr-r-r-p cr-r-r-p cr-r-r-p" went the cracked fiddle, and then both went in to do their best and win; but the keg, having got the lead, kept it, and the cracked fiddle was nowhere. When both had become well warmed up in the race, the Prince brought down his sea-boot again, making the old carpenter-shop fairly quake and tremble; then, with a shout which was probably taken for an American war-whoop, he seized Concordia by the waist; others followed his example, and never did "Pop goes the Weasel" do duty before to such a whirl as followed.

CONCORDIA DRESSED FOR THE BALL.

The ball was opened! The Prince and Concordia had gracefully done their duty, and satisfied the public expectation. They had given countenance to the revelry, and the revelry went on. To say that it never stopped, would be to exaggerate; but to say that it never would have stopped had there been something of what Dick Swiveller called "the rosy," might possibly be, to speak the truth, within bounds. The revellers certainly made "a night of it," if a night ever was made in a Greenland summer. As it was, the coffee had all given out, a whole box of tobacco had disappeared, the keg had resolved itself into its original staves, and the cracked fiddle had but one string left, and that had been twice tied, when the ladies, with their beautiful boots all knocked out of shape, began to drag their weary bodies off to their huts, and the sailors, with their coats on their arms, hailed for boats.

Meanwhile, much consternation had been produced by a report which was set in circulation, that a Parliamentarian had danced himself away, all but his cap; and a girl had, in like manner, disappeared, all but a ribbon. The consternation was allayed, however, when it was discovered that the two had stolen away together, and were getting married at the parson's.

Marcus never appeared again in the ball-room after his discomfiture; but I saw him crawling in the shadow of a rock, where he could look through the door and catch an occasional glimpse of his lady-love as she swung round in the Prince's arms. He beckoned me to him, and whispered in my ear, pointing to the gay and festive room from which the bright light was streaming out into the night, "He no good; me" (pointing to his breast) "son of head man of Bungetak." Saying which, he smiled in a self-satisfied and "bland-like" manner, and immediately drew himself deep within the shadow of the rock. Then I

F

went my way on board, marvelling how very much a man was half-savage Marcus.

As this was my last visit ashore, I had bidden my friends good-bye, after exchanging some little souvenirs with them. Early in the morning the anchor was tripped, and we were away. The little town in the wilderness was at our backs, and we were threading once more the winding fiord among the islands and icebergs, rejoiced at having seen a spot of earth so full of romantic associations; had beheld its ruins,

> "Trod upon them, and had set
> Our foot upon a rev'rend history."

"But these recede. Above me are the Alps,
The palaces of Nature, whose vast walls
Have pinnacled in clouds their snowy scalps,
And throned Eternity in icy halls
Of cold sublimity, where forms and falls
The avalanche—the thunderbolt of snow!
All that expands the spirit, yet appalls,
Gather around these summits, as to show
How Earth may pierce to Heaven, yet leave vain man below."
Childe Harold.

PART THE SECOND.
PALACES OF NATURE.

CHAPTER I.
ICE AND SNOW.

In the previous chapters we have traced the history of the Norman-Greenlanders from their first appearance to their decay. We have witnessed their early struggles, have observed them in their prosperity, and have stood beside the ruined edifices erected by their hands, and read there a mournful story of a fallen race.

Upon the causes of their fall we have, however, barely speculated. Among them all, none possess an interest to equal that one mighty cause which has been silently working there for countless ages. Beside those determined Northmen, Nature herself was erecting edifices which, by destroying the life-giving heat of the atmosphere, paved the way for poverty and death. With just propriety we may call these edifices palaces of Nature; and now to examine them will be our task. To do that, we leave the fiord of "the deserted homes" and steam into one that lies to the north of it. This is called the fiord of Sermitsialik, which signifies "the place of ice."

And here we will witness phenomena such as are not to be witnessed elsewhere in the whole known world. These phenomena exhibit results grand beyond any thing in or upon the earth, not excepting the earthquake and volcano.

This fiord of the ice is about of equal length with that of the "deserted homes." The two are separated from each other by a mountain-ridge which culminates in the Redkammen. The same ridge continues to the south, and, reaching the sea again, incloses the region of Ericsfiord, and the little earthly paradise where dwelt the kings of the sea in ancient times.

The mountain-ridge which thus encircles Ericsfiord like a horse-shoe has no break in it, and it is therefore a barrier. Northward of it there is another great ridge, and between the two there is a wide valley. This valley comes down to the sea at the head of the fiord of Sermitsialik, but it is not green like the valleys that lie beneath the shelter of the ridge of the Redkammen, but is filled with ice. This ice is in places more than a thousand feet in depth, and from two to four miles wide—occupying the valley completely.

The ice which thus fills the valley is called a glacier. *Ice-stream*, however, the Danes distinguish it, thus marking the difference between it and the *eis blinken*, which we call the *mer de glace*, or ice-sea.

The ice-sea is the great reservoir of ice which covers the interior of Greenland, and the glacier of the fiord of Sermitsialik is but a branch—a stream—that descends from it through the valley to the fiord. It is one of many hundreds of similar streams which are to be seen upon the Greenland coast, and by which the precipitations from the atmosphere are discharged into the ocean. They correspond to the rivers of other lands. These precipitations are in the form of snow. The air, which dispenses heat and cold, drought and moisture, life and death to the uttermost ends of the earth, is not neglectful of Greenland. The air soaks up the vapor from the sea, and drops it as snow-flakes upon the sides and summits of the Greenland mountains. These snow-flakes harden to ice, and the process goes on until the mountains are covered, as Mont Blanc of the Alps is covered, and the ice flowing down their sides has filled the lower lands between them. In many places this process has so long continued, that the valleys between the mountains here and there have become level with the summits of the mountains themselves, and there is a desert waste of whiteness, smooth almost as the sea, as void of life as Sahara, and more dreary to look upon.

I ascended once to such a level plane, reaching eighty miles from the coast, at an altitude of five thousand feet. This ascent was upon the glacier, at an angle, when I first set out, of about six degrees with the horizon; but afterwards, upon the *mer de glace*, it was by a scarcely perceptible acclivity. Unhappily I was set upon by a tempest. The temperature sank to thirty-four degrees below zero, having steadily fallen to that point as I climbed higher and higher in the air. Nothing could possibly be more terrible than a wind under such conditions, except, perhaps, a furnace-blast. Mercury hardened almost to the consistency of lead. The moisture of the breath froze on the beard in solid lumps of ice. The nose and cheeks grew white, and life was in danger. The drifting snow which came whirling along the icy plain was like the sand-clouds of the desert, which oftentimes overwhelm travellers. There was no chance for life except in flight. I was accompanied by five persons, who were all less accustomed to such exposure than myself. We turned our backs to the wind, and descended as rapidly as possible to the level of the sea, where the temperature was zero, at which degree of cold life is supported without inconvenience.

It would be difficult to inflict upon a man greater torture than to expose him to such a storm. The effect, after a time, is to make life undesirable. First comes alarm, then pain, then lack of perception. When one dies from freezing, it is the brain which first suffers eclipse. True, the cold has not solidified it, but has made it torpid, like certain animals in the winter-time, with which one may do any thing and they will not resist, being quite incapable of receiving an impression. One of my comrades said, " I can not go any farther; I do not want to; I am sleepy; I can not walk." Another said, "I am no longer cold; I am quite warm again; shall we not camp?" This proved that there was the greater need of haste and exertion, if we would not all be destroyed.

The whole continent of Greenland is, say, 1200 miles long by 600 broad. This gives 720,000 square miles of superficial area, and, assuming the ice, which covers the greater part of it, to have the very moderate average depth of 500 feet, we have a grand total of 70,000 cubic miles of ice—a result which seems almost fabulous.

It is not uninteresting to know that all this vast accumulation of ice is the property of Denmark. And there are probably few persons who understand fully the loss we suffered when we failed to purchase from that country the earthquake island of St. Thomas; for it was then in contemplation, should the Senate ratify the treaty of annexation, to open negotiations for buying up all these Greenland glaciers and the Iceland Yokuls besides. And there can be little doubt that the Danish king would have gladly sold out the whole of them. A king who does not appreciate the value of an earthquake can hardly be expected to bestow his confidence on glaciers.

CHAPTER II.
GLACIERS AND ICEBERGS.

BEFORE proceeding with our narrative we will dwell a little upon the great phenomena of nature to which the previous chapter called attention.

We have seen that the great sea of ice which covers Greenland, and makes it the Land of Desolation that it is, is formed from snow-flakes. That formation takes place only in certain conditions of temperature, which of course vary with the degrees of latitude.

The formation of glaciers has been for a long time a fruitful source of speculation among men of science. Into these we will not enter at any length, for my purpose is rather to give the results of personal observation and incidents of adventure, than to recite either the facts or reflections of others. Yet a few words of discussion may not be here out of place.

Every reader is aware that in the upper regions of the atmosphere the moisture which is precipitated on the mountain-top assumes the form of snow, while down at the mountain's base it is rain. In descending a mountain nothing is more common than to pass from one condition to the other—first a storm of dry snow, then moist snow, then water. In Greenland the snow falls dry. The mountains are lofty, and it never rains upon them at all. A fresh layer of snow is laid on every year. Should this continue uninterruptedly, of course the mountains would rise to an indefinite extent. Enormous quantities break loose and roll down the mountain-sides in avalanches; but this is but a small amount in comparison with the deposit. The glaciers are the means of drainage of these great snow-fields. These snow-fields are turned to ice by a very simple process, and the ice flows to the sea.

The surface snow on the mountain is white, dry, and light. Deeper down, it is hard; still deeper, it is clear transparent ice. The clear ice which forms such grand and beautiful arches of blue and green in the glaciers as seen along the Greenland coast, was once powdery snow upon the loftiest mountains, probably in the very interior of the continent. The transformation is an interesting process, and the movement of the ice itself from the mountain to the sea is one of the strange mysteries of nature. With respect to the former, Professor Tyndall has stated the case so clearly that I can not refrain from quoting the following passage from his excellent work entitled "The Glaciers of the Alps:"

"Could our vision penetrate into the body of the glacier, we should find that the change from white to blue essentially consists in the gradual expulsion of the air which was originally entangled in the meshes of the fallen snow. Whiteness always results from the intimate and irregular mixture of air and a transparent solid; a crushed diamond would resemble snow. If we pound the more transparent rock-salt into powder, we have a substance as white as the whitest culinary salt; and the colorless glass vessel which holds the salt would also, if pounded, give a powder as white as the salt itself. It is a law of light that, in passing from one substance to another possessing a different power of refraction, a portion of it is always reflected. Hence, when light falls upon a transparent solid mixed with air, at each passage of light from the air to the solid and from the solid to the air, a portion of it is reflected; and in the case of a powder, this reflection occurs so frequently that the passage of the light is practically cut off. Thus, from the mixture of two perfectly transparent substances we obtain an opaque one; from the intimate mixture of air and water we obtain foam. Clouds owe their opacity to the same principle; and the condensed steam of a locomotive casts a shadow upon the fields adjacent to the line, because the sunlight is wasted in echoes at the innumerable limiting surfaces of water and air.

"The snow which falls upon high mountain-eminences has often a temperature far below the freezing-point of water. Such snow is *dry*, and if it always continued so the formation of a glacier from it would be impossible. The first action of the summer's sun is to raise the temperature of the superficial snow to 32°, and afterwards to melt it. The water thus formed percolates through the colder mass underneath, and this I take to be the first active agency in expelling the air entangled in the snow. But as the liquid trickles over the surfaces of granules colder than itself, it is partially deposited in a solid form on the surfaces, thus augmenting the size of the granules, and cementing them together. When the mass thus formed is examined, the air within it is found as *round bubbles*. Now it is manifest that the air caught in the irregular interstices of the snow can have no tendency to assume this form so long as the snow remains solid; but the process to which I have referred—the saturation of the lower portions of the snow by the water produced by the melting of the superficial portions—enables the air to form itself into globules, and to give the ice of the *névé* its peculiar character. Thus we see that, though the sun can not get directly at the deeper portions of the snow, by liquefying the upper layer he charges it with heat, and makes it a messenger to the cold subjacent mass.

"The frost of the succeeding winter may, I think, or may not, according to circumstances, penetrate through this layer, and solidify the water which it still retains in its interstices. If the winter set in with clear frosty weather, the penetration will probably take place; but if heavy snow occur at the commencement of winter, thus throwing a protective covering over the *névé*, freezing to any great depth may be prevented. Mr. Huxley's idea seems to be quite within the range of possibility, that water-cells may be transmitted from the origin of the glacier to its end, retaining their contents always liquid."

We have thus briefly explained the process by which the mountain-snow changes its character, and, without actually melting and again freezing, the clearest ice may be formed from it, and go on accumulating, layer by layer, to an almost inconceivable extent.

I allude now to mountains generally, for Greenland is not the only ice-factory of the world. That country has by no means a monopoly of the business, for nearly all parts of the earth have their great reservoirs of ice formed in the same manner from snow as the ice of Greenland, only with this difference, that the climate and the temperature necessary to the formation of glaciers from snow is higher above the sea-level in most other places than in Greenland. This climate and temperature are found above what is called the "snow-line"—that is to say, a line above which the snow does not disappear in the summer, and is therefore perpetual. At the equator this snow-line is of course higher than either to the north or south of that point. Towards both poles it descends steadily. For instance, on the two great equatorial mountains of Chimborazo and Popocatapetl, it is about 15,000 feet; above which all is ice and snow, and below which vegetation, beginning with an arctic type, passes through all the stages of climate, until at its base we find the rich vegetation of the tropics. Frequently glaciers from that upper region descend into the lower regions of vegetation to a considerable distance, but they are gradually melted away at the end, and can not, therefore, go beyond a certain line, terminating in, or rather changing from streams of ice to rivers of water.

By the time we have gone so far north as Greenland we have discovered a great depression in this snow-line. In latitude 61° north, I have observed it to be 2400 feet. I

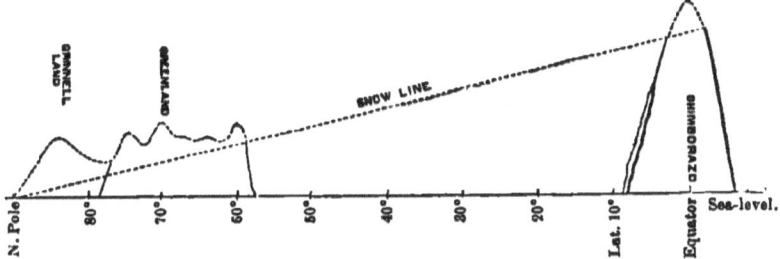

have found it to be 1700 feet at latitude 69°; at latitude 78°, it was 500; and at between 80° and 82° the snow-line appeared to touch the sea, having no belt whatever for vegetation.

The piling up of these mountain-snows is like the processes of a geological epoch in the steady growth by deposit. There is this difference, however, that ice formed in this manner is not, like rock, hard and unyielding, but, like putty, is, in a measure, ductile. In fact, it *flows* downward, and the superabundant accumulations find their way thus to the ocean. It is estimated that the snows of the Alps would increase the altitude of those mountains four thousand feet in a thousand years but for this strange ductile property of ice. As we have before seen, an ice-stream is, in effect, a frozen river, flowing at a very slow, but still at a very perceptible rate. The rate of flow in the Alps, variously estimated by different explorers and at different places, where there were different degrees of descent, is from six to fourteen inches daily. In Greenland the rate, as determined by me, is about from five to eight inches daily. The Greenland glaciers possess another marked difference from those of the Alps. The ends of the latter, descending into a lower and warmer level, are melted off, and disappear as the end of a tallow candle would disappear if held near a hot stove. Before this takes place, the ice, descending through the valley, conforms to all its inequalities, and the actual river which ultimately takes its rise from the glacier front does not more readily mould itself to the rocky bed over which it flows—widening and contracting, deepening or shoaling as the river-bed expands and narrows, or increases and diminishes its declination. An ice-stream, or glacier, like the river, has therefore its cascades, its rapids, its broad lagoons (so to speak), and its smooth, steady, even flow. It carries rocks along with it upon its surface (rocks which have fallen upon it from the cliffs along its sides), as the river carries sticks of wood; and, when the ice melts, these rocks fall in front, and, rolling down the valley, form *moraines*. But with the Greenland glaciers the result is different. The end of the glacier never descends into a level that is warm enough to melt away the end of it, as in the Alps, but it reaches the sea in all the glory of its cold and crystal hardness. When this happens, its end penetrates the water, and makes a coast-line of ice. The temperature of Greenland, down even to the water-level, is too low to allow of any considerable melting, but the result is the same. A fragment breaks off from the glacier and floats away upon the ocean, and is drifted to and fro with the ocean currents. Rocks which may have fallen upon the glacier from the cliffs are inclosed within it, or are carried upon the top of it.

The fragment which has been broken off, as above described, is known as an *iceberg*. This iceberg is dissolved but slowly as it drifts south with the arctic current, often reaching as far as the Banks of Newfoundland before it disappears entirely. Often it endangers vessels crossing the ocean, and it deposits at the bottom of the sea its burden of rock and sand, as it melts down. The Banks of Newfoundland have received constant accessions in this way. It was in like manner that those great boulders which we find upon plains, like our Western prairies, were deposited at a period when they were the bed of the ocean, and icebergs drifted that way from the Arctics.

And thus it will be seen that the Alpine glaciers and the Greenland glaciers, although disappearing by different direct processes, come to the same final end—the mountain-snows reach their natural home in the sea at last.

Many of the Greenland glaciers are of amazing extent. There is one sixty miles wide. Its front is in the water, and it is washed by the waves like any other coast-line. The rock-cliffs on either side of it are very lofty, from five hundred to a thousand feet. The ice-cliffs are from fifty to three hundred. Below the surface of the water this wall of ice extends downward to the bottom, and in places the depth is over two thousand feet. This great glacier, the largest known, lies at the head of Smith's Sound, and was discovered by Dr. Kane, who called it the Great Humboldt Glacier.

Another, twenty miles across, may be seen in North Greenland, in the fiord of Aukpadlartok. This I have surveyed, and shall have occasion to refer to it hereafter. There are several that are five miles over; others two and three, and indeed of every size, down to the very diminutive one that might be called an ice rivulet. Many of them have reached the sea, as already stated—some of them ages ago, others very recently; others have not yet flowed so far; but in all cases the flow is steady, and the accumulation within the inland reservoir goes on. The flow of a glacier may be likened to the great flood which sweeps down the valley from a broken dam. Though it comes very slowly, it comes very surely. It is irresistible. It moulds itself to the hill, it swells up over an acclivity, it pours over a cliff, and pursues its course with a strength and impulse that is grand and terrible to behold. And it is not noiseless, for its movement is attended with constant breaks, sometimes extending through its entire body. The sound occasioned thereby is truly appalling. The glacier is, therefore, often an object of real terror. The whole region is, in fact, full of startling wonders and novelties of nature. Its history is replete with violent convulsions. Once those were of fire, for the country shows evidence of volcanic heat; now they are of frost. The Land of Desolation is worthy of more consideration than it has ever yet received from the learned and curious, or even the adventurous.

CHAPTER III.

THE SOLITARY HOUSE OF PETER MOTZFELDT.

It is time now that I should recur again to the *Panther*, which we left steaming out of Ericsfiord.

When the revellers from the Julianashaab ball appeared after breakfast we were well away at sea. Most of them had either forgotten or had never been aware of the intention of the captain to sail so early in the day. When, however, they discovered where the steamer's head was pointed, they were well pleased with the sudden change, and found a lively satisfaction in the prospect of new fields for adventure; all except the Prince, who was (or at least so affected) much grieved that no opportunity was allowed him to go ashore after the ball. The captain may, indeed, have anticipated some possible mischief to the young gentleman, and so lifted his anchor when all were sound asleep. What, indeed, might possibly have happened may be readily guessed from an account of what actually transpired, according to our sagaman, who wrote the following description of it:

"It was a thousand pities, sure, to wound a tender youth in his most tender spot; the ship had sailed three hours when first he found that she was steaming off at least 'six knot.' The youth was furious, vowed he would go back, and cried, in anguish, 'Launch me that kayak.' The kayak was the pilot's, so he failed to sacrifice his very wretched life; then, after groaning once or twice, he hailed the steward: 'Here, man, as you love your wife, go quick and bring me paper, pen, and ink. I'll write a letter; then my will, I think.'

"Sad are these partings to the virgin heart—I mean the heart that never felt decay; when all the life has been the sunny part; no shadows flung into the gladsome day; and hard, indeed, it was upon our Prince; it was his first affair, and made him wince. No wonder! But the ink and pen were here; and so our hero grew more reconciled; he dashed away—they say it was a tear; and wrote, and wrote, and grew exceeding wild. Here's what it was, and, if you're so inclined, you may learn something of a tortured mind:

"'Concordia, dear! Concordia, dear! My heart is with thee on the lonely isle; I'm forced to say adieu to thee, I fear, for I am carried off; I slept the while; I did but sleep that I might dream of thee, and, sleeping, off they carried me to sea. Concordia, dear! Concordia, dear! Thou only on this earth my heart hast got. Oh, listen to me while I shed a tear, of which I have shed enough to fill a pot. I'd fill a dozen could I go to thee; then from this lonely isle away we'd flee, o'er the glad waters of the deep blue sea; our thoughts quite boundless, and our hopes quite glad. Those seal-skin breeches! oh, Concordia! they are bewitching, and they make me mad; and then that top-knot on thy head so fair, I've yards of ribbon for thy raven hair. My messmates all, hard-hearted fellows they! do call me spooney when my pain they see. Ah! who can tell my sufferings, thou away? I'll ever be a faithful spoon to thee. My image in thy bosom once install, I'll take them then, ay, breeches, boots, and all.'

"Which, and much more such stuff outlandish, our hero wrote unto his lady-love; doing it in very bad Greenlandish; he'd billed and cooed with her like turtle-dove; learning thereby a string of *koos* and *kahs*, and these he emphasized with ohs and ahs. A language which all maidens understand, of each and every nationality; you may write Greek and Choctaw with the hand; a maid will comprehend a sigh, you see; and every lover, be he green as grass, will wisely sigh, if he would catch his lass.

"The letter written, then the pilot went, bearing the missive with abundant warning, to take it safe and go where he was sent, and give it to the maiden in the morning. It must have touched her, Heaven only knows! the steamer steamed away; and thus it goes!—The tenderhearted must be torn away—sometimes it is 'stern parient,' sometimes steam. In this particular case you'd surely say, 'The Prince is certain now to kick the beam.' Oh no, not he! The youth but went below, slept, woke, then cried, 'Now for another go!'"

And another "go" he had, and we all had, sure enough, but of a very different character from the Julianashaab "go."

By keeping well inside the islands, which almost everywhere form a barrier along the Greenland coast, we managed to escape, in a great measure, the ice which had so much annoyed and alarmed us when we first "made" the Land of Desolation. Towards evening, our pilot, who had been on the bridge most of the day, approached the captain, and said:

"Captain, you see?"

"Yes," said the captain.

"Two icebergs there—go between."

"Yes," said the captain.

"Starboard then"—explaining further the route into the port—"no, hit rock—go for iceberg—port, no deep water—starboard, plenty ice—port, small—starboard, plenty—let go—Kraksimeut—you see?"

"Yes, pilot," said the captain, "certainly, clear as mud;" then, addressing himself to another quarter, he cried out, "For'ad, there!"

"Ay, ay, sir."

"Lay out on the jib-boom and keep a sharp look-out for rocks. Stand by to heave the lead."

"Ay, ay, sir."

And now, what with dodging first one way and then the other, and with taking the ice first on one bow and then on the other, with shaving the rocks most uncomfortably close, they managed, between the pilot and the captain, to give the *Panther* a pretty lively time of it, until we had finally come into a very narrow basin of water, where, in apparent danger of running our jib-boom into a solitary house, the order was given to "let go"—and we were at anchor in the harbor of Kraksimeut.

There was a great number of people about the solitary house. So far as appearances went, Kraksimeut comprised this one house only, and it was but one story high. Over it floated a Danish flag about the size of a pocket-handkerchief.

"My house," said our pilot. "Governor's house, Kraksimeut—me Governor."

Our pilot was Peter Motzfeldt, already mentioned in a previous chapter; and a right noble fellow is Peter Motzfeldt, if he does live in a solitary house, and *is* governor of Kraksimeut.

Kraksimeut stands upon a very small island, on the very outer extremity of the dividing ridge between the fiord which we had left and the fiord for which we were bound. In order to reach it, we have sailed north-west; to reach our next halting-place in the other fiord, we are to sail north-east. It is a good half-way station, and we resolve to spend the night there.

Peter Motzfeldt invites us ashore, and ashore we go to the government-house. The people we see are like those of Julianashaab; they smell of fish exceedingly. There is not another white man except Peter Motzfeldt. His wife is there, but she is a native, and has the inevitable native boots, and seal-skin pantaloons, and short jacket, and horn-like top-knot of hair, tied about with a profuse quantity of ribbons. Peter Motzfeldt's twenty odd children are there, including the two boat-loads heretofore mentioned, who had gone down to Julianashaab to see the sights, and have returned in anticipation of our arrival.

The scenery around this solitary house is dreary enough; there are only faint traces of vegetation in the crevasses of the rocks, and there is a glimpse of water only to be seen here and there among the icebergs and islands; but there is a golden sky above the setting sun, and golden splendors dropped from heaven upon the sparkling jewelry of the sea.

I took a walk about the island, and came back to the solitary house, after all my comrades had assembled there, to encounter a great surprise. Instead of finding this only white inhabitant of the place

"Steeped in poverty to the very lips,"

he was rejoicing in abundance. Eatables and drinkables were on the table in great profusion; pipes, tobacco, and even cigars, were circulating freely, and a livelier party than that which greeted me on my arrival would be difficult to imagine. They had literally taken possession of all there was to see of Kraksimeut, including Motzfeldt himself, whose genial face beamed upon me through the mists which arose from a steaming punch-bowl; and, as he stretched out a hand to give me welcome, he bowled down at least half a dozen bottles.

"Have a cigar?" said the Prince, passing along a box out of a smoky cloud. "Capital Havanas! plenty of the same sort left."

The Prince was clearly quite at home, as usual, and was already looking out generally for the public pleasures; for he continued:

"Lively times expected. Old chap there has sent for girls, and we're to have a dance."

And sure enough he had; for the girls came streaming in presently, and there was a repetition of the Julianashaab "break-down" (I know no better title by which to distinguish it). Of course, the Prince managed to pick out the prettiest girl, who had the advantage of being the daughter of Motzfeldt, and, by a pleasant coincidence, bore also the name of Concordia. This one had black hair and eyes, however. But, since there did not appear to be any Marcus to torment, the young gentleman clearly preferred the girl (with the auburn hair) he had left behind him.

Kraksimeut is one of the dozen principal outposts of the Julianashaab district, and the most remote one on the north; and it is, besides, one of the most productive. Its products are exclusively (if we except a little eider-down), the skins and blubber of seals; and during the season it is, according to all accounts, a very lively place. Peter Motzfeldt gets his pay out of the colony's production, upon which he receives five per cent. This, added to his salary (one hundred Danish dollars), makes his income over a thousand dollars of that money annually, and sometimes reaches fifteen hundred, which equals about seven hundred and fifty of ours. Upon this he has lived happily, as he says, and I do not doubt it, for fifty years. He has raised two families, and provides now for twenty-four persons, himself and wife included. This wife is a most tidy person, a native, with a slight mixture of Danish blood, and dresses always in the native costume. Indeed, there is not, and never was, a petticoat in Kraksimeut. From pitying Peter Motzfeldt, as I did at first, I began in the end to wonder whether he was not a most sensible fellow after all, when I discovered that his income was more than sufficient for his needs, and that even, although his family was large, he lacked for nothing that he wished to send for from Copenhagen. Really, it is not so bad after all, to be the solitary white man, in a solitary house, on a solitary island.

Besides the Motzfeldt family, there are about forty other inhabitants, all natives, who live in the usual native huts, that are scarcely distinguishable in the general waste of rock.

I found that an American had been at Kraksimeut before, and that Motzfeldt preserved the most lively recollection of the "Americana," who had taught him the little English he knew, and instructed him to sing "Yank Doodle" and "Hail Columby," which he repeated for us with variations not originally made and provided. This American was Colonel Shaffner, who some years ago, after the first failure of the Atlantic Cable, interested himself to establish a line by way of the Faröe Islands, Iceland, Greenland, and Labrador; and it was a pity that his scheme was impossible of success. You would think so at least if you heard Peter Motzfeldt praise him; and I doubt not that he well deserved it all, for there have been few more spirited enterprises set on foot this many a day. I say it was impossible of success; not that the cable might not be laid and the shore-end secured, but it would be simply absurd to think of keeping it in a sea where icebergs ground in two or three hundred fathoms water.

On board the steamship *Panther* there was a man, common enough in point of rank, but the like of which never was seen before with respect to qualities. He was the *mate*. Why he was ever put there in that capacity, unless it was to "try our virtue by affliction," I can not imagine.

He would beat a "reformer" any day for wrong-headedness, or a discontented donkey for obstinacy. As if these qualities were not enough, he was afflicted with the curiosity of a magpie. But the particular direction of his curiosity was aquatic. He was great on finding bottom. Upon one occasion he tried to find it by dropping overboard a gun; on another he got into a kayak and shoved off from the ship's side, to find himself very quickly head downward, with the boat fast to his heels; and he would have been as certain of drowning as if he had undertaken to swim with his feet fast to a bladder, had his head not struck bottom, where luckily there was a lot of sea-weed, which he grasped and drew himself out among the shells and slime; there he got a footing, and, the water being shoal, he came right side up, with a great deal of water and very little breath in him. Had his disposition to find the bottom with the top of his head terminated there, it would have been well; but unhappily his weakness extended to the *Panther's* keel. If there was the remotest chance of putting her on the rocks at any time, he was sure to make the effort. And he was, moreover, very sly. He always waited until the captain was down below or had gone ashore, before he gave his mind to it. At Kraksimeut, he waited until the captain was well enveloped in a cloud of smoke, in the house of Peter Motzfeldt, before he tried the depth of the water in the harbor. Slacking up a rope, or neglecting to put out one, it matters not which, he let the *Panther* swing with the tide, and her stern slid up as nicely on a rock as if she were coming to her bearings in a dry-dock. This astonishing mate then, with great apparent satisfaction, looked over the stern, and amidst the mud and sea-weed, which had been loosened, and which was bubbling up about the rudder-post, there read XIV.; and thus he had found the depth of

Kraksimeut harbor, and was satisfied. Then he smoked his pipe while waiting for the water to fall; and we came on board to find the *Panther's* stern going steadily out of the sea, with great danger of breaking her unfortunate back. Meanwhile the mate was never before known to be in such capital spirits.

Fortunately, as it happened, the *Panther* was not materially damaged, owing to her amazing strength of backbone; but we were detained nearly a whole tide beyond our time. But when at length under way, we had a splendid sail among the islands, until we struck the open water of the fiord of Sermitsialik, when we stood fairly up midway between its lofty banks, directly for the glacier.

For a time we could not see the object that our eyes so eagerly sought, owing to a bend in the fiord, but, passing this, a great long line of whiteness came gradually out against the sky, and beneath it dropped a white curtain to the sea. As we proceeded this seeming curtain became a solid wall.

G

CHAPTER IV.

THE GLACIER.

How shall I describe the scene which steadily opened to us as we steamed rapidly up the fiord.

Imagine it! The fiord is two miles wide; the valley beyond is of corresponding width, and the glacier fills it perfectly. How thick it is, of course, can not be told, but hundreds of feet it must be everywhere; it is probably from one to two thousand feet in many places. The banks of the fiord continued to be the banks of the glacier for about ten miles, gradually vanishing to a wedge-like point, and merging then into the great *mer de glace*, which, expanding to the right and left above the highest hills, carries the eye away upon its boundless surface as upon the ocean.

At length the inclined plane was lost; the distant line of the *mer de glace* was lost also, and we were beneath a line of ice-cliffs from one to two hundred feet high, as clear as the purest crystal, and emblazoned with all the hues of heaven.

A cold shudder crept over me as the vessel steamed in close to the front of this great reservoir of frost. The sound of falling waters filled the air, and ever and anon deep sounds, which seemed like convulsions of the earth, were emitted from it. The falling waters were of melted snow and ice from the surface of the glacier, which, gathering into streams of considerable size, leaped over the cliffs, and sent a cloud of spray floating away upon the air to resolve the sun's rays, giving back to the eye the fluttering

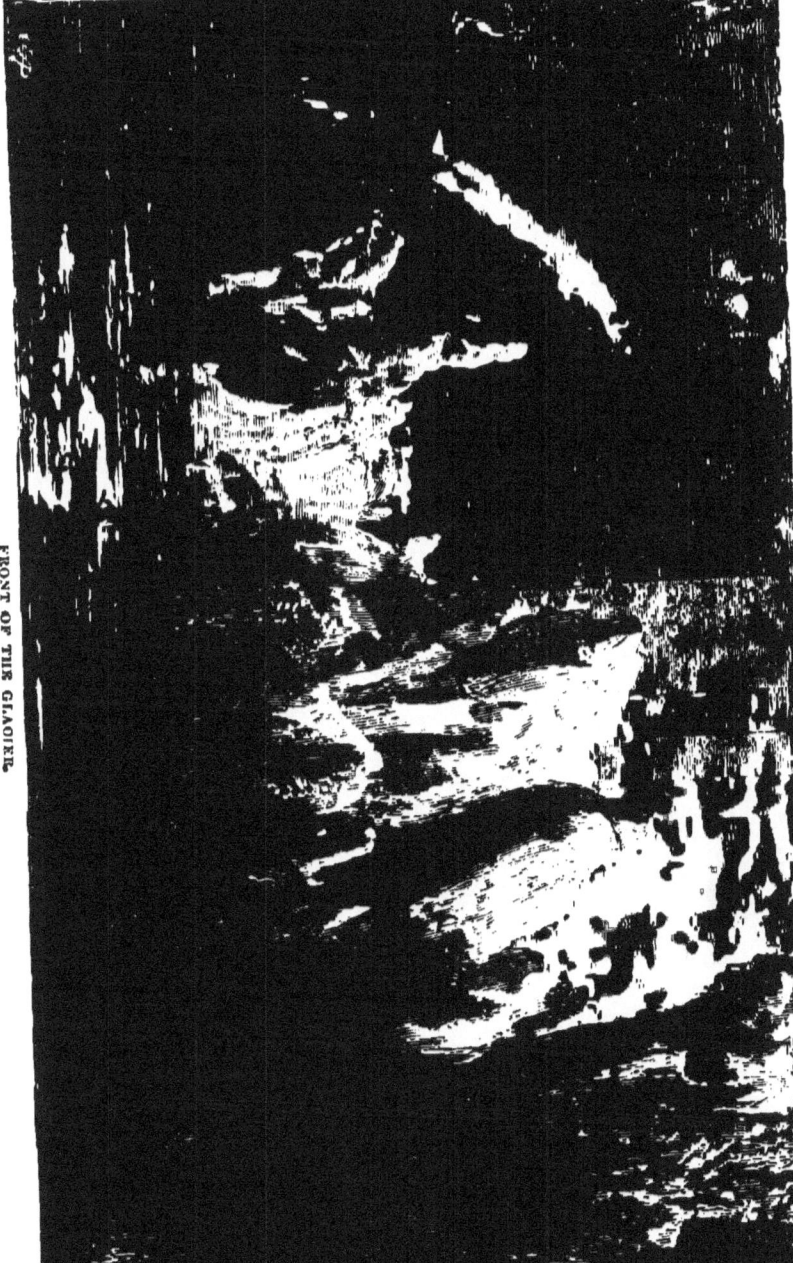

FRONT OF THE GLACIER.

fragment of a rainbow. The sounds were occasioned by the movement of the glacier in its bed, and the resulting chasms which opened from time to time in the ice.

We probably enjoyed here an opportunity such as was never enjoyed by any previous explorer. I know of no glacier accessible as this is, for the reason that the fiords are interrupted either with islands or shoals, which, by preventing the free discharge of the icebergs that break from the glacier front, render the navigation of the waters quite impossible, even to a boat. Such is the character of the glacier of Jacobshavn, in Disco Bay, North Greenland, which I have made the most strenuous efforts to ascend, and which is crowded with a perfect wilderness of icebergs for the space of nearly thirty miles, often being so tightly packed together as to be scarcely distinguishable from the surface of the glacier itself, even when one looks down upon the fiord from an elevation of a thousand feet.

But the fiord of Sermitsialik presents no such embarrassing feature. The water steadily deepens from the glacier front (where in one place it is 270 fathoms) towards the sea; and the current being rapid, owing to causes which I shall presently have occasion to explain, the icebergs float away as fast as formed. While coming up, we passed several of large and many of small size, but none of them were aground, and all were hurrying out to the ocean, as if in haste to mingle their crystal particles with the rolling waves, and once more enjoy the freedom of the boundless sea.

We approached the glacier to the left, and when so near that we had barely more than room to wheel about we changed our course, and slowly steamed over to the opposite side, a distance, as I have before observed, of nearly two miles.

I have spoken of the glacier front as a wall, a cliff, and a coast-line. As a coast-line it is winding; as a wall or cliff it is perfectly vertical; but it is far from smooth. On the contrary, it presents the most fantastic collection of forms that can be conceived of—caves that are apparently limitless, peaks like church spires in symmetry, Gothic arches, clefts that wind away until they are lost in deep blue. And in this blue we see the most perfect of all transparent hues, changing too with every moment, and subtle as the colors of the opal. Talk of painting it! the "light of a dark eye in woman" would not be more difficult. The green of the caves is not less subtle, nor less beautiful. This green is observed wherever the ice overhangs the water. In the sunlight the surface is pure white, except where there has occurred a recent fracture; and the effect is that of the most delicate satin, in all its changes of surface, produced by the different angles in which the light is reflected to the eye.

We enjoyed a most excellent opportunity of observing all these phenomena while passing over, as we went only at half speed, and spent almost an hour in reaching the opposite side. Near the centre, and not far from the front of the glacier, we found the deepest water, the color of which changed, soon after passing the centre, from a light green to a dirty brown. The cause of this was soon explained. The eastern side of the valley, in which the glacier rests, is much deeper than the other side, and the waters from the surface of the *mer de glace*, and the glacier itself, which find their way down through the chasms, gather in the deepest portion of the valley, and, rushing on over the rocks beneath the ice, reach, finally, the front of the glacier, where they bubble up like a huge, seething caldron—a Stygian pool of fearful aspect. This muddy water discolors that side of the fiord all the way to the sea; a circumstance which I was quite at a loss to account for until I had actually witnessed the cause of it, and seen the *Panther* carried, by the force of the current, bodily off from the glacier against the action of her helm.

I have mentioned the irregularity of the line of the glacier front. It presented numerous projecting angles. Near the centre, it forms almost a right angle. Thus do we observe how much more rapidly the centre of the glacier moves than its sides.

Having reached the southern shore, we discovered the water to shoal very rapidly at thirty fathoms from the rocks, showing that there was a wide shelf there; and, upon ascertaining that it was good holding-ground, and finding nineteen fathoms, we anchored, and swung into the stream, which was there found to flow at the rate of four knots, thus accounting for our inability to cross over without drifting away from the glacier. Our anchorage was a hundred fathoms only from the ice-cliff, and this rising two hundred feet above the surface of the water, it seemed, at that short distance, to be hanging almost over us. To one at all familiar with the tricks of glaciers it was evident, from the first, that the situation was one of danger. But the captain, who was solely responsible for the vessel, appeared to like his holding-ground, which was thick mud, and said that if we were going to stay at the glacier, there's where the *Panther* must continue, for there was no other anchorage, as he could see. It was accordingly determined to take the risks, such as they might be, and hold on there until the morning, at the least.

We went ashore after supper and, climbing over the rugged rocks, ascended to the summit of a hill twelve hundred feet above the sea, and saw the sun go down behind the mountains; and against the brightness of the sky, in the lingering twilight, we beheld the great ice-sea of Greenland, lighted with the gorgeous tintings of the clouds. Oh, what a sight it was!—that desert waste—its cold, hard surface glittering with a borrowed splendor, and taking to itself the robes of heaven, as if to cheat the memory of its right to hold it as the very type of what might ever bear the name of Desolate.

CHAPTER V.

CROSSING THE GLACIER.

THE night did not prove promising for the safety of the *Panther*. At intervals alarming sounds proceeded from the glacier, and now and then a quick sharp crack, followed by a heavy thud, would tell us that a mass had split from it and fallen to the sea, which in the morning was covered with small fragments that had been thus disengaged; and masses, some of them of considerable size, were drifting past the vessel with the current.

At an early hour I set out to cross the fiord, accompanied by the captain, with the purpose of seeking a harbor, or at least a more safe anchorage. Owing to the loose ice, the passage was not accomplished without difficulty. In many places the boat could not be propelled with oars, and we were obliged to push our way along by main force, using the boat-hooks and the oars as poles.

The scene had greatly changed in every respect from the day before. Besides the fragments of ice upon the sea that had been broken off during the night, the sky was leaden, and there was a perfect absence of color everywhere. The ice was a dull cold gray, the atmosphere was chilly, and, although our labors were by no means light, overcoats were not uncomfortably warm. The sun had scarcely risen above the hills when we reached our destination, where we were fortunate enough to find a good anchoring-ground, with plenty of room to swing, in a bay where there was no current and very little ice. There being only five fathoms water, there was no chance of any large pieces of ice coming down upon us. Accordingly it was determined to shift our ground; but, since we had come so far, we concluded that we would go farther; and so we landed, to find ourselves upon a green slope, with the side of the glacier to our right, a cliff to our left, and a gorge in front. Over the green slope we walked half a mile, then through the gorge a mile farther; and, having arrived at this point, we concluded to cross the glacier, and to return to the opposite side of the fiord on foot rather than by boat. So we sent back our crew and set out upon a hazardous adventure.

The captain, always ready for any proposition of an adventurous nature, had quickly responded to my own desires; in fact, he was the only man on board who was always prepared for whatever might turn up. Such another captain there never was, as I believe. Brave almost to temerity; yet, possessing excellent judgment, he was just the man to get into a difficulty, and the very man to get out of it. Although only twenty-five years old, he had, nevertheless, been eight years in command of one sort of craft or another, and was a thorough sailor. Buoyant and clever besides, he was always good company; but on a journey his indefatigable zeal and long legs were apt to lead his companions a lively race.

We had no difficulty in climbing the side of the glacier, at a point where the slope was almost thirty degrees. The ice here contained much foreign matter—stones and sand—which deprived it entirely of a slippery character. In a few minutes we were on the summit, and a dreary scene it was that met us there. Imagine the rapids above Niagara Falls congealed to the very bottom; the falls and river frozen everywhere, and Lake Erie solid: then imagine the banks above the falls lofty like those below, and yourself standing on the rapids. Imagine Lake Erie so near that you can see its frozen surface, and you have, on a small scale, the *mer de glace* which we saw when looking at the glacier. The frozen rapids are the glacier itself; the falls below, the glacier's front (with the horseshoe reversed); the river sweeping down to Lake Ontario is the fiord; and Ontario itself the ocean, into which the icebergs drift that break away from the glacier, and go off with the current.

There is this great difference, however—the river, from bank to bank, is straight upon the surface, while the glacier curves. The accompanying cuts will better illustrate my meaning.

It was along the gorge formed by the curve of the glacier on the one side, and the slope of the land on the other, that we made our way up from the sea, all except the first half mile, which, as I have said before, was over a green slope, formed by the lofty land breaking away and leaving a beautiful spot which is one day destined to be completely covered with the ice-flood. And it was such a beautiful spot that I could but regret its ultimate blotting out; for, notwithstanding the wall of ice that was so close to it, it was covered with thick brush-wood, consisting of birch, dwarf-willow, and juniper; among which were matted tufts of heather, crake-berry, and whortleberry; and many bright flowers were here and there scattered over a rich turf of grass and moss. A greater contrast could hardly be imagined than between this spot of green which we had left and the glacier upon which we stood.

Here the glacier is two and a half miles wide. To cross it was no easy matter; nor was the effort without danger, for it was full of cracks, into which we were constantly in dread of falling from the slippery ridges which separated them. These cracks, or crevasses, were, in a general way, parallel, running inward and upward from the shore at angles varying with the locality, but averaging about forty degrees. In places they were very near together, being separated by only a few yards; in other places they were twenty or thirty yards apart. But they were continually running into and crossing each other, although pursuing a general sameness of direction. It was this circumstance that gave to our journey its dangerous character; for as we followed the ridges in their course inward and upward we were, from time to time, brought to a stand at a sharp point where the two chasms united. We had then to spring over an unfathomable abyss, or to retrace our steps and seek a better track. Sometimes we did the one, sometimes the other. Luckily we were both sure of foot; yet the leaps were often such as could only have been made under the spur of curiosity to see, or the no less common one of unwillingness to abandon an undertaking.

Towards the middle the travelling became better. Here, for the space of a couple of miles, there was a dead level, and the ice was very little disturbed; while above, where the glacier appeared to have poured over a precipice, or at least down a very rapid descent, there was the most wonderful jumble that can be conceived of. The crevasses there ran in every direction, though the prevailing one was, as in other places, inward and upward. The ice appeared at one point to have been let down by successive stages, forming a series of terraces, or escalades, which might be likened to the steps of some giant temple. Indeed, it was a stairway befitting the grand palaces of nature which lie away upon the mountain-tops beyond.

I never tread these ice-wildernesses without awe. One sees so much, and yet so little. There is nothing to withdraw the attention from one sole manifestation of nature. In other places as in the forest, where there is life in various forms; by the sea-shore, where there is perceptible movement, and at all times something suggestive of life; anywhere, indeed, almost, the thoughts are not concentrated upon one, and only one, peculiar force. There is something almost terrible in this boundless desolation. God seems nearer in these deserts; His laws, which never change, are not hidden from the consciousness by delighted senses; and the mind is there inspired with a lofty emotion when contemplating the simple grandeur of His handiwork.

I was particularly impressed on the present occasion. The groaning of the mighty river of ice, which could not have been less than a thousand feet in depth, was constant, and proceeded from every side; even beneath my feet there seemed to be an uneasy trembling; and how much soever I might have been alarmed, I would not have been surprised had a yawning chasm opened beside me or underneath me at any moment.

These deep voices of the ice were, however, not the only sounds that greeted the ear; for rivulets meandered here and there over the icy plain. In one place many of these uniting formed a considerable stream, that ultimately found a crack into which it fell roaring and hissing down through all the vast depth of ice to the glacier's bed, there to help swell the stream which, as before described, pours out from beneath the glacier into the fiord.

By this time the sun was well up, and the day was growing warm. Even here, upon the summit of the glacier, the temperature was not at all chilly or uncomfortable. The ice and snow were melting rapidly, and our inconvenience was rather from dampness than from cold, for we were often, in our efforts to get along, compelled to crawl upon all-fours, or even flat upon our bellies, to get over treacherous places, so that our clothing was soon thoroughly water-soaked.

In crossing the middle part of the glacier we experienced little difficulty; but when we had begun to descend towards the opposite shore from where we had started, our troubles of the beginning were renewed, and even magnified. It became often a serious question whether we could proceed at all—whether we would not, after all our labor, be compelled to return. The crevasses were then of great width, much too wide for us to spring over, and, after winding to and fro, springing here and there, we were several times forced to take our leaps over again on the backward track, as there was no place to be found where a leap forward seemed possible. At length, as we neared the shore, the case became desperate. After much effort we found ourselves out upon a very acute angle, with a deep chasm on each side. Two crevasses had here crossed; but from the two sharp points there appeared to be a bridge, or at least a connecting link. When the cracks were formed a large mass of ice had apparently fallen off, and become wedged between the walls as one sometimes sees a rock in a mountain gorge. It had not fallen far, and was not difficult of access, but it was sharp like a house-roof, and slippery as a house-roof when covered with sleet. It was, clearly, take this natural bridge, or turn back and return over all the tedious distance which we had already traversed. This, however, was not to be thought of while there was a possible chance; so we tossed hats for the first venture, and the lot fell to me.

CROSSING THE CREVASSE ON AN ICE BRIDGE.

Getting down on all-fours, I crawled out as far as I could go in that way. I then bestrode the ridge, and propelled myself along upon my bare hands, making a few inches headway with each effort. On either side there was a bridge, with a yawning depth of blue beneath me melting into "darkness most profound," from which came the roar of falling waters. It fairly made my head swim as I clung insecurely to the sharp, narrow, slippery bridge and looked down first one side, then the other, into the abyss. Retreat I could not, even if so disposed, for I had descended from the start, and could not back myself up with my hands, nor could I turn round. There was nothing to do but push ahead; and this I did, cheered on by the captain's shouts to be careful and not break down the bridge, for he wanted the use of it. Finally, the effort was rewarded with success, and as I scrambled up the slope and along the ridge of the other side to a place where I could sit down and rest myself, I experienced a profound sensation of relief. The captain followed, and, after accomplishing the feat successfully, as I had done, he said, looking back at the dangerous pass, "Well, I don't want any more of that sort of thing," a sentiment which I very heartily echoed. But the very next crack we took, although having much less the appearance of risk, had like to have proved fatal to me, for, on a leap of about eight feet I partly missed my footing, and fell short of my intended mark. When I felt myself going back I experienced that horrid sinking feeling which comes over one only with the prospect of immediate death, without the chance for a struggle. So far as I could know, I was gone; and in an instant more I should have been plunging down into the chasm, had not my foot brought up on a slight projection, which gave me an opportunity to use my hands; and the captain coming now to my assistance,

I scrambled up to a place of safety. After this we encountered no more serious difficulties, and, discovering a smooth slope, we descended by it to the shore, which we reached very wet, very sore, and much fatigued.

We were about two miles now from the vessel, which distance was traversed through a gorge corresponding to that by which we had ascended on the opposite side of the glacier. It was, however, much rougher, and the shore being more abrupt, the disturbance, both of rock and ice, was much greater. And here we observe a most interesting feature of the glacier movement and formation.

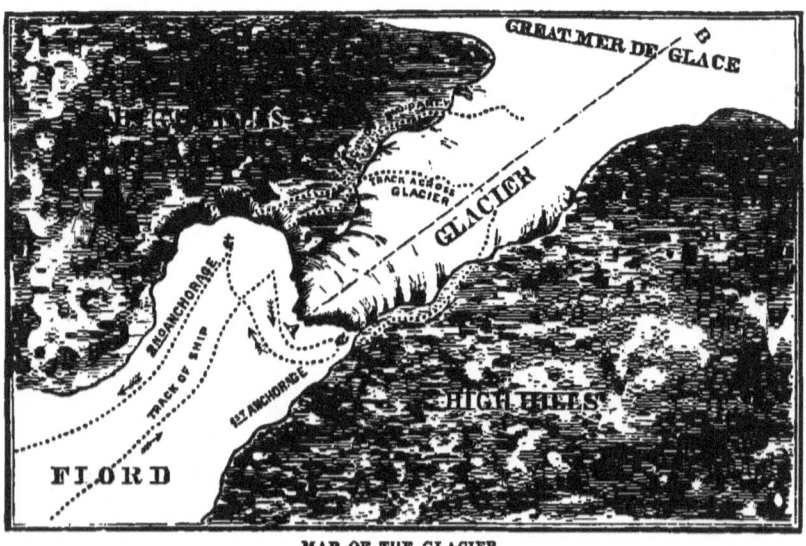

MAP OF THE GLACIER.

The glacier, in its progress down the valley into the fiord, must necessarily adapt itself to every inequality of the bank. But this is not done without serious resistance. Thousands and millions of tons of earth, sand, and rock are rooted up, and pushed aside when the glacier expands into the side valleys, and, when a solid cliff receives the pressure, the crushed and disturbed condition of the ice, as the glacier impinges against the rock, shows how immensely powerful is the force. Something must give way before this irresistible flood. In one place there was a ridge rolled up to the height of fifty feet, and rocks weighing hundreds of tons were treated as if they were the merest pebbles turned over and scattered by the mould-board of a plough.

Our descent through the gorge was not without interest of another character. Down near the fiord the disturbance of the ice had been greatest in consequence of passing over a more rapid declivity, and here several cracks opened from the bottom, and, closing more or less perfectly at about fifty feet altitude, appeared like the mouths to great caverns. Inspired by curiosity, I entered one of these, to find myself scrambling along over rocks and through deep mud, while water dropped down upon my head in torrents, for a distance of about thirty yards, when I came upon the border of a rushing stream of muddy water. This was the stream already mentioned, which gushes out from beneath the glacier's front.

Of all the signs and tokens of watery tumult that I have ever witnessed this excelled them all. The roar of the fast-flowing stream as it dashed down the steep declivity over the rocks beneath, and against the ice above, breaking around the enormous boulders upon which the glacier was supported, was perfectly deafening. I had come in alongside of a ledge of a rock about ten feet high, upon which the ice rested firmly. This ledge, terminating where I stood, formed a protecting barrier, behind which I could witness the spectacle in perfect security, though not with comfort, for to be drenched with ice-water is not at all agreeable.

As I stood here, I realized more perfectly than ever before the process by which have been formed those markings on the rocks which Professor Agassiz has so conspicuously pointed out in regions which were once covered with ice during the glacial epoch. The effect of this enormous pressure of these hundreds of feet of ice that were above my head, sliding down over the rocks, and rolling upon the boulders, was there evident to the senses. The movable rocks were being rounded or ground to powder, and the bed was being scarred with deep and ineffaceable scratches. Below me the bottom of the cavern allowed of my continuing down beside the stream about fifty feet to a point where both a stream of light and a stream of water were admitted into the blackness through a wide crevasse.

Curiosity once satisfied, I began to realize the perilous situation into which I had thus voluntarily come. The darkness through which I was groping made it not improbable that I might stumble and plunge headlong into the muddy river and be borne away by the

"Dark water that tumbled through the gloom."

Then it seemed as if the great arch might give way and bury me in its ruins, or a mass might break off from above, and, falling upon my head, crush me to death; and while creeping cautiously along, with my face turned towards the opening by which I had rashly entered, and with no longer an unsatisfied longing to quiet my fears, I could not but accuse myself of an absurd temerity, when I suffered myself to be led into a place where,

"Bellowing, there groaned
A voice as of a sea in tempest torn
By warring winds."

I was soon, however, in the open air again, and as thoroughly water-soaked as if I had fallen bodily into the sea; and being perfectly chilled, I did not long delay in finding my way down to the beach, where I joined the captain, who was awaiting me. He had hailed for a boat, and I was soon out of my shivering condition, but not soon enough to prevent me from moralizing over the unfathomable depths of human folly, while yet reflecting upon the wonders we had seen, and the unusual adventures we had experienced during our morning walk; for be it known we had started off without breakfast, and after six hours' continuous labor we were returning at eleven o'clock, with stomachs which could not be beaten for emptiness. It is only in such a bracing air as that of the Arctic regions that one can endure such continued exposure without suffering severe prostration. The idea that people necessarily consume more food in that region than another, is a popular error. Excessive feeding is everywhere a habit and not a necessity; but as "the sleep of the laboring man is sweet," so is his appetite vigorous everywhere.

CHAPTER VI.

SPECULATIONS.

I TRUST that I have made plain, even to the least scientific of my readers, the nature of the glacier which we are visiting, as well as the general principles of glacier formation and movement. Why ice, a solid, firm substance, should move in obedience to the same laws which govern the movements of fluids; why, for instance, a glacier should, like a river, move more rapidly at its centre than near its banks, is a question which the wisest philosophers have sufficiently discussed without my attempting it here. Taking the fact for granted, and knowing that the vast reservoir of ice in the interior of Greenland is the great source of supply to all the glaciers that pour to the sea through the mountain-passes, we may here, I think, not inappropriately, pause a little to watch the progress of this glacier of Sermitsialik.

Even within the period of a generation it has undergone very perceptible changes. Peter Motzfeldt has told me that fifty years ago he walked across the valley in front of it, and plucked whortleberries upon the identical spot where I had gone into the ice-cavern to hear the waters rushing to the sea. He pointed out to me the line of the glacier front at that time, so far as he could remember it (and the memory of such men is apt to be accurate); and, accepting his memory as correct, the movement of the glacier from that time to the present has been about seven (7) inches daily, the distance being a fraction over two miles.

THE GLACIER OF SERMITSIALIK.

With this positive assurance before us we may, in imagination, witness the spectacle of this glacier's growth. Going back to the time when it first emerged from the *mer de giace* (to the time when the ice first began to bulge downward into the valley which it now fills completely), we see the valley clothed with verdure, sparrows chirruping among the branches of the stunted trees, herds of reindeer browsing upon its abundant pastures, and drinking from a stream of limpid water which, melting from the glacier, pours down over the same precipices, and through the same defiles which the ice now fills and covers. This must have been about two hundred and fifty years ago, since the distance from the sea to where the break occurs in the mountain-chain through which the ice-stream emerges into the valley is about ten miles. We see it then just appearing, and we watch its progress through this long time. Its front is hundreds of feet high and miles across. We observe the icy flood moving steadily and irresistibly onward, over precipices, down steep declivities, upon level plains—sometimes advancing with comparative rapidity, sometimes slowly, but steadily, year by year, coming towards the fiord. We see it swallowing up rocks and pastures; we see the deer retire farther and farther down the valley with each returning year; we see the hillocks within the valley overwhelmed with the flood of ice, the crystal stream pouring over and around them as if it were some semi-fluid substance; we hear the cracking of the ice as the strain here and there becomes too great; and we hear, too, the echoing sound of the avalanche of ice- and snow, crumbling from its front, and crashing down into the plain beneath. We thus watch the ice-stream until the front of it has reached the fiord. But here it does not stop. The bed of the sea is but a continuation of the same inclined plain as the bed of the

H

valley, and its onward course is continued. It pushes back the water; it makes a coast-line of ice where there had been a beach; and a white wall now stretches from one side of the fiord to the other. As it flows onward, it gets into deeper and deeper water, its foot still resting on the bottom of the sea. Thus the icy wall sinks gradually down as it moves along, and in course of time it has almost gone out of sight. Then it gets beyond its depth.

When fresh ice floats freely in sea-water, there is one-eighth of it above the surface to seven-eighths below. If these proportions become disturbed—that is to say, if the glacier should project far enough out into the sea and

VERTICAL SECTION OF GLACIER.

deep water to present more than seven-eighths below to one-eighth above, then the buoyancy of the water will lift the end of the ice-stream until it attains its natural equilibrium. To do this, of course, a break must occur, as the ice will not bend. But for a long time the continuity of the ice is not interrupted — so great is its depth (many hundreds of feet), so great is its width (two miles). But finally it is compelled to give way; the force applied becomes too great for its powers of resistance. A crack, beginning at the bottom, is opened, with a fearful crash. The crack widens, and when it is completed to the top a fragment is detached. This fragment is buoyed up to its proper level; and while the loud noise of the disruption is echoing among the hills, and the great waves of its creating are rolling away, the monstrous mass is coming slowly to rest, ready to float off with the current to the ocean. This fragment, as we have already seen, is the *iceberg*. Its birth, as we shall presently notice, is attended with the most violent disturbance of the sea and air, and presents a magnificent spectacle.

The accompanying vertical section of the glacier of Sermitsialik, run up its axis from the fiord to its junction with the *mer de glace* (a distance of ten miles), will illustrate the fact I wish to prove, and the theory I wish to illustrate. The view of the same glacier, on page 147, will still further aid the reader; and this, examined in connection with the small map on page 162, will explain what any number of words would fail to make clear. This vertical section shows an iceberg just broken off and floating away. The line of the section is from A to B, as shown on the map.

CHAPTER VII.

MEASUREMENT OF GLACIERS.

As we have seen, the glacier does not accommodate itself to the bed in which it rests very readily. The substance, though possessing a sort of ductility, is not sufficiently plastic to mould itself with much rapidity. A sudden squall will snap a twig, or uproot a tree which a gale would only bend. In like manner, the pressure upon the ice becomes in places too great, and, unable to bear it, the ice snaps. Professor Tyndall has said — and this is borne out by my own experience—" By pressure ice can be moulded to any shape, while the same ice snaps sharply asunder if subjected to tension." Hence arise the great crevasses which so much embarrassed the captain and myself while crossing over the glacier of Sermitsialik. These cracks are therefore continually occurring. Beginning as a loud and alarming peal, they become in the end a crash. This particularly happens when the glacier, flowing over a quick descent, moves rapidly.

In this manner are opened those crevasses already mentioned as running inward and upward from the shore, and pursuing a general parallelism. The force is not that of pressure, but of tension. The sides hang more or less upon the shore, while the centre moves on, and thus the ice is drawn apart. The shore-ice thus lags behind, and the total amount of that lagging is told in the aggregate width of the crevasses.

I have mentioned that the rate of progress of the centre of the glacier of Sermitsialik must have been about seven inches daily. Others move at the rate of five. The process for this determination is simple enough. I have performed it many times, and may thus briefly describe it.

After climbing to the surface of the glacier, I staked off a base-line near the centre, and parallel with its sides. I then set up a theodolite, first at one, then at the other end of this base-line, and, having connected it by careful angular measurement with some well-defined object (readily again recognized) on the land, at the side of the glacier, the work was done. After an interval of weeks or months, the process was repeated, and then a very simple trigonometrical computation revealed the fact that the base-line was moving down the valley, and the rate was determined to a small fraction.

The unequal movement between the centre and the sides was shown by quite another method. A line of stakes was set up across the glacier from shore to shore. After a few weeks this line became a slight curve; after a few months the curve was very perceptible. Could the observation have been continued through years, it would have been like a well-bent bow, or the letter U.

Such measurements as these I once made upon a glacier at Port Foulke, North Greenland. The top of the glacier was reached, after much difficulty, by cutting steps with an axe. The cracks were not, however, found to be so wide or so numerous as those of the glacier of Sermitsialik, but they were sufficient to inspire me with a lively sense of the danger of such exploration. When my first experiments were made, there was a strong wind howling down from the *mer de glace*, bringing with it sharp, cutting snow-drifts. The brass instrument which I used froze to the eye, and had to be covered with buckskin. The moisture of the breath condensed upon the lenses, and I had to breathe through a tube while observing. The men who carried the chain "scorched" their fingers with the cold metal. Under such circumstances the pursuit of science becomes a species of martyrdom, and is therefore not much in favor.

In the movement shown by these measurements we have conclusively exhibited the likeness of the glacier to a river, and the assertion that it is but a flowing river of ice is fully borne out and proved by observation with mathematical nicety. In my own experiments upon the Greenland glaciers I have but followed the example and practised the methods of Professors Agassiz, Forbes, Tyndall, and others, not forgetting the experts of the Alpine Club, whose explorations of the glaciers of the Alps have latterly become so familiar to the public.

CHAPTER VIII.

THE BIRTH OF AN ICEBERG.

I CAN imagine no more grand and imposing spectacle than the birth of an iceberg; and we have now, I think, gone far enough in the examination of glaciers and their movements to contemplate such a spectacle, which, whatever it may seem to the reader, was to me most thrilling. It did not happen in connection with the *Panther*, and may at first, therefore, seem to be a little out of place; but as it serves my purpose, I make free to use it, by way of illustration.

The scene was in a fiord ten times wider than that of Sermitsialik, though not much longer. Unlike that of Sermitsialik, it was studded with islands and shoal places. The glacier which terminated it was twenty miles across, although not quite uniformly; for the ice had poured down into the sea, and, while having blotted out some of the islands, it had barely touched others; otherwise the coast-line of ice was perfect and continuous. The islands and shoal places in the fiord arrest the icebergs; and within ten miles or more of the glacier it is almost impossible to go. With great difficulty I came within five, in a boat. Farther I could not force my way by any possibility; and, accordingly, we made the land and climbed a lofty hill for a view.

The fiord which I thus describe is known as the fiord of Aukpadlartok, a native word signifying "the place of the red rocks." I had gone up the fiord from Upernavik to the hut of a hunter, who was the bestyrere of a small settlement of that name belonging to the Upernavik district.

It was a grand spectacle that met my eye as I stood upon the hill-top overlooking the fiord, with its thousands of icebergs, its dark rocky islands, and the immense quantity of loose ice which filled up the space between the bergs and islands, until there was scarcely a patch of water to be seen anywhere as large as a good-sized duck-pond. Very different from the fiord of Sermitsialik, where there were no islands nor shoals to arrest the ice in its progress down the fiord.

I was accompanied by the bestyrere of Aukpadlartok, whose name was Philip. We stood together looking at the glacier and the great sea of ice which stretched away into the interior, blending mountains and valleys into a vast plain, when Philip said, "Listen! the glacier is going to 'calve;'" for that is the name by which they distinguish the breaking off of a fragment.

I heard a loud report, but I could not at once distinguish the source of it. An instant afterward it was repeated, now louder than before. It resembled the first warning sound of a coming earthquake.

Philip had detected the spot whence the sound proceeded, and said, "Look! it is rising."

I could now see that a portion of the glacier was being lifted by the water. A great wave was rolled back with this upward movement, and dashed fiercely against the icebergs that lay farther down the fiord. Another instant, and the sound, which was before so deep and loud, broke through the air with a crash that was like the discharge of heavy artillery near at hand. I knew now that a crack had opened in the ice-stream, and that a mass had been disengaged.

The position of the crack was quickly apparent, and we

could see that a fragment of enormous proportions had been set at liberty. It first reared itself aloft as if it were some huge leviathan of the deep indued with life, and was sporting its unwieldy bulk in the hitherto undisturbed waters. The crack had now opened wide. The detached fragment plunged forward; the front, which had been rising, then sunk down, while the inner side rose up, and volumes of water that had been lifted with the sudden motion poured from its sides, hissing, into the foaming and agitated sea.

Thus an iceberg had been born.

It would be impossible with mere words alone to convey any adequate idea of the action of this new-born child of the Arctic frosts. Think of a solid lump of ice, a third of a mile deep, and more than half a mile in lateral diameter, hurled like a mere toy away into the water and set to rolling to and fro by the impetus of the act—as if it were Nature's merest foot-ball—now down one side, until the huge bulk was nearly capsized; then back again; then down the other side once more, with the same unresisting force; and so on, up and down, and down and up, swashing to and fro for hours before it comes finally to rest. Picture this, and you will have an image of power not to be seen by the action of any other forces upon the earth.

The disturbance of the water was inconceivably fine. Waves of enormous magnitude were rolled up with great violence against the glacier, covering it with spray; and billows came tearing down the fiord, their progress marked by the crackling and crumbling ice, which was everywhere in a state of wildest agitation for the space of several miles. Over the smaller icebergs the water broke completely, as if a tempest were piling up the seas and heaving them fiercely against the shore. Then, to add still further to the commotion thus occasioned, the great wallowing iceberg, which was the cause of it all, was dropping fragments from its sides with each oscillation, the reports of the rupture reaching the ear above the general din and clamor. Other bergs were set in motion by the waves, and these also dropped pieces from their sides; and at last, as if it were the grand *finale* of the piece—the clash of cymbals and the big bass-drum of nature's grand orchestra—a monstrous berg near the middle of the fiord split in two, and, above the sound of breaking waters and falling ice, this last disruption filled the air with a peal that rang among the bergs and crags, and, echoing from hill to hill, died away only in the void beyond the mountain-tops; while to the noisy tune the icebergs of the fiord danced their wild ungainly dance upon the waters.

It was many hours before this state of wild unrest was succeeded by the calm which had preceded the commencement of it; and when at length the iceberg that had been born came quietly to rest, and the other icebergs had ceased their dance upon the troubled sea, and the waves had ceased their lashings, it seemed to me that, in beholding this birth of an iceberg, I had beheld one of the most sublime exhibitions of the great forces of nature. It was in truth a convulsion.

CHAPTER IX.
A NARROW ESCAPE.

The birth of the iceberg described in the preceding chapter will better enable the reader to comprehend a much more fearful event which happened in the fiord of Sermitsialik.

During the absence of the captain and myself from the vessel the artists had not been idle. They had landed near the glacier, and with brush and camera had begun their work. The day was warm, the mercury rising to 68° in the shade, and the sun, coming around to the south, blazed upon the cold, icy wall. This must have produced some difference of temperature between the ice touched by the solar rays and that of the interior, which was in all probability several degrees below the freezing-point, for towards noon there was an incessant crackling along the entire front of ice. Small pieces were split off with explosive violence, and, falling to the sea, produced a fine effect as the spray and water spurted from the spot where they struck. Scarcely an instant passed without a disturbance occurring of this kind. It was like a fusillade of artillery. Now and then a mass of considerable size would break loose, producing an impression both upon the eye and ear that was very startling.

By one o'clock every body had come on board to dinner, and for a while we all stood on deck watching the spectacle and noting the changes that took place with interest. It was observed, among other curious phenomena, that when the ice broke off the fractured surface was deep blue, and that if any ice, as sometimes happened, came up from beneath the water, it bore the same color; but after a short exposurse to the sun, the surface changed, and became almost pure white, with the satin glitter before described. Our situation for a view could not have been better chosen, and it is not likely that such an opportunity was ever enjoyed before by explorers, since it is not probable that a vessel ever rode before at her anchor so near a glacier.

After dinner the work was to be resumed. The photographers hastened ashore, hoping to catch an instantaneous view of some tumbling fragment, which if they could have done would certainly have exceeded in interest any other view they had secured. The question of moving our anchorage was deferred to the captain, who decided to go over to the other side when the artists had been put ashore with their tools. Steam was indeed already up.

The boat had reached the shore for this purpose, and had shoved off for the ship, leaving the artists on the beach; and the order had been given by the captain to "up anchor," when loud reports were heard one after another in quick succession. A number of large pieces had broken off, and their fall disturbed the sea to such an extent that the vessel began to roll quite perceptibly, and waves broke with considerable force upon the shore. Then, without a moment's warning, there was a report louder than any we had yet heard. It was evident that some unusual event was about to happen, and a feeling of alarm was generally experienced.

Casting my eyes in the direction from which the sound proceeded, the cause of it was at once explained. The very centre or extreme point of the glacier was in a state of apparent disintegration. Here the ice was peculiarly picturesque, and we had never ceased to admire it, and sketch and photograph it. A perfect forest of Gothic spires, more or less symmetrical, gave it the appearance of a vast cathedral, fashioned by the hands of man. The origin of these spires will be readily understood to be in consequence, first, of the formation of crevasses far up on the glacier; and secondly, by the spaces between them widening, and sharpening and rounding off by the action of the sun as the glacier steadily approaches the sea. At the base of these spires there were several pointed arches, some of them almost perfect in form, which still further strengthened the illusion that they might be of human and not of natural creation. At the extreme point there was one spire that stood out quite detached, almost from the water's edge to its summit. This could not have been much less than two hundred feet high. I had passed very near this while crossing over in the boat, and the front of it appeared to extend vertically down to the bottom. In the clear green water (for the muddy water of the southern side did not reach over so far) I could trace it a long way into the sea. I had little idea then how treacherous an object it was, or I would not have ventured so near, for I was not more than a boat's length from it.

The last and loudest report, as above mentioned, came from this wonderful spire, which was sinking down. It seemed, indeed, as if the foundations of the earth were giving way, and that the spire was descending into the yawning depths below. The effect was magnificent. It did not topple over and fall headlong, but went down bodily, and in doing so crumbled into numberless pieces. The process was not instantaneous, but lasted for the space of at least a quarter of a minute. It broke up as if it were composed of scales, the fastenings of which had given way, layer after layer, until the very core was reached, and there was nothing left of it. But we could not witness this process of disintegration in detail after the first few moments, for the whole glacier almost to its summit became enveloped in spray — a semi-transparent cloud through which the crumbling of the ice could be faintly seen. Shouts of admiration and astonishment burst from the ship's company. The greatest danger would scarcely have been sufficient to withdraw the eye from the fascinating spectacle. But when the summit of the spire began to sink away amidst the great white mass of foam and mist, into which it finally disappeared, the enthusiasm was unbounded.

By this time, however, other portions of the glacier were undergoing a similar transformation, influenced, no doubt, by the shock which had been communicated by this first disruption. Other spires, less perfect in their form, disappeared in the same manner, and great scales peeling from the glacier in various places fell into the sea with a prolonged crash, and followed by a loud hissing and crackling sound. Then, in the general confusion, all particular reports were swallowed up in one universal roar, which woke the echoes of the hills and spread consternation to the people on the *Panther's* deck.

This consternation increased with every moment; for the roar of the falling and crumbling ice was drowned in a peal, compared to which the loudest thunder of the heavens would be but a feeble sound. It seemed as if the foundations of the earth, which had given way to admit the sinking ice, were now rent asunder, and the world seemed to tremble. From the commencement of the crumbling to this moment the increase of sound was steady and uninterrupted. It was like the wind, which, moaning through the trees before a storm, elevates its voice with its multiplying strength, and lays the forest low in the crash of the tempest.

The whole glacier about the place where these disturbances were occurring was enveloped in a cloud, which rose up over the glacier as one sees the mist rising from the abyss below Niagara, and, receiving the rays of the sun, hold a rainbow fluttering above the vortex.

While the fearful sound was pealing forth, I saw a blue mass rising through the cloud, at first slowly, then with a bound; and now, from out the foam and mist, a wave of vast proportions rolled away in a widening semicircle. I could watch the glacier no more. The instinct of self-preservation drove me to seize the first firm object I could lay my hands upon, and grasp it with all my strength. The wave came down upon us with the speed of the wind. The swell occasioned by an earthquake can alone compare with it in magnitude. It rolled beneath the *Panther*, lifted her upon its crest, and swept her towards the rocks. An instant more and I was flat upon the deck, borne down by the stroke of falling water. The wave had broken on the abrupt shore, and, after touching the rocks with its crest a hundred feet above our heads, had curled backward, and, striking the ship with terrific force, had deluged the decks. A second wave followed before the shock of the first had fairly ceased, and broke over us in like manner. Another and another came after in quick succession; but each was smaller than the one preceding it. The *Panther* was driven within two fathoms of the shore, but she did not strike. Thank Heaven, our anchor held, or our ship would have been knocked to pieces, or landed high and dry with the first great wave that rolled under us.

When it became evident that we were safe, our thoughts naturally flew to our comrades on the shore. To our great joy, they too were safe; but they had not had time to clamber up the steep acclivity before the first wave had buried them. Flinging themselves flat upon the ground when they discovered that escape was hopeless, and clinging to each other and to the rocks, they prevented themselves from being carried off or seriously hurt. One had been lifted from his feet and hurled with much force against a rock, but, excepting a few bruises, he was not injured, and with much fervor thanked Heaven that it was no worse. He had, indeed, abundant cause. Had the party not been favored by the rocks, which were of such formation that they could readily spring up from ledge to ledge, they must all have perished. The wave, before it reached them, had expended much of its force. If they had been upon the beach and received the full force of the blow, they would inevitably have been killed outright or drowned in the under-tow. Their implements —bottles, plates, every thing—were either gone, or were a perfect wreck. Fortunately, their cameras were upon the hill-side, and beyond the reach of the wave, where they had used them in the morning. The boat, also, was safe; she had been hauled out some distance from the shore, and by putting her head to the waves she rode in security.

The agitation of the sea continued for half an hour after the first wave broke upon us. This was partly a prolongation of the first disturbance, but proceeded mainly from the original cause still operating. The iceberg had been born amidst the great confusion, and as it was the rolling up of the vast mass which sent that first wave away in a widening semicircle, so it was the rocking to and fro of the monster that continued the agitation of the sea; for this new-born child of the Arctic frosts seemed loath to come to rest in its watery cradle. And what an azure gem it was! glittering while it moved there in the bright sunshine like a mammoth *lapis lazuli* set in a sea of chased silver, for the waters all around were but one mass of foam.

I measured this iceberg afterwards and found its height above the surface of the water to be one hundred and forty feet, which, supposing the same proportions to continue all the way down, would give a total depth of eleven hundred and twenty feet, since the proportion of ice below to that above is as one to seven. Its circumference was almost a mile. No wonder that its birth was attended with such fearful consequences.

The part which had been the top of the glacier had become the bottom of the iceberg. The fragment, when it broke off, had performed an entire half-revolution. Hence it was that no part of it was white. But as the day wore on the delicate hue which it first showed vanished, and before the berg finally disappeared down the fiord it wore the usual opaque white which distinguishes its older brothers who have drifted in Baffin's Bay for perhaps a score of years.

As may well be supposed, we did not wait for another iceberg to catch us in such a defenseless situation. Our jolly captain was now quite content to own that he held glaciers in profound respect, and lost no time, therefore, in picking up his anchor. Then, as soon as our bruised and thoroughly drenched artists were brought aboard, the *Panther* wheeled upon her heel and steamed over to the opposite side, where, at a more respectful distance, anchorage was found which promised safety if the glacier should take upon itself once more to perform such fantastic freaks as the one of which we had like to have been victims; and we had no mind now for another such dangerous encounter.

CHAPTER X.

ICEBERGS CRITICALLY EXAMINED.

WE named our new harbor "Panther Bay," and, while resting there until another day comes to invite us to new work and new adventures, let us, more critically than we have had opportunity to do before, examine into the character of these icebergs of the Arctic Sea.

It is, perhaps, not surprising that so few people should really understand what an iceberg is, seeing how few people go where they come from. The icebergs of the Northern hemisphere have but one birthplace: they all come from Greenland—at least all of any magnitude. There are many glaciers in Spitzbergen, some of which reach the sea; but they are of diminutive proportions, and the fragments broken from them are few in number and very small. There are many glaciers in Iceland, but they are confined to the mountains. There are also glaciers upon some of the lands north of Hudson's Bay; but, like those of Spitzbergen, they occupy a small space compared with the vast accumulations of Greenland. And from Greenland they discharge mostly on the Baffin's Bay side. In a former chapter we have observed how the ocean current comes from the north along the eastern coast of Greenland, freighted with ice-fields (not bergs), sometimes bearing trees from the Siberian forests. This current sweeps thence around Cape Farewell, and continues north along the Greenland coast, with greater or less velocity, to almost the seventy-fifth or seventy-sixth parallel of latitude, before taking a westerly course, and then again a southerly one to the coasts of Labrador, Newfoundland, and the United States. The icebergs are discharged by the fiords into this current, and the result is that, unless there should be a prevalence of strong northerly winds for a considerable time, sufficient to force them against or across the current and out into the Atlantic, their drift is northerly at all parts of the coast up as far as Melville Bay. The easterly winds, however, affect them; and they are in great numbers blown across Baffin's Bay until they touch the southerly-setting current, when they drift down into the North Atlantic, as if for no other purpose than to annoy the crews and captains of Liverpool packets and other craft sailing in those waters.

It will thus be seen that, unless driven by the wind, they never leave the great Polar current of the Spitzbergen and Greenland seas, and the waters of the Labrador—a current which is a mighty one and has worked mighty changes on the surface of the earth. We all know and can trace its course now, but that course was once very different. In a remote geological age it must have swept over the greater part of what is now North America, when that land was the bed of the ocean, just as at the present time it sweeps over the growing Banks of Newfoundland. Then Lake Superior discharged into it as a gulf: afterwards, when this gulf became an inland sea, Huron and Michigan were the outlets; afterwards Erie, then Ontario, now the Gulf of St. Lawrence, which latter will, no doubt, in the course of time, form another freshwater lake of the great chain, as the sea becomes more and more filled up.

We have seen already that many of the icebergs that drift down with this current carry imbedded in them vast quantities of rock and sand, which are, necessarily, deposited at the bottom of the sea when the iceberg melts.

Thus do they add something every year, as we have also seen, to the Newfoundland shoals, and likewise strew the ocean bed along their path with gatherings from the Greenland hills. When these now submerged regions come to be elevated above the sea, the geologists of that day will have less trouble to account for the boulders being there than our forefathers had to explain the presence of similar masses of rock on the Illinois prairie, or in the valleys of the Mohawk and Connecticut rivers.

The melting of an iceberg is far from rapid. Many years are required to mingle its crystals with the waters of the ocean. Yet its rate of drift being slow (and it may be held for years grounded among a cluster of islands or among shoals), and the distance great, by the time it has reached the track of vessels the largest part of it has disappeared; and, immense though they sometimes appear to be when seen from the decks of ships crossing to and fro between America and Europe, they are then but a fragment of their former greatness. Indeed, very few of them ever reach so low a latitude at all, going to pieces, little by little, long before the current has carried them so far.

A very homely illustration will bring an iceberg more clearly to the mind of the reader who has never seen one than the most elaborate description.

Observe the little bit of ice that clinks in your tumbler at dinner-time. Observe it closely, and you will perceive how very small a part of it floats above the surface of the water. That part is about one-tenth, but it floats in fresh water. Change it to sea-water, and the part above would be one-eighth. Now this little bit of ice is an iceberg in miniature — an iceberg in every essential feature except that it did not in all human probability come from Greenland. In form, in general transparency, in the play of light upon it, in its prismatic character, in the shape of its projecting tongues which lie beneath the surface of the water, in the delicate mist which plays around it in the warm air, it is the very image, on a small scale, of those great monoliths of the Arctic frost which come sailing down Baffin's Bay with the Polar current in all their stately grandeur and magnificence.

It is difficult for the imagination to conceive of the great magnitude of some of these Greenland icebergs; and yet, as we have seen, they are but comparatively trifling pieces, torn by the sea from glaciers. The iceberg is indeed as the paring of a finger-nail to the whole body, when compared to the quantity of ice in the reservoir from which it came. Magnify the bit of ice in your tumbler until it becomes to your imagination half a mile in diameter each way, and you have a mass that is far from uncommon. Add to this a mile, two miles of length, and you have what may be sometimes seen. I have sailed alongside of an iceberg two miles and a quarter before coming to the end of it. Yet this is not greater, in proportion to the entire Greenland accumulation, than the little bit of ice in your tumbler is to the immense stores which the ice monopolists have in their store-house when they stand ready to avow, and do avow, that the stock is nearly exhausted, and that they propose to double their charges on you just when the hottest weather oppresses the city.

The name iceberg signifies ice-mountain, and mountainous it truly is in size. Lift it out of the water, and it becomes a mountain five hundred, a thousand, two thousand, or three thousand feet high. In dimensions it is as if the city of New York were turned adrift in the Atlantic, or the Central Park were cut out and launched in the same place. And an iceberg of the dimensions of Central Park is far from unusual. In general outline of surface the resemblance is often equally good. It is undulating like the Park, and craggy, and is crossed by ravines and dotted with lakes—the waters of which are formed from the melted snows of the late winter, which have fallen upon it, and also of the ice itself, after the snows have disappeared before the rays of the summer's sun. In such a lake I have even once bathed, although, I am glad to say, but once, and that was in "the days of other years," when the youthful impulse was strong to *say* "I have done it!"—a disease which I believe to be amenable only to that treatment popularly known as "sad experience." Skating on an iceberg lake is more satisfactory and sensible, though it is just as well to give an iceberg as wide a berth as possible, and have as little to do with it as you can at all times, for it is liable to go to pieces (though this rarely happens in winter) when you are least expecting it. I have often climbed them, however, and with different motives; sometimes to aid in watering the ship (for the lakes upon them are of the best and purest water); sometimes to obtain a distant view; at other times for the mere purpose of curiosity and adventure. Ordinarily, a slope may be found by which the ascent can be made without difficulty, but sometimes spikes in the heels and a boat-hook in the hand become necessary. Frequently, however, the sides are quite vertical all around, and it can not be scaled at all. On one occasion, I measured an iceberg that presented on one of its sides a vertical wall that rose three hundred and fifteen feet above the level of the sea. Another one that I saw in the upper part of Baffin's Bay, and measured carefully, I will describe minutely. The sea was quite smooth, and the day calm, so that I enjoyed a most excellent opportunity, such an one as I never had before, and probably shall never have again.

This iceberg was not only remarkable for its size, but

for its great variety of feature. I rowed all the way around it, and measured it as carefully as possible. One of its sides was nearly straight and regular, having the appearance of being recently broken from the glacier. When facing the sun, it glistened marvellously. This side was six thousand five hundred feet long—over a mile and a quarter. At one end it was two hundred and forty feet high, rising squarely from the sea. At the centre the height was less, being only one hundred and sixty feet; at the other end it was one hundred and ninety.

These measurements were made with as much accuracy as was attainable under the circumstances, and are quite reliable within small limits. The log-line and chronometer—the one to measure distance, the other to note time—were of necessity the means of obtaining the length. For the height I dropped the "chip" at the base of the berg, and then, rowing out a hundred fathoms, I had a tolerably good base-line for obtaining the altitude—a pocket-sextant giving me the necessary angles. Say that I made a mistake of twenty-five feet, it is yet near enough for all practical purposes. It was big enough in all conscience, any way.

In measuring my lengths I was not so liable to error, and in the same manner as before I found one end of the berg to be eighteen hundred feet across. Here it terminated in a rounded bluff that was one hundred and twenty feet high.

Turning at the base of this rounded bluff, I came upon a side wholly different from the one I had before measured. It had evidently been for a long time the front of the glacier—perhaps for a period of fifteen or twenty years, or even more. It was everywhere irregular. In places it was cliff-like, as was the other, but for the most part it was worn into all sorts of irregular shapes. This had been done partly by the washings of the sea, partly by the sun, and partly by the streams of water which poured from the glacier while this iceberg was a part of it. There were bays in the side of it large enough to float a frigate. The *Panther* might have gone in and turned around upon her heel without fear of striking.

In another place there was a considerable bay, with two ice islands in it that were very peculiar. To this bay they were as Governor's Island and Ellis's Island to the bay of New York, and they had as firm a foundation, but the bottom upon which they rested was ice. They were mere hummocks, and the water on the berg was quite shoal. Yet we went in at least a hundred yards before we reached the shore of it, all the while being really *on* the iceberg, for the ice projected away out beneath us; and as I looked over the side of the boat down through the clear bright water, which we were shoaling constantly, I thought I had never seen any thing more exquisitely soft, tender, and transparent in color than the green of the sea, nor had I ever seen a more perfectly graduated tint than that from the deep water when we first came over the ice to the margin of the bay. It was as if we sailed through liquid emerald.

I "landed" upon the shore of this bay and climbed the iceberg. It was not an easy climb, even with the aid of steel spikes in my heels and a boat-hook in my hand. In places the ascent was very steep, and had I lost my footing I should have slid down at a fearful pace into the sea.

Upon reaching the surface I found it to be rolling, and much broken. There were two conspicuous hills upon it, one of which was two hundred and ninety, the other two hundred and seventy feet above the sea-level. At least this was the record of my barometer. Between these hills and among others less conspicuous, I discovered a lake a quarter of a mile long. Its course was winding like the lake of Central Park, which it resembled in size. I followed along its shore until I found the outlet, and there, through a narrow gorge, the overflow of the lake was rushing over a crystal bed in a rapid torrent, until coming at length to the side of the berg the pure cold stream leaped wildly down into the ocean, roaring like a youthful Niagara, and breaking into spray. On every side there were indeed streams, most of them quite small, so that the whole iceberg was shedding water on every side, and the constant sound of innumerable cascades charmed the ear with their ceaseless roar.

From the lake I wandered about among the icy hills until I grew bewildered, and I found my way back to the place of ascent not without embarrassment. The cause of this was partially explained—the iceberg was revolving; and, as I steered my course back by the sun, I naturally mistook the direction until I had discovered what was wrong, when I began to look for the two hills first mentioned, by which I recovered my bearings, and was soon on the right track again. Upon climbing these ice-hills, I obtained a grand view. The whole sea was studded with icebergs—hundreds of them there must have been—of every conceivable shape, from the great wall-sided mass that looked like a huge castle to the colossal effigy of some winged monster floating upon the sea.

Although on an iceberg, I was not without life to keep me company. A flock of kittiwake gulls flew about my head, and, perching upon a hill, set up their noisy chatter; and one old burgomaster gull, who had caught a fish, came there to swallow it in peace. But, to his evident surprise and sad disgust, he was suddenly pounced upon by a predatory jager, who had seemingly been hovering round for just such a chance; and, with an angry scream, the burgomaster, who had started off when he saw his enemy, gave up his prize, which the jager quickly caught in mid-air.

It was altogether a strange sensation, afloat at so great an elevation on an ice-mountain in the sea. Yet my footstool was firm and solid as the eternal hills.

Had time and circumstances admitted, I should gladly have carried up my camp-fixtures and remained there for a day or so watching the grand panorama of the hills and sea, while the sun, like a golden wheel in the blue sky, rolled around me, changing from hour to hour the aspect of every object within the range of vision—now silvering an iceberg, now coloring it, while it floated sometimes in a sea of blue, and again of green; now blazing with red the rugged cliffs of the fiord; now throwing them in shadow, as if they were the gloomy walls encompassing the abyss of Dante's Giants; now gilding the distant mountains, now robing them in purple; now silvering the far-off *mer de glace*, then melting it into a sea of rubies, or blending it with the blue sky; for such scenes I have often witnessed in the Arctic seas, though not from the summit of an iceberg.

But this camp on the iceberg was not possible; so, when I had found my way, I descended from my lofty elevation to the boat, and then, pulling on around the berg, completed my survey of it.

The scenery was much varied as we passed along. At one time we were beneath a dismantled tower; at another time, a ruined spire; then a deep cleft of blue or a dark cavern of green, in which the slow-moving billows were caught and confined, until, as if tired of their imprisonment, their hollow voices came gurgling out like the loud breathing of some mighty monster of the deep exhausted with his efforts to move the mountain from his path.

The side along which we were now passing proved to be six thousand feet in length. The end beyond was thirty-five hundred. Thus, in making the complete circuit of the iceberg, we had pulled almost three and a half miles.

The altitude of the berg I averaged at one hundred and eighty feet above the sea-level, which would give a total average depth of fourteen hundred and forty feet, or more than a quarter of a mile. Multiply these figures, and we obtain a total cubical contents of 23,850,000,000 feet. Convert this into tons, and all the carrying capacity of all the ships in the world are as nothing to it. Freight them all with ice cut from it, and an impression would hardly be made upon it. It is only by such figuring that we can form any thing like an adequate idea of the enormous magnitude of this huge vagrant of the Arctic seas. Its beauties are not defined so readily. Solid and mighty, it is yet a subtle object. The light plays through it as through the opal. Flashes of every color come from it. Here we see the emerald, there chalcedony; and again transparent quartz or sapphire, the topaz or the ruby, as the sun's rays dart through its sharp angles, or the tintings of the clouds are reflected from its sides.

More than this I can not say of the floating ice-mountain. Words fail utterly in the description of such a mighty work of nature—fail us as completely as do the pigments of the painter. Who could paint or who describe the leap of Niagara, or the roar that rises from the great abyss? At best, the effort of the artist gives but a vague idea of the truth. The iceberg—in its birth, growth, and immensity; in the varying phases which it presents at different times; the subtle quality of the light and color which play around it—is utterly beyond the reach of art. And who could paint, or who describe its age? Nothing but actual observation will even so much as suggest the long period occupied in its formation. Close inspection will reveal an infinite number of lines of stratification, which, like the multiplied rings of the old forest oak, mark the years of its increase, and tell of the untold ages during which it was growing in the parent glacier; but there is nothing in it or about it to fix the period when the hardened snow-flakes which compose it were first dropped upon the Greenland hills; nothing to show its steady growth through the recurring cycles of time.

CHAPTER XI.
MAN *VERSUS* MOSQUITOES.

ON the morning after we had anchored in Panther Bay I went ashore to stake off a base-line, preliminary to a survey of the glacier and surrounding region, in which operation I was kindly assisted by two of my shipmates and Peter Motzfeldt. We had a clear level space of half a mile for our work; but the operation was attended with some difficulty on account of the willow and birch bushes, which were about four feet high—too high to clamber through readily, and too thick to allow of crawling. But this was not the worst. When the sun was fairly up we were sweltering in heat, and the mosquitoes, coming out in swarms, excelled any thing I have ever seen. We persevered, however, and reached the glacier, close beside which we put up our last stake and fixed our last station. To observe with the instrument was, however, not possible. The eye was blinded by mosquitoes, the lenses were covered with them; the air was positively thick with them. They were in the mouth, they were in the nostrils, they were down the neck, they were everywhere, inside and outside the body. We breathed mosquitoes into the lungs and took them into the stomach. It was not that a swarm rose here and there from the marshy places or from among the bushes, but they hovered over the plain in a misty cloud.

I tried to return upon my track and take some sights, but the thing was impossible. Human nature could bear it no longer. I turned back, and, joining my comrades, together we made a break for the glacier, and, clambering up its sloping side, we found a convenient perch, and from our cool retreat looked down upon the scene of our recent battle, and, in peace, soothed our wounds. Our enemies did not dare venture on the ice, and we had got the best of them at last.

And we had besides a very convenient situation for observing the movements of our friends, the artists, who were ashore photographing and sketching the glacier from every available point. They had their heads covered with mosquito nettings at first; but that did not appear to make any difference. The mosquitoes got through and under them, in one way or another, and the nettings were torn off. Then they flirted them about their heads, and for an instant cleared a breathing space, but as soon as the work was resumed, back they came. The oil sketches of the artists became like geological formations which represent innumerable trilobites imbedded in the strata. Blob was so confused with his incessant efforts to keep his eyes cleared out, that he actually could not tell sky from water, nor ice from rock, when he came to expose his sketches in the cabin.

But the photographers had the worst of it; the "colonel" (who was first operator) especially, for he had to focus his instrument, which proceeding required time and care; and the agony of that interval of enforced quiet was most intense, if we might judge from the fierce pawing, and stamping, and running to and fro that followed, all of which would have been very amusing, had we not known by experience that it was very distressing and very painful. Then the insects got into the instrument and ruined the plates, which was a still further aggravation. The "major," who was second operator, could do nothing satisfactorily in "developing," for they filled his tent in place of air. Like ourselves, they were all finally forced to own defeat, and, darting for our perch upon the ice, escaped the torture. From this safe retreat we managed to raise signals of distress, and a boat coming to the shore, we made a bold dash for the beach, and, getting on board, were at last in safety, for they did not venture so far out to sea. Our faces were swollen, like a prize-fighter's fresh from battle.

Here, so close to such a great body of ice, we thought it strange, at first, to find the temperature so high; but, in that locality, to be attacked by mosquitoes surprised as much as it disgusted us. They were even much worse than at the ruins in Ericsfiord, where there was no ice at all.

Late in the day, when the sun was getting low, and the heat was less, the work was resumed under better auspices, and in the morning the labor was finished. I had in my port-folio as complete a map as was needful for my purposes, excepting some sights that I wished from the summit of the glacier, and these we proposed to obtain immediately.

While we were fighting the mosquitoes several icebergs broke away from the glacier with a very grand effect; but we were too much distressed to enjoy the scene fully, as we had been before too much alarmed. So, after all, although we had very lively impressions of the commotion caused by the birth of an iceberg, there was always some disturbing element to make the scene something less than perfect. However, after our ignominious retreat from fighting the mosquitoes, when, from our new anchorage, we could watch the glacier with perfect security, we had the good-fortune to see a berg somewhat larger than the first, broken off in the midst of much the same grand disturbance of the sea. Having no occasion now to look to our safety, we watched the crash, and listened to the loud reports with the eagerness of fascination. We saw the waves rolling away to the shore and sweeping over the ice that lay scattered upon the fiord; we observed the newly-liberated iceberg wallowing in the sea, and admired it as it floated off, slowly gathering to itself a white cloak, as if its tints were too delicate to bear the light of day.

CHAPTER XII.

A PICNIC ON THE GLACIER.

Two oomiaks loaded with women, and half a dozen men in kayaks, had followed us up from Kraksimeut; and they pitched their camp upon the shore as near our vessel as they could. An old seal-skin tent gave them shelter; the andromeda-leaves furnished fuel, and, in consideration for some trifling service, the stores of the *Panther* supplied them with food. They were not in any respect an attractive party, and, even with the best intentions in the world to play the amiable, I doubt if the Prince ever made the slightest effort to prove himself agreeable to these Kraksimeut ladies of the oars. They were not to be compared to Maria and Concordia, and the rest of them at Julianashaab.

One difficulty, however, was, that their camp was unapproachable on account of the mosquitoes, which, however, did not appear to disturb them. They were sometimes seen to brush off the insects when they settled too heavily on one spot; but otherwise they might bite their fiercest and remain unnoticed. They had grown so accustomed to them that even the blood did not seem to be poisoned.

These people were, however, useful to us in one way. On the last day of our stay in the fiord, it was determined to scale the glacier in a body, seeing that it might be possible, after the experience of the captain and myself. Accordingly, a party was made up, and these native men and women, whose boots were better adapted for climbing upon the ice than ours, were engaged to carry our luggage, consisting of surveying instruments, artists' materials, provisions, and cooking-fixtures.

After crossing the mosquito-infested plain, we entered the gorge between the glacier and the rocks, where we were free from our pestiferous enemies. Thence we clambered along for a little over two miles before we ventured to climb the ice. This was almost a mile beyond where the captain and I had before ascended.

The ascent was made with no further difficulty than would be experienced in climbing any steep hill. Here we were not much embarrassed by crevasses, for we were approaching the level plain mentioned in the former description, where there had been very little disturbance of the ice. The amount of foreign material was immense. Rocks weighing many tons were imbedded in the glacier, or were lying loose upon the surface, owing to the ice having melted away and left them free. These we amused ourselves with rolling down the declivity; for some of them were much rounded by ice-action, and were not so large but that they could be raised with a lever and two or three pairs of hands.

When upon the surface, we experienced something of the same difficulty that had been encountered before by the captain and myself. In one place only, however, was the track so rough as ours. Here there were clefts of such fearful character that it fairly made one shudder to look into them as they yawned before us at every few steps.. In order to get on at all, however, it was necessary that some one should take the risk of the first leap. This usually fell to the lot of the captain by his own election; for, being both vigorous and fearless, he was usually at the head of the party; and when any place more than ordinarily dangerous was encountered, he was heard to cry out (from the opposite side of the danger), "Come on!" But not every body could come on, especially those who carried burdens; so a rope was thrown across and secured, and a safe passage was obtained for the entire party. Once only was an accident seriously threatened. This occurred to a man who had put something in him to make his legs unsteady; and but for the captain's rope he certainly would have disappeared into the bowels of the glacier. He was hauled up in a lively state of wonder as to "how we all got down there?" Our "fair" companions in the seal-skin pantaloons required very little assistance, and in their soft-leather boots were more sure-footed than we. They seemed quite surprised at our gallant offers of assistance; for they had been in the habit not only of helping themselves, but their lords as well, in every thing where help was possible—a practice universal among savages and half-civilized people. Gallantry is a fine art, the sentiment not being natural to man.

When at length we had reached the level part of the glacier, for which we had directed our course, and every body that had any particular business to attend to had gone about it, the romance of a picnic was illustrated in form, if not in fact, by an improvised dance. The Prince of course led off, saying, "What's a picnic without a dance?" and never did couples "trip the light fantastic toe" upon a spot apparently less adapted for it. Yet, if many of the conditions of a first-class summer entertainment in the open air were wanting, we did not lack a warm sun, nor merriment, nor singing. The dancing did not amount to much, it must be owned. As for the accompaniments to the singing, there was the music of a babbling brook which flowed near by, across the icy plain; and right in front of us it dashed down into a cleft, to seek the glacier bed, and there mingle with the sub-glacial river which carries to the sea the summer meltings of the *mer de glace.*

The view from our camp was one that I shall long remember. From the midst of the motley group of men and women that surround me, I look to right and left, and there rise the dark, rugged, rocky shores of the glacier, and then, continuing away to the south-west, become the shores of the fiord, which, dotted with icebergs, winds away like a noble river, and, in the distance, melts into the ocean. Turning in the opposite direction, I scan these same coasts for a few miles, and, like two wedges, there they sink into the white slope which rises above them and vanishes in the limitless distance.

We were not at any time cold. Our dinner was capital, abundant, and much enjoyed, and it was not the less appreciated that the labors of the day were over, and that it was prepared without the aid of the ship's cook and steward. The artists had accomplished all they came for; and with the same assistants, who, as before, had aided me, I had staked off a base-line, taken my angles, and obtained every sight that was necessary to connect my measurements with the same hill-tops that had been my guides in the survey on the mosquito-plain. And thus I had all needful materials to complete the map which appears on page 162, and the section on page 170. Then, amidst much enthusiasm, we flung our flag to the Arctic breeze.

The reader may, perhaps, regret, as I did, that there was so little of thrilling interest to mark the day's adventure. It was simply a novel experience; an unusual place for a picnic—an unusual place to stand on a warm midsummer's day.

Such as the day was, I have, however, recorded it, leaving the reader's imagination to supply whatever may be lacking in the sentiment of the solitude and desolation of our surroundings. He may, perhaps, fancy that women, dancing, and festivity were strange accompaniments to such a scene, as they surely were.

We did not, however, care to make the venture quite complete by sleeping on the ice. Gathering up our traps, therefore, we made our way back as we had come, and, arriving all safe on board, we picked up our anchor, and, as we steamed down the fiord, the wonderful ice-stream, which had afforded us so many adventures, melted away in the gathering twilight of the evening.

CHAPTER XIII.
BOUND FOR THE ARCTIC CIRCLE.

Having our pilot, Peter Motzfeldt, on board, we were obliged to put into Kraksimeut. After passing a few hours there, we made a direct course for the open sea. Motzfeldt, in the generosity of his heart, insisted upon it that we should rob him; but even the professional habits of our trader would not suffer a gift without a quid pro quo; and I trust that this worthy inhabitant of the solitary house on the dreary island may not have been damaged by our visit.

Passing along near the coast, we had a fine view of the mountains which rise there directly out of the sea; and, after rounding the south-western cape of Greenland, which bears the name of Cape Desolation, we shaped our course for Arsut fiord, where the famous kryolite mine is situated, at a place called Iviktut. The entrance to this fiord is often seriously obstructed with ice-fields. We were fortunate enough to find it free, and, aided by our excellent Danish charts, we got in without trouble.

A man with a very sailor-like rig boarded us, and, addressing us in English, said he was Captain Abel Reynolds, of Boston, agent of the American Company.

This great kryolite mine is managed after a most inconvenient fashion. In the first place, it is a monopoly of the Danish crown, which has leased it to a Danish company for a period of years, to work upon a royalty of twenty per cent. This Danish company have sold to the Pennsylvania Salt Company the exclusive right in America

THE KRYOLITE MINE AT IVIKTUT, ARSUT FIORD.

to the disposal of the ore, if such it may be, for convenience, called, to the extent of one half the production of the mine. This Pennsylvania Salt Company, having no means of transportation of its own, lets out that part of its business to a company in Boston, the Messrs. Ryder & Crowley, and Captain Reynolds is their Greenland agent. Then the Danish Government has its *Regjeringens Controlleur*, Captain Harold Saxtorph; the company has its superintendent, Herr S. Fritz; its assistant-superintendent, Herr H. Stockfelth; and its surgeon, Herr E. C. Nobel; and a right good set of fellows they proved to be, if rather numerous for the business. The American agent made us snug as possible in the worst anchorage that ever was; the controller entertained us hospitably; while his wife treated us to the music of a Yankee sewing-machine. To the superintendent we were indebted for the offer of any amount of coals, which he had there in abundance for the use of the engines which he employs to pump the water from his mine; and personally I had to thank him for much useful information, and for the gift of the only fine specimens of kryolite crystals that I have ever seen; and to his assistant I owed more than thanks for a superb photographic plate of the mine and Arsut fiord, taken by himself, and other similar favors. Nor was the doctor lacking in the offer of his services; but luckily none of us required his professional attention, a circumstance which imposed a double share of thankful acknowledgment.

This kryolite mine is really a wonderful affair. Why Nature should have ever taken it into her head to drop this valuable mineral in Greenland, and nowhere else, is a puzzling matter. The mineral is a fluorate of sodium and aluminum (mostly the former), the best specimens containing ninety-nine, the worst ninety per cent. Besides these, I found iron, tin, lead, silver, copper, arsenic, and molybdenum; but none of these latter exist in sufficient quantities to make the working of them profitable.

The soda is the product which makes the mine (or rather quarry) valuable. And a mine of riches it would be, truly, were it anywhere else almost in the whole wide world. Its great distance from manufacturing marts; the extraordinary dangers attending the shipment of it, owing to the ice; the high royalty which the Government imposes; and the shortness of the season during which the miners can work, make it comparatively of little importance in a commercial point of view. Yet one-half the product of the mine (six thousand tons) is annually shipped to Philadelphia, in from fifteen to twenty vessels, whence it is carried by rail to Pittsburg, to be converted into commercial soda by the Pennsylvania Salt Company, who would, but for this mine at Iviktut, be compelled to make their soda from artificial sources.

The discovery of the mineral was made by the natives many years ago. It is said they used it in a powdered state, as civilized men do snuff. At first it showed itself as a little round, yellowish hummock above the general gray of the metamorphic rock which inclosed it. Upon coming to the knowledge of the world, only a few fragments were brought away; and I can remember the time, when my mineralogical studies first commenced, that to obtain the smallest fragment, even, of the Greenland kryolite was to add to a collection one of its most rare and costly minerals. Now it has no other value than to boil down into soda for ordinary commercial uses.

The mine has been in operation under the present company about twelve years. An effort to work it had been previously made, but failed for want of capital, and under the present management it has only lately been profitable. The mineral appears to exist as a sort of conical injection through the overlying rock. It is now worked down until the mine, or quarry, is about sixty yards in diameter and fifty feet deep, forty of which are below the sea-level; and since the solid rock is interrupted for a short distance on the sea-side, the water has constantly endangered the mine by flooding—a catastrophe only prevented by the admirable engineering skill of Mr. Fritz.

The number of miners employed is about one hundred, and since there are no settlements in the neighborhood, and therefore no natives to bring them supplies, their provisioning is entirely done from home. The miners were a well-contented-looking people, and, so far as I could see, did not suffer in their isolated situation any thing worse than the torment of mosquitoes, which there, as in all other parts of South Greenland, where the ice does not overrun the land, are thick as the sands on the sea-shore.

The kryolite is the only mineral product of Greenland that has proved of any commercial value. Yet, judging from the appearance of the country, one might think Greenland abounded in mineral wealth, and, if properly explored, a profitable return would certainly be obtained. An unsuccessful effort was made to work a plumbago vein near Upernavik, but to this and the kryolite the mining operations of Greenland have, I believe, been confined.

Unfortunately, the day of our visit to Iviktut was as dirty and disagreeable an one as ever was seen even in that country—rain, hail, snow, wind, cold, every thing possible almost in the way of badness. We did not, therefore, remain long, but, picking up our anchor again, we steamed away once more, and, passing through a narrow gate-way at the foot of the Great Kunak, or Arsut mountain, as it is sometimes called, we were soon out at sea, heading northward for the Arctic Circle, to find the midnight sun.

The midnight sun! A word of strange import! A new

existence was to open for us now, in a summer of perpetual brightness. For days and weeks together lamps would be held in great contempt; we would be careless of the hours; there would be "no morn, no noon, no night—no any time of day;" no time for "turning in" or "turning out," except as the ticking clock might show us what to do,

> "In that strange, mysterious clime, where springs
> Are but the twilights of the summer day;
> Where summer an eternal sunshine brings;
> The winter, darkness and sublimity—
> Where reigns dread solitude, and rolls the Polar Sea."

"The lands are there sun-gilded at the hour
When other lands are silvered by the moon—
The midnight hour, when down the sun doth pour
A blaze of light, as elsewhere at the noon."

PART THE THIRD.
UNDER THE MIDNIGHT SUN.

CHAPTER I.
ACROSS THE ARCTIC CIRCLE.

When we came to cross the Arctic Circle, instead of having the midnight sun, we had no sun at all; for one of those villainous fogs, so prevalent during the summer in the Arctic regions, set upon us and hung about us, hiding every thing for several days.

It rolled over us like a great wave, submerging us in damp and darkness. The wind was southerly, and the air was charged with moisture, which was precipitated by the cold water and icebergs over which it passed. I verily believe there never was such another fog. A thin layer of mist rested on the sea, above which one could climb and sit upon the royal yard and be in sunshine, and from that delightful elevation overlook the great waste of rolling vapor, and watch the glittering icebergs now and then protruding through it into the light; and in the distance trace the great white mountain peaks, and illimitable glaciers of Greenland. This was the sublime aspect of it; but down on deck there was nothing to be seen at all. Three ship's lengths away the atmosphere was as impenetrable to vision as a stone wall. From the quarter-deck we could scarcely see the look-out on the forecastle. The fog trailed about the rigging, sometimes in great streaks like festoons of white "illusion," and down upon the deck came dripping a perfect shower of the condensed vapor. In five minutes every thing was as wet as if the clouds had been dropping rain. The *Panther* was bewildered. Her compasses, never reliable at the best of times, were here, in the far North, utterly worthless. Every compass seemed to have an idea of its own as to where North was, and only changed its mind on being vigorously joggled; and no two of them agreeing after they were joggled. The situation was rather embarrassing; but for all the captain would not heave to. He would keep going somewhere, at any rate. The danger was that he might hit an iceberg. The sea was dotted all over with them. "All right," said the captain; "I don't think we'll hurt it much!"

That we should have a chance of proving it seemed the most likely thing in the world; for we sometimes heard from them as the billows broke against their sides or rolled within their wave-worn caverns, and their smothered voices were often painfully near; yet we did not see any of the bergs themselves, until suddenly there came a thrilling cry from the look-out, "Ice close aboard—dead ahead!" This warning went through the ship as if it had been "breakers"—the worst of all sounds to hear. The captain said never a word, but rang his bell, "Stop her"—"Back astern"—"Full speed!"

The cabin was cleared in a twinkling, and the people rushed on deck in a violent state of alarm, to see before them a huge mass of whiteness looming through the fog. It seemed impossible that we should escape it. Notwithstanding the reversal of the screw, we were yet forging ahead. The moments were like that terrible interval on a railway train, between the first thump of the car off the track and on the ties, and the crash which follows, scattering death and destruction. It was one of those short periods of one's life when the memory is apt to be remarkably fresh respecting misspent time. Happily, this was the worst of it. The ship slewed to starboard, which saved her jib-boom, and by that time the headway was stopped, and we began to go astern. But we were then in the very vortex of the breaking waves—in the hissing foam of the angry sea.

A few moments more, and the iceberg that had caused us such a fright was swallowed up in the gloom; and, giving it a wide berth this time, we steamed on more cautiously at "dead slow," groping through the worse than darkness of the night.

We had no further adventures of that description; but the uncertain currents of the sea, and the unreliable state of our compasses, caused us to become bewildered in our course. We did not once get even a glimpse of the sun for three days, and of course were running wholly by dead reckoning. The fog had become so deep that we could no longer climb above it and sit in the sun on the royal yard. "I'd give my old gun," said the captain, weary with watching, and disgusted with uncertainty—"I'd give my old gun (a rare instrument) to know where we are."

Now the captain had just come into the little cabin, which for the cruise we had "shoved up" on the main-deck amidships. The window overlooked the bulwarks, and the noises of the deck and of the machinery were kept away—a lucky circumstance, for at the very instant of the captain's speech my ear caught an ominous sound. I listened again to make quite sure, and then told the captain that if he kept on three minutes longer at the present rate of speed I would claim the gun. "Where would we be, then?" inquired the captain, somewhat incredulously. "On the rocks?"

The sound was unmistakable. The low murmur that

comes from the shore is very different from the loud roar from the waves breaking on the iceberg in the deep sea, and the practised ear can quickly distinguish the one from the other. The headway of the ship was arrested as soon as possible, and the fog lifting a little, we could faintly see the fatal line of surf. But we had still twenty fathoms water under us, and had plenty of room to wheel round, and crawl back upon our old track until we were beyond soundings, when we returned to our old trade of groping for another day, at the end of which, to our great joy and relief, and with the sudden bound of a mouse popping from its dark hole, we slid from under the oppressive canopy of vapor into the bright sunshine. Indeed, the limit of the fog was almost like a wall—sharp and well-defined; and while the quarter-deck was still in shadow, the forecastle was brightly illuminated. Fearful now that the fog might roll over us again, the *Panther* was made to do her best, and we steamed on into a scene of a very different description—still, however, among the icebergs—but now in a bright, instead of a cloudy atmosphere.

It was fortunate that the fog terminated when it did, for otherwise we would have been in great jeopardy. The icebergs were, in fact, so numerous, that the horizon was for a time quite obliterated. We turned and twisted among them to right and left, as one would follow the zigzags of the Boston streets, from Brattle Square to—well, any other place you choose to mention.

We might have been in a state of constant terror had we not been in a state of constant admiration. The atmosphere from a wonderful fog changed to a wonderful brightness. I have rarely seen any thing to compare with it. The hour was approaching midnight, and the sun, nearing the north, gradually dipped until it had touched and finally passed close to the horizon, with its upper limb just above the line of waters. For some time previous the sky had been peculiarly brilliant; but when the sun went fairly down, the little clouds, which had before been tipped with crimson, melted away, and the whole sky became uniformly golden; while the sea, quite motionless, unruffled by even the slightest breath of air, reflected the gorgeous color like a mirror; and the icebergs, of every size, from the puny fragment a few fathoms only in diameter to the enormous block hundreds of feet in height, and of every shape, from the wall-sided semblance of a giant citadel to the spired effigy of a huge cathedral, presented an aspect of indescribable brilliancy as they floated there in the golden sea.

In color they were wonderfully varied — against the brilliant sky dark purple, shading away to left and right into amethyst, and then into green and blue and pearly white; and away behind us, against the dark fog-bank which lay upon the waters, chased silver; while everywhere around were flecks of lustrous splendor stolen from the sky.

Emerging from this dazzling brightness, we glided on through the night in view of some of the finest coast scenery of a region where the scenery is never tame. First we passed under the gloomy, cavernous Black Hook; and then near the stupendous cliffs of the main-land, which, cut by deep gorges, seemed like grim old time-worn columns holding up against the sky a vast white entablature—the great ice-sea of Greenland. Then we came beneath one of the noblest landmarks of the coast — a cone-shaped mountain rising from the sea, which we had seen some sixty miles or more away. At first it was but a dark hummock against the sunset; now, through the breaks in a fleecy cloud which girdled it, we caught occasional glimpses of its crest brightened by the morning sun.

With helm a-port, we wheeled in on the south side of the mountain, and entered, close beside its base, a narrow, winding fiord as the sun was dropping his earliest rays down upon a silvery thread of ice-incumbered waters that wound between cliffs of unparalleled magnificence. The base of the mountain formed the cliffs on our left, and, as I afterwards determined, they were at one point 2870 feet high, rising so squarely from the water that it seemed almost as if one might drop a plumb-line from the summit into it.

The mountain is an island some ten miles in diameter east and west, by six north and south. This line of cliffs is almost uniform around its base, above which the conical top ascends quite regularly to an altitude of 4500 feet. This is the Kresarsoak—the "big mountain" of the natives—the "Sanderson's Hope" of old John Davis, who sighted it in 1585, soon after he had first discovered this Land of Desolation and been so nearly wrecked among the ice that beset it.

The cliffs upon our right were not less lofty nor less gloomy than those of the mountain's base. The fiord widened a little by-and-by, and we opened a more cheerful spot, where, for a short distance, the cliffs at the base of the mountain are broken away, and the slope of the mountain itself extends down in an almost unbroken descent from the crest to the sea. Here there are some signs of life. Up to about five hundred feet elevation the slope is in places green—little patches of mountain heather, and moss and stunted grass, which some flowers speckle with white and yellow. It seems like a green curtain hung across the entrance to the interior of the mountain, where, according to native tradition, dwell mountain giants. By this same legend the mountain is but a shell, the whole interior being one great cave, which, if true,

THE PEAK OF KRESARSOAK.

gives the giants plenty of room. Had we been wholly unused to Greenland scenery, we might have imagined ourselves steaming into some mysterious region where creatures of a supernatural sort actually held possession of land and sea in their own right; for, as we came near the base of the cliff, and directly under the peak of Kresarsoak, we detected something moving upon the water, and loud noises came floating on the air. Slacking our speed, until there was barely headway enough to keep us free from the icebergs, we were soon surrounded by a perfect swarm of amphibious creatures, in all essential particulars like that marine centaur of a pilot we had fished up out of Ericsfiord. Despite the colder climate (for we were now seven hundred miles nearer the North Pole than then), they bore no further appearance than he had done of being cold, wet though they were. They gathered about us on every side, and accompanied us with every manifestation of delight. Afterwards a boat came off with four of the same fishy-looking creatures at the oars, and a white man at the tiller, who was not slow to announce himself as the "governor" of a settlement called Karsuk, lying at the base of the mountain, on the very green slope which had attracted our attention. Esac was his name. A sorry-looking governor, to be sure, was Governor Esac; but then it would never do to allow a governor of any sort to pull alongside; so we hove to and hauled him aboard, and then let his boat drop astern in tow.

Governor Esac was in a very bad way. He had the rheumatism, for which what seemed to be a suitable prescription (as he thought at least) was administered, and when he finally left us he carried off a bottle of the same, a gift from the doctor. The medicine worked like a charm, for the patient soon ceased his complaints, and declared himself in possession of the very thing he stood most in need of, which seemed very likely, seeing how happy he looked, and great as the prospect appeared of his being more so.

Esac's rheumatism being provided for, we pushed on towards our place of destination, which was a great trun-

ENTERING THE FIORD.

cated cone standing in the middle of the fiord, and right before us. This truncated cone we came to know right well afterwards. Its height is 2300 feet. Its sides slope a little only from the perpendicular, and at our position, when Esac left us, there was no perceptible break in the line of the cliff to an altitude of 1400 feet. Above, the top is more or less ragged, yet the crest is nearly level, and the whole aspect of the rock is one of such great symmetry that it seems almost as if it were carved by man for a gigantic monumental pile.

Only by a close inspection of it can one realize its immense height. Even after having visited and examined it, I was quite amazed when I came to measure its dimensions. We were, indeed, all much deceived, and none more so than the captain, who, when a full mile away from it, thought he was quite as near as it was safe to go; and accordingly he hauled the *Panther* up alongside of an iceberg, and tied her fast.

How rejoiced were we all now to get once more out of the ship! A "landing" on the iceberg was easily effected, and we ran about over it as if it had been dry land. It was comparatively small, being not over a hundred yards in diameter by fifty feet in height, and it was undulating on the top. In the little valleys the water which the warm sun had formed of the pure fresh ice had gathered, and from one of these little pools we filled our water-tanks.

Satisfied that this was a place for birds, I persuaded the captain to take a boat with me and row towards the cliff, which, owing to a strange optical illusion, appeared to be only a few rods distant. To the captain's great amazement we had a pull of twenty minutes before reaching it. The sight then, up or down, was grand. Upward the cliff rose nearly half a mile above our heads: downward its image was repeated in the clear, bright waters.

THE LUMME OF THE ARCTIC SEAS.

A strange feature of this cliff, and others of like geological formation, is that the rock is fractured here and there horizontally, and that scales have splintered off from time to time, leaving a series of narrow ledges, or steps, which extend from the very bottom to the top; and these ledges are in the summer-time the home of myriads of birds.

These birds are the well-known "bacaloo bird" of Newfoundland and Labrador, and the St. Lawrence region generally, where they winter. They are the lumme of the Arctic seas, and the *Uria Brunichii* of the naturalist—a species of what are popularly known as "divers."

When about half a mile away from the cliff we began for the first time to perceive something of its character. Then birds came flying over us in considerable numbers. Many of them were on the water, and, like all the divers, who rise with difficulty, they made a great noise about us as they prepared to take the wing, flapping along close over the surface of the sea. As we kept nearing the cliff they became still more numerous.

Presently we heard a murmuring sound like that of distant falling waters. When we had arrived under the cliff, this sound increased in volume, and became so loud that we were obliged to elevate our voices to make ourselves heard by each other. This result was caused by the constant fluttering of innumerable birds, and their incessant screaming. Some of the ledges, or shelves, on which they sat were very narrow, others were two or three feet wide; some were but a few yards in length, others were many rods; some were in pretty regular order, one above another, others were sloping and irregular; but upon all of them, from near the water's edge to the summit of the cliff, birds were sitting, packed close together, and facing outward—sitting bolt upright, row above row, crowded into the smallest possible compass, and looking for all the world like soldiers with white coats and black caps standing shoulder to shoulder on parade. Low down the birds were easily counted; but higher up they melted away into scarcely distinguishable lines of whiteness, and higher still they disappeared from sight altogether.

At first it puzzled me to account for their strange attitude; but when I discovered that each female bird lays but one egg, it was readily explained.

They make no nest whatever, but lay their single egg upon the naked rock. The bird can only cover it, therefore, by placing it upon its end, which is accomplished

SHOOTING LUMME.

with the bill, and then she sits down upon it as if it were a stool.

After listening a while to their strange cries, and watching their movements, we remembered that we had come out to try our luck at shooting. Our guns were fired simultaneously, and down came plump into the water birds enough to make a meal for the whole ship's company. But what a change now there was in the aspect of the cliff! Following the discharge of the guns there was an instant of calm. It seemed as if every scolding voice was hushed. Every bird had leaped into the air; and now the wild flutter of their wings, as they darted away from the rock, was like the rush of a tornado; while they were so numerous as they passed over that they threw a shadow on us like a cloud. Having sprung from their eggs so quickly, many of them were left insecure, and a perfect shower came spattering down the cliffs.

But the birds did not long keep the air. They soon lit upon the water, with a great splash, about a quarter of a mile from the cliff, perfectly blackening its surface. Some of them did not even go so far; but, wheeling about in mid-air, they put back in haste to get once more upon their eggs before they had time to cool; and those who took the water quickly came back, despite the danger, to shelter their precious treasure of a single egg.

Many of the birds were now observed to be in a state of violent anger with their nearest neighbors, and, as they sat there upon their stools, they reminded me of angry fishwives. With ruffled feathers they were continually scolding each other at the very top of their shrill voices; and, not satisfied with this, they plucked out each other's feathers, and tried to gouge out each other's eyes. When it is borne in mind that the birds must have numbered millions, the volume of sound may be well imagined. It was at first difficult to account for all this disturbance, except upon the ground of pure love of fight. Presently, however, I observed that there was a deeper cause at the bottom of much of the difficulty. Many of the birds were in fact arrant thieves, and were guilty of all manner of dishonest devices to cover up their crimes. In short, they stole each other's eggs, seemingly without compunction of conscience. The bird must sometimes leave her egg, for she can not remain there and starve to death while the chick is hatching. She may be a careless bird, and as she leaves the ledge, her precious egg may roll off the cliff after her and thus be destroyed; or her neighbors may roll it off while quarrelling. Upon her return she looks for her egg, but does not find it; she at once suspects that it is lost, and knowing that to remain virtuous is to be chickless, she instantly decides in favor of theft, and steals the first egg she can lay her bill upon; and then down she sits upon it with as much coolness and unconcern as if it had belonged to her from the beginning. When the true owner of this stolen egg comes back, she may steal in like manner, or she may accuse some other bird with the theft. Perhaps she may accuse the right one; but right or wrong, if there is an accusation, there is sure to be a fight; and perhaps, before the fight is ended, the egg which is the cause of the quarrel may roll down the cliff; and then both birds get even by turning thieves again. But the egg is not always left without a protector, for the male bird sometimes sits upon it while his mate goes off to feed. The poor fellow, however, likes this business little enough, and I observed that the female did not trust to his faithfulness to the family interest holding out very long, for she invariably caught her breakfast (small shrimps) as speedily as possible, gave herself a hasty dip in the sea by way of a morning bath, and hurried back; whereupon the uncomfortable benedict of a lumme betook himself to freedom with a scream and a rush that is very enlivening.

It did not require a great many shots to satisfy us with lumme-shooting. It was a barbarous sort of sport, and verily, in the sportsman's sense of the word, there was no sport in it at all. Having knocked over about twelve dozen, we returned on board, leaving the poor frightened birds at such peace as they might find in the confused state of the private property which must have resulted from our so often driving them from their family stools.

ESAO.

Upon our return to the *Panther* every boat was at once manned, and the hunters all set out for the cliffs. The day was calm and pleasantly warm, and at its close we were the richer by almost half a ton of birds, after which successful raid upon the feathered inhabitants of the cliffs we cast off from the iceberg, and steamed over to the little bay of Karsuk, where we found good anchorage with sandy bottom, and paid a visit to "Governor" Esac, who proved to be the only white person there.

The Government-house at Karsuk is of the uniform style of architecture that prevails throughout the village (and, indeed, throughout Greenland generally), and differs only from the others in its superior size, increased comfort, and greater ornamentation—that is to say, the vestibule is not so long as that of the others, and does not, therefore, accommodate so many snarling dogs and litters of puppies, the owner being rich enough to afford a separate shelter for those ordinary members of a Greenland family. Then this same vestibule is four instead of three feet high, and you run a correspondingly less risk of knocking your brains out as you go in. The interior—roof, floor and wall—is lined and covered with planed boards, which Esac has obtained from the Government stores at Upernavik.

The house has but one room, it is true, but then it is sixteen by twenty feet, while the native houses are only ten by twelve, and their walls are lined with seal-skins instead of boards, and the floor is covered with flat stones. As for the walls, they are all built alike, six feet high and four feet thick, of stones and turf. There is a roof of rough timbers and boards; then the whole, roof and walls, are covered with heavy sods, which grow green, and convert the hut into a sort of mound. At fifty yards you could hardly distinguish Esac's house from the general green of the hill-side but for the Government stove-pipe which projects through the roof, and the smoke of Danish coal that comes from it, for it must be understood that this country produces no fuel save dried moss and blubber, of which the natives make, in an open dish of soap-stone, their only fire.

Esac had made good use of the doctor's prescription, for he seemed to be now entirely free from pain—at least he did not once mention it; but he pointed to an empty bot-

ESAU'S HUT.

tle with one hand, while extending the other to welcome us. Then he introduced us to his wife, and invited us to be seated, with immense decorum, and with a high appreciation of the rights of hospitality. Half the floor was raised a foot above the other half, and down we sat on this, along with the different members of his family, including a son recently married and his blushing bride—at least it is fair to suppose that she was doing what brides always do, as a matter of course, only she was too dark to allow the blushes to be visible. Along the back part of this raised place, or dais, there were piled up great bags of eider-down, which are spread out at night, and there the numerous family of Esac would bestow themselves to sleep, after such fashion and in such place as they found most suited to the taste and convenience. There being no partitions, the choice was limited only by the walls and certain claims of modesty, which drove the females all to one corner, and the males to the other.

Esac's wife was a thorough-bred Esquimaux, and when we entered she was seated beside a lamp, over which hung a steaming kettle that gave forth the pleasing aroma of coffee.

This housewife was a woman worth knowing. She wore yellow boots of extraordinary length, seal-skin pantaloons, a Scotch plaid jacket lined with fawn-skin, and hair twisted into a top-knot after the native fashion. Altogether she looked neat and matronly; of course also after the native fashion. Esac's approbation left no doubt on that score. "Mine frau!" said he, pointing to the lady of the yellow boots. "Mine frau—all same you speakum vife." He had been on board many a whale-ship, and had, with the singular facility of the Danes everywhere, picked up a little English. Then he continued: "Very good vife she. Plenty vurks;" and with his right forefinger he counted this item number one off upon his left forefinger; "plenty good cooks" (finger number two); "plenty good coffee makum" (finger number three); "plenty sew" (finger number four); and then, after a pause, and dropping his fingers, evidently regarding them as of no further account, he threw back his head, sniffed the air, and said, triumphantly, and as if there was no use talking further, "No smell."

But if Esac's frau did not smell, the Government-house did, so that we remained only long enough to pat the babies, bestow some presents, and receive some in return, when we took to the open air for relief; not, however, until we had partaken of a really excellent cup of coffee of this estimable lady's preparing—coffee being the universal and, besides the pipe, almost the only luxury of these Arctic wilds.

It is offered to you everywhere, in every hut and tent even of the lowest savage. It has, of course, only been in use since the Christians came there; but now it is a national beverage, and one of the principal articles used in trade. In the Upernavik district alone the annual consumption is about six thousand pounds among a total population of less than seven hundred souls—nearly ten pounds to each man, woman, and child. And every man, woman, and child has free access to the Government store-rooms, when they go provided with blubber, walrus or narwhal ivory, eider-down, or some other merchantable commodity; and in return he receives every needful article of civilized comfort and convenience, save and except only, as I have before observed in my relation of Julianashaab, the villainous "fire-water." The exclusion of spirits from the Greenland natives is but one of many evidences of the paternal care which the Danish Government exercises over these children of nature. The whole system being devised with the view of making the natives useful subjects, instead of reducing them to dependents, and, while causing them to be taught Christian doctrines, inculcating at the same time the practice of Christian virtues in conformity therewith, a circumstance not so usual as to be unworthy of mention. It is thus that, finding no conflict between precept and example, the Greenlanders have embraced Christianity, with its churches and its schools, and present an exceptional example of the current of a savage nature being turned into the stream of modern civilization.

We were bound to the colony of Upernavik, capital of the Upernavik District; and having accomplished our business in the fiord, we steamed around the base of the "big mountain," and in a couple of hours were at anchor again in a most uncomfortable situation, among a great quantity of drift-ice, directly off the little town, which, perched upon the naked, treeless rocks, presented a most woe-begone appearance. Yet hearty hospitality and a warm welcome were in store for us, as I knew they would be; and we soon forgot the desolate surroundings, as one would forget the desert in the wild flower that he finds growing by the way. My good old friend of former years, C. N. Rudolph, M.D., Bataillonschir, and governor of the Upernavik District, was there to greet us; and his great ancestor, the father of all the Hapsburgs, could not have welcomed guest with more lordly courtesy than did this true-hearted gentleman offer us the freedom of his house.

And his house was snug and comfortable. Two children and a kindly, gentle wife comprised the family; and, after seeing them, we needed not to see the fragrant flowers growing in the windows, nor to eat an excellent dinner, to convince us that we were in a home as happy as it

THE GOVERNOR AND FAMILY.

was refined. The wild winds might whistle as they would over the boundless wilderness beyond the window-panes —they could not disturb the peace and comfort that reigned within.

I never shall grow weary with recalling the tender love of flowers that I witnessed everywhere in Greenland. I never saw there a Danish house without them. They would not bear, throughout the entire length of any single day, exposure to the open air; but then, dear souvenirs of love and love's sweet offices, they keep them safe behind the glass, and nurse them as they nurse within their hearts the kindly ties that bind their lives and memories to sunny skies and summer gardens far away.

CHAPTER IL.
BEYOND CIVILIZATION.

UPERNAVIK DISTRICT extends from about latitude 70° to latitude 74°, and enjoys the pre-eminent distinction of being the most northern spot of all the earth where civilized industry is carried on. The settlements comprised within this most northern of the Greenland Districts are, Upernavik (which is the capital), Proven, South Proven, Karsuk (the home of Esac), Aukpadlartok, Kresarsoak, Kryatok, and Tessuisak. Of these, the latter is the most northern, and is, moreover, the most northern spot of earth where any Christian people dwell. It lies some fifty miles to the northward of Upernavik, in latitude 73° 35'. There, after leaving Upernavik, and twisting for many hours about among a perfect maze of islands, we made our next halt. The place differs in its general features from Karsuk, already described, only in having for its trader, governor, or bestyrere, whichever you like to call him, a man of more intelligence than Esac, and altogether of very different character. This governor's wife is Danish, and he brought her with him from Copenhagen to this last boundary of the Christian world, and he lives in a comfortable little house of civilized construction. His wife, when she first came here, was a fresh young bride; and here four children have been born to them. One of these sleeps in its cold grave among the stones.

The town itself is otherwise not unlike Karsuk, and has about the same number of native inhabitants, an equal number of yelping dogs (I should say about a hundred),

VIEW OF UPERNAVIK AND KRESARSOAK.

and the average proportion of the filth and stench inseparable from a town of such description. Among it all the trader's little whitewashed house loomed up cheerily, and, like a light-house in a dirty fog, it was a pleasant thing to look upon. It was late at night when we dropped our anchor, but the photographers had time to get out their camera and bath; and as the clock struck twelve they made a picture of it—the most northern house upon the globe, *photographed by the light of the midnight sun!* a feat well suited to the place and the romantic circumstances of our situation. We carried the picture off as a pleasant souvenir.

But, unhappily, the proprietor of this house was not there, nor his family. They had all gone off reindeer-shooting—the entire family camping out in the open air—a circumstance which I regretted the more that the man had served me before as interpreter and dog-manager in 1860-'61, and I was naturally desirous to see him. We sent off a native courier, but the courier missed him, and after remaining twelve hours, and the case appearing hopeless, the *Panther* was headed once more northward, and over the classic ground of the whalers we were soon passing Wedge Island and Cone Island, and Horse's Head, and Cape Shackleton; and finally we fetched up at the Duck Islands, sixty miles beyond Tessuisak.

The Duck Islands were in former years a sort of whalemen's rendezvous. To this point they fought their way among the great ice-fields along the Greenland coast; and here they are beyond the Danish colonies, and beyond the reach of human succor if misfortune happens them. Ahead of them lies Melville Bay, and the "middle ice" or "pack," which they are bold to enter, and if lucky enough, in the end, to pass, they are pretty sure to find an ample reward in the cargo of whale blubber and whalebone which they will gather in the northern and western waters of Baffin's Bay. In former times this fleet numbered something like a hundred sail; but now about a dozen steamers do the work of the noble old sailing ships, of which the recently destroyed *True Love* was the last. As the fleet "take the ice" here early in June or late in May, we were of course too late for them.

When a little more than half-way between the first and second of the Duck Islands we ran, at nearly full speed, upon a sunken rock not laid down on the charts—perhaps for the reason that nobody ever hit it before, but more probably, as it seemed, because of the disposition of our mate to allow no opportunity to be lost for sounding Baffin's Bay with the keel of the *Panther*. We struck it first with the stem, and fortunately glanced off to port, thus easing the shock, and, by somewhat deadening the headway of the steamer, the better enabled us to take the rock again and get fast aground.

The shock was, I need hardly say, rather startling. The worst results were, not without reason, anticipated. The timber-heads were of course, as everybody supposed, started and glaring wide open; of course the ship had sprung a leak; of course we would have to take to our boats, and make our way as best we could to Tessuisak and Upernavik, and there meet the Danish ship, and reach home by way of Copenhagen, leaving the *Panther* to go to pieces on the rocks. It was not a pleasant prospect, but there was no help for it. The artists were in a great stew about the "negatives." Our special artist (the very lively young gentleman, much given to caricature, already mentioned, who, for short, bore the cheering name of "Blob") was much alarmed for the safety of his numerous sketches. "The Professor" bemoaned the fate of his collection of specimens. But to every body's great surprise, and to the utter destruction of every body's well-laid plans of misfortune, a careful examination proved that no harm had been done whatever, except to the cabin furniture. The shock set our cups and plates shying about the deck in a very fragmentary state, and sent our cabin-boy, who was, as usual, asleep in the pantry, head foremost through the door, where he tripped up the steward, who was bringing in a pot of boiled mush, all of which the unhappy boy received on the abdominal region, and for the first, last, and only time during the cruise got thoroughly waked up.

It was none of our (that is to say, the passengers') business whether the *Panther* got off the rocks or not. That was the captain's affair; and therefore, when we learned that no hole had been made in her bottom, we were eager to get ashore, and after the birds. "The Professor" was easy in his mind about the specimens; "Blob" was relieved about his caricatures, and the "negatives" were safe. What was to prevent us? Nothing but the settlement of the question of responsibility as to whose fault it was that we hit the rock. The mate said it wasn't his. Oh no! who ever was at fault when any mischief was done? But the captain declared it was; and the mate, with equal zeal, repeated that it was not. But the second mate was against him, and every body else appeared to be; so he protested very loudly that it was no part of his duty to keep the run of all the rocks in Baffin's Bay; which was rather hard upon the captain, who kept the charts, and, if there were any rocks lying around loose, should know about it.

This home-thrust incensed the captain greatly; and, without making any secret of it, he advised the mate to go home to his mother (which he would, no doubt, have been glad enough to do), and, with a consistency peculiar to maritime people, told him, with the same breath, that he had better go and scrape the rust off the anchor, as that was all he was fit for. This settled the matter; and the matter being settled, a calm followed on the heels of the storm; and, upon the first lull, we got a boat off the davits, and got ourselves and our guns and heavy shot,

EIDER-DUCKS.

for the promiscuous slaughter of ducks, landed on the beach. Then we all filed off to left and right, and marched inland, the ducks very obligingly getting up before us as we went along, and hurrying away with a terrible flapping of wings and quacking with fright—at least, such as we did not bring down—and, since they rose superbly, any body with half a hand could have knocked over his bird. The sport was good, and by all odds the best we had yet enjoyed.

The islands proved, indeed, to have been well named. The birds were the famous eider-duck, close kindred of our much prized canvas-back, though much larger, and, feeding on shrimps, their flesh is not so well flavored.

The whole aspect of the place was forbidding in the extreme—too bleak and desolate to make one think of looking there for game did he not know better beforehand. But there were, towards the centre of the island, some small pools or lakes of snow-water, which furnished moisture for the growth of great quantities of moss; and in this moss, after the waters had subsided and left it dry, the birds had built their nests, lining them with the delicate down which grows upon the breast. This the bird plucks off with her bill to the extent of a good handful, leaving the feathers intact; and when she quits her nest to feed, she covers her eggs with this warm material to keep them warm. In regions farther south the Greenlanders make descents upon the islands, and carry off this fine lining of the nests, which, when cleaned, becomes the well-known and very valuable "eider-down" of commerce. "Live down" is the commercial name for it; and it is a singular fact that the same material plucked from the bird even an instant after death is worthless. The wonderful elasticity which gives such great value to the " live down" is wholly wanting in the dead.

During the early part of the season the ducks go in pairs, and the contrast between the two is very great— the female bird being brown and homely, while the male is black, with cream-colored breast and neck, and has the most beautiful tints of green upon his head. If the nest is robbed of down, and the female's own supply is exhausted, the male will sometimes obligingly pluck himself to accommodate her; but after she begins to "sit" he is seldom seen about her nest or in her company, and, indeed, is not allowed there except when she has been robbed, and wants his help to refresh the family nest. The males then flock together — like hen-pecked husbands at the clubs—and are very wild. To get within range of them at all one must lie low behind the rocks, and wait for them to fly overhead. In this manner we shot quite a number, and found their flesh a little fishy, but very fair. We enjoyed the afternoon's sport immensely, and perhaps not the less that the captain had come ashore very soon after we landed to convey the pleasing intelligence that, the tide having risen, the *Panther* was afloat and all right. And apart from this, we liked to have the captain on all hunting expeditions. He was generally the best shot, which detracted something, of course, since he was pretty sure to be the winner. But then he was always gay and lively; and he carried a gun which nobody but a tall, powerful man like himself could possibly have used—one of those Newfoundland sealing-guns—long enough, ordinarily, to knock a bird over without firing. But the captain was too fond of sport for work of that sort, and he invariably allowed the bird to get beyond the muzzle before he pulled trigger. Fifteen dozen birds rewarded us well for some fatigue, undergone in a temperature warm enough to enable us to dispense with coats, even although we were in latitude 74°, and surrounded on every side by ice.

The islands were so full of interest, and possessed so many romantic associations, that I wandered about them, from one to the other, rather in pursuit of my own fancy than of game. Everywhere that I went there appeared traces of the whalemen—at one place a flag-staff, at another place the fragment of a wreck; here they had built a fire, and there they had made a camp; and upon the very summit of the outer island, five hundred feet above the sea, we discovered the walls of an old look-out station, behind which many a hardy mariner whose ship was "beset" among the ice had come and watched, perhaps for days, waiting and hoping for some favorable change of wind and weather to bring a change of ice and change of fortune.

On another part of this same island we came upon seven graves. They were about fifty yards from the beach, on a rapidly sloping hill-side facing the west, beneath a great tall cliff, which forms a conspicuous landmark for vessels approaching from that direction.

Never was place of human sepulture more desolate. Here there were no birds; there was not even a blade of grass, nor a bit of moss—not a living thing—nothing but a waste of naked rocks and loose stones, that had been tumbled by the frosts of winter from the cliffs above. The dead had been laid in some convenient place among the rocks, and the stones had been heaped upon the coffins; and at the head of each rude sepulchre there had been placed a board on which the shipmates of the dead sailor had carved his name and age, and the place of his nativity, his ship, and rank, and day of death.

There was something very touching in the evident care with which the last sad offices of the living to the dead had been performed. But even there, in the drear solitude, other men had followed after the mourners, and graves which the wild beasts had respected, and which showed such signs of tender solicitude, had been most barbarously desecrated. The graves themselves remained as they had been originally prepared, but the head-boards, on which careful hands had carved the brief record of a career that the grave closed over, were broken into splinters, and strewn upon the rocks around. A party from some whale-ship (it could be no other) had landed there, and, using the head-boards of the graves for targets, had blown them all to pieces with ball and shot. Not a single one remained intact, and the resting-place which each was meant to tell of could not possibly be identified. Nor could much be made of the splinters that I found. The records on two of these ran thus :

"Of the ship Jane, of Hull, died April 28, 1832:"

"Who died on board of the ship Alexander, of Dundee, June 21, 1842, adged 42 years."

But to neither of these was any name attached; and even this much was deciphered with difficulty, so effectual had been the aim of the vandals. Another splinter told that
"Wm. Hardy, aged 59,"
had died, but I could not make out the name of his ship or the date of his death. Even about the "Wm." there was uncertainty. The only perfect one ran thus:

"To the memory of Thos. Roberts, seaman, Leith, who died on board the Alphen, of Peterhead, July 6th, 1825, aged 37 years."

It was late in the afternoon when we brought up at the summit of the island in the whalers' old look-out station, where we commanded a superb view of the surrounding region. How grandly the mountains and glaciers of Greenland loomed up on our right! How splendid was the sea around, speckled with ice, while here and there appeared a dark rocky island among the general whiteness. How tempting Melville Bay ahead, with its interminable " pack."

CHAPTER III.

ICE-NAVIGATION.

WHILE the chain is clicking in the hawse-hole, let us take a quiet view of the situation. There is no need, however, to describe with much minuteness the "Melville Bay pack" which lay before us. The ice freshly broken up in any large river is a sufficient illustration, provided the imagination will stretch the river to three hundred miles in width, and magnify the drifting fields of ice in proportion. In the early part of the season this ice is very hard, and many feet in thickness; but by August (which was the time of our being there) it has become porous, its thickness has been greatly reduced, much of it is on the eve of disappearing altogether, and still more of it has quite melted away. Almost all the fields, or the "floes," as they are called by the whalers, have been eaten through in places; and over all there are pools of water formed of melted snow, which give them a mottled appearance.

In the month of August this "pack" is mostly confined to the Melville Bay region; hence the name of "Melville Bay pack," which I have used before. At that season the navigation is not particularly difficult or dangerous. By keeping well away from the land the passage can then always be made with safety. It was by following the opposite course that Captain Sir Francis M'Clintock found himself delayed in 1857, with his ship firmly frozen fast, and with no alternative but to pass the winter drifting with the "pack" in a most uncomfortable and hazardous situation. Had he followed the example and advice of Dr. Kane, he might have won his knightly spurs a year sooner, and with less discomfort.

Earlier in the summer the pack extends far down Baffin's Bay; and south of the Arctic Circle it stretches away to the coasts of Labrador and Newfoundland. And it is here that commerce profits by it, for the seals flock to it the moment it has ceased to be the solid ice of the winter, and become the "pack" ice of the spring. Of these seals there are many varieties. Some are permanent denizens of the North; others are migratory. These last only are found so low as Newfoundland and Labrador. Seeking the ice in the month of March, they crawl upon it, and there bring forth their young. These seals come up from the South—from the St. Lawrence region and along the shores of New Brunswick and Maine, where they have wintered—and with the ice they drift back south again until it melts away. Other varieties (the true Arctic seals) adhere to the solid ice, as far as possible, and, if drifted off southward with the pack, return north again to winter, and then, in order to breathe (for the seals are not fish, and can not breathe under water), they are compelled to keep holes open in the ice with their sharp claws. These true Arctic seals are not so numerous as the southern varieties, of which latter millions may sometimes be seen at one time upon the drifting ice. It is the young of these (when from two to three weeks old) that are slaughtered in such great numbers by the seal-fishers. The vessels, usually small schooners, but sometimes steamers like our *Panther* (which was built for that service), enter the pack, and the crew, scattering to right and left over the ice, gather up the seals as they go along, the vessel merely keeping pace with them. Upon the first attack the old ones abandon their young to their fate, and the

THE POLAR BEAR.

innocent, whining "baby seals," too young to appreciate danger, are captured without difficulty—a tap on the nose with the toe of a boot or with a boat's "gaff" robbing them quickly of what little life they have.

From the seals let us pass to their enemies, the bears— I mean, of course, the true Arctic bears, known in different localities by different names—"ice-bears" they are usually called in the far north, because they are not found elsewhere than on the ice. But farther south this is not always true of them, since both from choice and necessity they often take the water, and are generally known on "the Labrador" as "water-bears." They are often carried off from the pack upon a single ice-field, which, going to pieces under them, forces them to swim, perhaps, many miles before reaching another. I have seen one swimming in a heavy sea, where there was not a piece of ice in sight. They seldom take to the land, and never voluntarily. Their food has either failed them on the ice, or they are pursued by enemies, or the ice has all melted away and left them no alternative. The naturalist's name, *Ursus maritimus*—"the bear of the sea"—expresses their character perfectly. In color they are yellowish-white—quite dark, indeed, when contrasted with the snow. "White bear" is therefore a misnomer, as is also "Polar bear;" but this latter is the name most commonly in use, and is the one, therefore, which I shall employ whenever referring to them.

The food of the seal consists of those low forms of marine life known to us as shrimps, and to naturalists as *invertebrata*, and sometimes certain varieties of *mollusca*. The former exist in vast numbers in the icy waters of the North; and it is this abundant supply of food which attracts to that quarter of the world not seals alone, but those enormous flights of birds of which we read, and some idea of which was given in former chapters of this book. On the other hand, the food of the bear is the seal. Therefore, wherever ice is seen seals may be expected; and where seals are seen, you may look out for bears.

We had seen seals and we had seen the "pack," and thus bears were suggested; and the suggestion was peculiarly welcome to the people of the *Panther*. The anchor was aweigh in almost no time at all, and, steam being up, the *Panther* was pointed northward, in the calm

SEALS.

evening. The sun was in the west, a good way above the horizon, and a pleasant glow was over sea, and land, and glacier.

We steer for Wilcox Point, fifteen miles in a north-easterly direction from the Duck Islands, and it is a very lofty, noble headland. We spread out the map on deck to see what comes next, and where we are to go. Eastward from Wilcox Point we observe that the coast trends some miles, and then comes a mountain called "The Devil's Thumb;" and as we subsequently see it, it has very much the appearance of a thumb projecting vertically above the hand when it is placed edgewise on the table, with the little finger down. We afterwards discover the hand to be an island, and the thumb the centre of it, but we did not know it then. Why the Devil's Thumb, rather than the thumb of some more respectable character, might seem puzzling; but I fancy that that dark spirit of evil was complimented with this monument on account of his supposed influence over the neighboring sea. The sea is there, indeed, very perilous, and no part of Baffin's Bay is so much dreaded as that vicinity. The icebergs are so numerous that the locality is often called "Bergy Hole;" and the currents are so swift that a sailing vessel, once becalmed off "The Thumb," is very likely to be sucked in and whirled about, as if there were some secret and supernatural influence at work upon the waters; and if the ship escapes without getting battered against an iceberg or so, and being much damaged in consequence, she is very lucky. Dr. Kane's brig, the *Advance*, got whirled into this dangerous situation, and I shall not soon forget the struggle of hours at the oars, by which means the brig was saved, though not until every body was thoroughly worn out, and ready to drop down with fatigue.

In a north-westerly direction from the Devil's Thumb, and distant from it about two hundred miles, lies Cape York, and between these two points the coast makes a deep curve, and the space thus embraced is Melville Bay —though the name has really a wider significance—the term Melville Bay being usually meant to signify that part of Baffin's Bay west of it, where the "middle ice" is always lying. The entire sweep of Melville Bay is one vast line of glaciers, wholly unapproachable, and from which are cast off an incredible number of icebergs, that are scattered over Baffin's Bay in all directions, and by accumulating in greater numbers year by year, gather the ice-field about them more and more, and thus render navigation each year more difficult and perilous. Since ships first penetrated Melville Bay a very perceptible change has taken place.

Most of which information we gather from the map; and while gathering it the *Panther* is coming, bows on, to the very first field-ice we have seen. There it is before us —a great, long, level plain of white and blue, stretching beyond the line of vision. It does not look so very formidable, after all, and is rather disappointing, until the ship takes a projecting tongue, and, by the shock that it gives us, shows there is more body to the ice than first appeared. In fact, from seven-eighths to nine-tenths of it lies below the surface of the water; and not until the *Panther* had split a fragment off and turned it up on its edge, as the bow slid over it, did we appreciate its really solid quality.

But this was a brush not worth mentioning; and on went the *Panther* beyond and across clear water until we approached another great field, which had at first appeared to be a part of the one which we had passed; but the event proved that there was a wide streak of open water stretching to the northward, which a whaleman would call a "lead;" and, seeing that our farther progress in the direction we had chosen was cut off, we bore away from Wilcox Point, and steamed north at great speed between the "floes."

Very soon there was no water to be seen except the lead we were in — everywhere limitless ice — unless we went aloft, when other leads were visible, meandering among the floes in all directions. The lead we had entered was at first at least a mile wide; but as we proceeded it gradually narrowed, then became crooked; loose floes of small size were lying here and there upon it. The mate, who was aloft, kept the man at the wheel busy enough with his "starboards" and "ports" and "steadys," until it was reported that our lead was a blind one, and we were coming to the end of it. An immense floe lay between the two great floes to right and left of us, jammed tight, and squeezed and broken up upon its sides. This was the report from aloft, and the mate cried, " Starboard ! —hard a-starboard !"

"What's that for?" shouted the captain, with stentorian voice. "What do you want to starboard for?"

"Jammed tight everywhere, and we must go back," said the mate.

"Is there no opening anywhere?"

"None; but the ice looks weak on the port hand."

"Keep her for it, and put her in," roared the captain.

"Ay, ay, sir! Starboard a little; steady—steady as she goes."

And down we bore upon the ice, the rakish bow and stem of the *Panther* well up out of the water, and looking defiant, as if it were a matter of no kind of consequence to her what amount of ice lay before her. It seemed as if she could crush it down, and trample on it, and ride over it rough-shod, and never wink until the affair was finished. Perhaps the captain's threat—seemingly made in earnest—to "put her through, or knock her bloody eyes out," may have had some effect upon her, and have inspired her with additional resolution.

We were soon so near the ice that the opening could be seen from the bridge, and the mate was called below. "Mind your helm, Mick," said the captain to the man at the wheel; "mind your helm there!"

And still on we went, still rushing towards the ice at full speed, the screw grinding fiercely, and making the ship tremble in every timber. It was soon too late to check her headway, even if the captain should have desired it; to wheel round now was quite impossible. We braced ourselves for the shock that was coming—every man catching hold of something to steady himself with. The captain watched the point he wished to make ahead. "Port—port a little—steady, steady, as she goes."

Cr-r-r-r-ash—the solid iron cut-water of the *Panther* has taken the ice. She cuts into it, slides upon it, and crushes it down; the ship rides up again, and sinks, and buries herself one full length in the body of the floe; but still she slides up once more and crushes the ice farther on, but going slower now; and then she stops and settles down to her proper level, and the groaning of the ice seems to be a cry of relief and satisfaction from the noble ship, which only wants a little breathing-time before she begins again.

She isn't hurt—not in the least. Her masts are all standing right, her bows are sound as ever, her solid, iron-bound sides have not a scratch. Pretty well for a first beginning; and no one now doubts the *Panther's* ability for any thing.

"Back astern," shouts the captain; and we haul out into clear water a hundred fathoms or so, and butt away into the opening we have made before. We ride over the broken ice; the cut-water strikes again; again we feel the ship going up forward; again she sinks and rises, and then she settles down again at rest. Then we go below, in great glee, to supper, and the captain tells the watch-officer to "keep her at it;" and the screw, thumping against the ice that has come about the stern, is kept revolving, and the wedge-shaped *Panther* is pushing in between the floes, forcing them asunder.

When we come on deck again the crack is opening. The jar and steady pressure have had their effect; the floes have been set in motion, the crack widens, and we grind through into clear, open water.

This bold dash into the very teeth of the enemy saved us a wide detour, and brought us by a short cut into an extensive area of open water, which gave us a free passage northward as far as the eye could see. But still we had

THE DEVIL'S THUMB.

heavy floes on the starboard hand, which prevented us from hauling in, as we desired, close under Wilcox Point. We had, however, a fine view of the noble headland at a distance of five miles.

Running now along the edge of an old floe that lay to

our right, all eyes were strained, and all glasses were doing service in search of bears. Men were in the rigging and up aloft. We soon opened Melville Bay, the tall spire of the Devil's Thumb coming in view through a blaze of sunshine exactly at midnight.

It was a midnight long to be remembered. The bright sun stood in the heavens before us but a little way above the horizon, glittering upon the icebergs and flinging gems broadcast upon the floes. The great glaciers that climbed up from the sea at the bend of the bay, until they were lost in a line of purple against a belt of golden light, reflected the light from their glassy terraces; the cavernous old cape which towered above our heads was warmed and reddened by the glow; upon the summit of the Devil's Thumb there lingered a brilliant ray; and, as the lofty column rose from out a vast cluster of icebergs, it seemed as if it were a church spire mounting to heaven above some nameless city.

CHAPTER IV.
HUNTING BY STEAM.

At length there came the cry of "Bears! bears!" which had been so long eagerly desired. With the first alarm the people swarmed up from below, and the deck was alive in an instant, every body shouting "Where?" And "Where? where?" rang through the ship loud enough, as one would think, to have frightened all the bears of Melville Bay into fits.

But there were the bears, sure enough; and they appeared to be the very ones we were looking for. Clearly they had seen the *Panther* long before we had discovered them; but they did not appear to be at all frightened, but stood their ground boldly, looking at us evidently with more curiosity than alarm. There were three of them, an old mother and two cubs, standing about three or four hundred yards distant from us, and quite still. The mother was in the middle, with a cub on either side, in a very cool and composed manner. They appeared to be an affectionate sort of family, and were a very odd sight as they stood upon the old ice-field, the only living things on that desolate waste. It seemed, indeed, a pity to disturb these denizens of the Polar wilderness.

The steamer was stopped as quickly as possible, and we lay there watching them, and they us, both parties endeavoring to make up their minds what the other was going to do. The bears probably did not see us—only the steamer—since we kept our heads as much as possible below the bulwarks; and whatever wind there was being from the north, they had not discovered an enemy with their noses. The steamer was but a black curiosity, and we were well pleased when they manifested a disposition for a nearer inspection and a closer acquaintance. The old mother led off, and the two young ones came shuffling along beside her, very slowly and cautiously, edging away, however, towards the vessel's stern, manifestly for the purpose of coming as far as possible around to the leeward of us. And here the ice favored the old bear's design, for a long tongue projected far out from the general line of the floe. If they should reach the end of it they would be able to discover us, but then they would be at the same time in a trap of their own making. In this design we encouraged them by lying low behind the bulwarks. It did not seem to be in accordance with the rules of the hunt to allow your game to crawl around where he could wind you, and this it was, of course, within our power to prevent; but since the captain had the management of his own vessel, and knew what he could do with her, he became the master hunter by virtue of his office. "We'll get the whole lot of them now," said he, "if they only crawl along out on that point a little farther." And he told the engineer to go ahead at half-speed, and told Mick to shove his helm hard a-port. The action wheeled the *Panther* around upon her heel, and she now stood upon the dead waters facing the bears, who still, slowly and cautiously, were going out on the tongue of the old floe.

"Why, captain, what are you going to do now? The moment the bears scent us they will take off!" exclaimed an anxious hunter.

"But before they do," replied the captain, "I can cut in behind and head them."

"But the ice, the ice, man You will surely not drive her into a floe like that?"

"That I will," said the captain, promptly; "drive her into an iceberg, if necessary."

So now it was the skill and strength of the *Panther* against the skill and fleetness of the bears.

Bears are not graceful animals in their movements. Their enormous legs are carried along as if they had no joints in them, and their immense feet are lifted in a manner to suggest their being mounted on snow-shoes. The long, tapering neck is the only graceful thing about them.

I was particularly struck with the old mother's excessive caution. She would not come near, and yet she would not go away. Had she taken to her heels when she first discovered us she could, of course, have defied pursuit, for the ice-field was so extensive that we could never have overtaken her. But she seemed to be fascinated with the steamer, and her curiosity got the better of her discretion. It is not the first time that this same quality, inherent in all living creatures, has involved its possessor in trouble.

She moved along with great deliberation. She appeared to be a well-fed bear, and probably had breakfasted recently and felt lazy; for she did not once attempt to run, nor did she wade through the pools of water which were on the ice, but deliberately walked around them, as if indisposed even to wet her feet. Sometimes she would turn her back towards us, sometimes her front; often she would stop, stretch out her long neck and sniff the air all round, turning her head to right and left, throwing her nose as high up as she could get it, and then dropping it on the ice as if she might discover something there. Meanwhile, the little ones were cutting all sorts of antics about her. Seeing that she was not alarmed, they were in great glee, evidently regarding the *Panther* as a very wonderful show, got up by their mother for their special benefit. They chased each other like a pair of kittens;

raced round and round the old bear, rolled each other over on the ice, using their paws and teeth upon each other after the usual innocent and playful fashion natural to dumb animals in their youthful state. They splashed the water right and left as they ran through the pools; and altogether they appeared to be a pair of very lively, and highly delighted young bears, who regarded the present occasion as rather a jolly sort of entertainment.

It took this family party somewhere near half an hour to get around to where the old one wanted to be, to satisfy herself as to whether the *Panther* was a friend or a foe. Once she seemed irresolute, and turned about as if she would retrace her steps and make off; but then she turned back again, and for some minutes after seemed to be dragged by two antagonistic impulses, first one way and then the other, with a general gain of force, however, on the string which drew her out to the point of ice.

By-and-by she got where she seemed to be satisfied, for she suddenly stopped short, threw up her head, gave a tremendous snort, wheeling around at the same time in a state of alarm, and looking about as if for some means of escape. After a moment's reflection she took the back track. The alarm spread to the little ones, and the lively creatures ran around their mother as if they would inquire what the matter was, and if the show was over, and they were to have no more of it, while she seemed to be encouraging them by assurances that it was no great affair, but that it was necessary for them to use their legs as nimbly as possible, for they must get out of that. So their gambols were ended, and the little things whined piteously, and did their best. They appeared to be as unhappy as children caught in a thunder-shower on their way from a country fair. It was now not less amusing to watch them than before. In the confused state of their

THE PANTHER AFTER THE BEARS.

minds they grew utterly careless of what they were about, and they often sprang upon rotten places in the ice, and broke through, and by the time they had crawled out again the mother was some distance ahead, and was obliged to wait, and often to run back, if not actually to render assistance to her cubs, at least to encourage them. As for herself, she could readily have escaped; and she appeared to be quite conscious of the fact; but she would not leave her young: her devotion to them was indeed touching, and worthy of all admiration.

Meanwhile the *Panther* had not been idle. The moment the old bear got the wind of us, and began to show symptoms of alarm, the captain rang his bell, "Ahead, full speed." The screw began to revolve, and at the top of her speed the vessel bore down upon the ice, across the line of the bears' retreat.

This was the captain's plan from the beginning, and it now became a mere question of time; though on the *Panther's* part there was in the minds of most of us a question of strength and power.

We came upon the ice as before with a grand crash, striking what appeared to be the weakest spot. The shock was worse than any thing we had yet felt, the ice being firmer than before; but the solid iron cut-water opened her way into it as formerly, and she rode up on it and crushed it down, and rode up again and settled once more; and in the conflict every body was very uneasy on his legs. The jar made lively work in the pantry, where the cabin-boy had retired when he had shouted "bergs" instead of bears, and, quite exhausted by the effort, had fallen fast asleep there, and was aroused by the soup-tureen coming down and landing, bottom up, on the crown of his head, which nearly cracked his skull, but saved the crockery, and in a measure woke up the young man.

"Blob," who was standing beside the coamings of the main hatch, making a sketch of the bears, turned a somerset into the coal-hole, where his picture was turned into a black bear instead of a white one. Otherwise no damage was done; but the ruse was altogether successful, as the captain had anticipated; for the force of the shock started the ice, and a crack opened right through in front of us to the water on the other side. The point to which the bears had gone was thus broken from the main body of the floe, and the game was now on a raft, and at our mercy.

The crack, opening very rapidly before the steady pressure of the vessel, gave us a free passage through, and seeing themselves thus headed off, and the steamer bearing down across their line of retreat, they took the back track, and now, all thoroughly frightened, ran across to the opposite side, behind us, thus compelling us to wheel about and return through the crack. At this moment the photographers came rushing on deck demanding the right of a "first shot." Quick as a flash the camera was down and focused, a slide with a little hole in it was dropped before the lens, and the family group of polar bears was taken at a distance of about two hundred yards. To accomplish this feat required the very first degree of enterprise and skill. The camera was stationed upon the top-gallant forecastle, and the impression was obtained while both ship and bears were in motion. The brightness of the light, of course, greatly favored the success of this altogether novel experiment in the photographic art. The artists (Mr. John Dunmore, of Boston, and Mr. George Critcherson, of Worcester) deserve the highest commendation for their successful accomplishment of so difficult a feat. The bears now took the water with the manifest intention of swimming to the solid floe; but here we again anticipated them, and they wheeled about again, and swam back towards the ice which they had left but a few moments before. Putting the helm a-starboard, we now came directly in upon their wake, and when within fifty yards of them slackened speed.

At this moment they presented a magnificent sight, their beautiful long hair waving gracefully in the clear blue water, and their round, buoyant bodies floating along swiftly towards the ice and hoped-for safety. The tender regard of the mother for her offspring was here as strikingly apparent as when on the ice. She would not abandon them; but, on the contrary, the nearer we approached the more she stuck by and encouraged them, still, as before, with one on either side. Once she invited them to dive, and, imitating her example, the three went down together and paddled themselves along for some distance about twenty feet below the surface, where we could easily see them striking out for dear life. When they came up we gave them a volley from our rifles, and the old mother and one of the cubs lay lifeless upon the blood-stained water.

The other cub, by some mischance, escaped with only a slight scratch, and reached the floe, where, as he rose, another ball entered his side, and sent him off with a mortal wound, whining piteously. The captain now jammed his steamer into the ice, and, clambering down over the bob-stays, gave chase. The bear soon stopped and hid himself behind a hummock, and when the captain came up with him he was disposed to make fight. His whine was converted into a defiant growl, and he charged his pursuer; but a well-aimed shot brought the game down and completed the hunt.

It only remained now to get the animals aboard, to weigh and measure them, to award the skins to the rifles which had given them death-wounds. This last was no easy matter; but finally, after much discussion and some rather animated assertions, such as usually take place on like occasions, the award was finally made, and we tied up to an iceberg that promised us a chance for watering ship, and, after the excitement and exposure of the night, we were well prepared to enjoy a good breakfast of the game we had brought from the Duck Islands.

Casting off from the iceberg next day, we set out to look for further game, steaming up in a north-easterly direction through a wide lead. Presently we saw something dark on the edge of the ice, and soon made it out to be a seal, a very large one, of the barbed species. We knew from former experience how very wild they were, and, slacking speed, we approached cautiously. At first he appeared to be asleep, dozing lazily in the warm sun; but if so, the noise of the steamer awoke him, and he grew restive and alarmed. Evidently he was not to be caught as the bears had been, and if we would shoot him we must exercise great care; so the headway of the steamer was slackened still further, and we all lay low behind the bulwarks as we glided slowly along, thus stalking the animal in a somewhat unusual fashion. But he was too old to be cheated, and when still two rifle-shots away he threw up head and tail, and floundered into the water. Then he swam off, and brought his almost human-looking face above the surface not twenty yards away, then took a deliberate look at us, and before a rifle could be aimed he had apparently satisfied himself, for he turned heels over head, and with a terrific splash disappeared to be seen no more.

This little incident would not be worth naming, since it was an entirely unsuccessful feat of hunting, had it not been that at the very moment the seal disappeared from the ice an immense bear sprang out from behind a ridge of hummocks, along which he had evidently been crawling, stalking the very same seal that we were after. We had clearly robbed the beast of his breakfast, and he appeared to be more disgusted with the circumstance than alarmed by us. Yet he was not quite so unsuspicious as the bears we had before encountered. He was the largest bear I had ever seen, and we wanted him badly. He looked splendid as he stood there upon the floe. The moment he saw the *Panther* he came to a dead stand, and made no further movement than to turn his head first to one side and then to the other, in a sort of measured oscillation. There was evidently upon his mind a feeling of irresolution that was constantly increasing; yet it did not seem as if he was willing to own to himself that he was afraid, until the steamer coming in contact quite unavoidably with a piece of ice made a considerable crash, which settled the bear into a suspicion that the object he was looking at was hardly to be trusted. He wheeled suddenly round on his hind-legs, like a horse wheeling at play in a pasture, made a most magnificent bound across a pool of water, and then took himself off quite leisurely, turning his head back over his shoulder with every step, to have a further look at us. Occasionally he would give a snort, attended with an extra leap, and then go waddling on again at the same stiff-legged and snow-shoe pace as before described in the case of the other bears which we had hitherto pursued and captured. But for all he had still clearly some lingering doubts of the *Panther's* hostile disposition, and, allowing this feeling to get the better of him, he came to a dead stand, and squared himself round to have a better look at us; then he advanced a few paces, stopped and fixed his gaze upon us steadily. Meanwhile the *Panther* lay still upon the waters, and appeared to have her eye upon him, and the two stood, as if trying to stare each other out of countenance, for some minutes. The bear seemed at length to be getting charmed, for he advanced a hundred yards or so with the greatest coolness and deliberation; and then, as if suddenly recollecting his previous prudential notions, he wheeled short around as before, took a huge leap, and went upon the back track again.

To look at the animal now and watch all his antics, one would think him as mad as a March hare. He turned first to the right and then to the left, after he had gone a little way, and then he began to move up and down in front of us, like a sentry on post, acting very deliberately all the while, poking out his head and drawing it in again like a turtle, elevating his nose as high as he could, and then depressing it again close down upon the ice, occasionally stopping short and looking at the *Panther* sideways.

All of these manœuvres, it must be understood, were for the special benefit of the *Panther*, for we on board of her were closely hidden behind the bulwarks, with nothing but our eyes exposed. Up to this time it was clear enough that the bear had not been seriously frightened. Like the others, he was in some doubt and uncertainty about the meaning of the dark object, and was filled with curiosity. We had, therefore, great hopes that he would become reconciled to the *Panther*, and be inclined to closer acquaintance. It is not an uncommon thing for a bear in Melville Bay to leave the ice and swim off to a vessel. I have known them to come deliberately alongside, attracted thither, no doubt, by the smell of bones which were burning in the galley—a whaleman's device for attracting the bears. But the sight or smell of a human being, or of a dog, alarms them at once, and they instantly make off.

In the burning bones they find, no doubt, something savory and suggestive of food.

We felt greatly encouraged when we saw the bear begin to march up and down in front of us, as if standing guard; but unfortunately the *Panther* could not forever hold her breath, and with the first gush of steam through the escape-pipe old Bruin bounded up in the air as if possessed, gave a fierce snort, and ran away as fast as his legs would carry him; and in order that he might make the best time possible, and show off his points to the best advantage, we fired a volley from our rifles after him, without the least hope or chance of doing him any damage, owing to the great distance. He did not now pause until he was a good quarter of a mile away from us, when he faced round once more, seemed to bestow upon us an approving nod, and then, with much deliberation, made for the opposite side of the floe, where we now busied our minds with devising ways and means of reaching him. But no way could we see but once more to put the *Panther* into the ice—no very difficult matter; but here the ice was unusually thick, and there did not appear to be much chance of breaking through it. To go around the floe was to make a circuit of several miles, and long before we could reach the point towards which the bear was going he would be far enough away.

Running down a little way near the edge of the floe, we discovered a narrow isthmus, against which the captain put the vessel, as before, under full headway, but with less happy results. Only a few fathoms of the ice were broken away. Owing to this circumstance the shock was greater than on either of the former occasions; but, nothing daunted, the captain backed her out and put her in four successive times, and was rewarded in the end by starting a crack, through which the steamer was forced.

We were now in the same lead for which the bear was making, and we could with our glasses still see him upon the ice, though very near the water, which by this time he could readily have reached had he done his best. We bore down upon him with all possible haste. Presently he disappeared. He had taken the water, and was making for the opposite ice, which was very solid, and was held firm and fast by a great number of icebergs, which were imbedded in it. If he once reached this the game was up.

The second mate was sent aloft, and detected him in the water heading for a point which, instead of being low and flat, as is usual, was rough and hummocky. The *Panther* was pointed there also, with the view of cutting off his retreat. This once accomplished, the bear was of course ours. Seeing our purpose, the animal, now evidently in a great state of terror, swam away for dear life, making a splendid spectacle of himself as he floated along with his nose only above the surface, and was clearly in much the condition of the soldiers who swam the river from the battle of Ball's Bluff—he was not hurt, but fearfully demoralized.

We were only about sixty yards away when he reached the point, and we now felt sure of him. We had not succeeded in cutting off his line of retreat, but we had come within easy range; and since the vessel was forging ahead, we should be almost atop of the animal by the time he got out of the water. The *Panther* was going fairly for the ice, and we were all ready to fire the moment he showed himself. But the animal was too cunning for us. The rough hummocks of the point hid from our view a bight on the opposite side, into which the bear swam for safety; and now, thoroughly sheltered behind the ice for which we were making, he was getting the

THE CAPTAIN AFTER THE BEAR.

better of us. With that quickness of perception characteristic of the skillful sailor, the captain grasped the situation, and, seeing that to round the point was to lose the bear for certain, he shouted to the man at the wheel to put his helm hard a-port, which caused us to bring up with a terrific thump a short distance from the point, where the ice was comparatively thin. The moment the ship struck and buried herself a little, the captain let himself down by a rope from the cat-head, and, followed by two other rifles, ran over the floe towards the bend of the bight for which the bear was making, but not in time to intercept him. He reached the ice, and drew his enormous body out of the water a hundred yards from the riflemen, and bounded away with the speed of the wind, not stopping even long enough to shake himself of the great quantity of water in his long hair. Every body fired at him, of course, but none of our balls took effect; at least none of them produced any impression upon his speed. The captain thought he saw blood, and kept up the race for half a mile, hoping to see him drop or halt, as the one he had chased before, mortally wounded; but the animal was soon out of sight among the icebergs, and our eagerly coveted game was gone.

We were all much chagrined by this mishap. Every man had regarded him as his own particular prize, and felt quite sure of him. We had even taken the measurement and weight of his body. One was going to have his skin spread out for a mat, with his head stuffed and his paws on. Another was going to drive four-in-hand in the Park, and have him for a sleigh-robe; another was going to sell him for two hundred and fifty dollars currency, and he knew where to place the article; but all these bright anticipations came to a most lamentable end when the bear carried off his own skin in his own four-in-hand fashion.

We were soon consoled for this disappointment by another alarm. It came from the look-out up aloft, and was answered with a universal "Where away?" which was answered in turn by the most satisfactory assurance that they were down on the extreme point of a long, narrow floe, and were apparently easily accessible. They were three in number. We bore down upon them without delay, the man aloft conning the ship, until they were seen from the deck, when the captain, as usual, gave his own orders.

The ice upon which the bears were proved this time to be very thin and rotten, as was evidenced by the fact that the animals frequently broke through. They could not, therefore, travel very fast, even if they should become frightened; and then, besides, as we came nearer to them we perceived that, no matter how fast they might travel, there was but little chance of their escaping us, for in whatever direction they might attempt to go we could follow them; and when in the water they would be easily overtaken, as they would have at least a quarter of a mile to swim before reaching another floe.

The *Panther* tore through the ice this time without difficulty; and she actually broke the ice up with such facility, and approached the bears with such rapidity, that they were almost dropped into the water — at least a crack was forced open ahead of us, almost underneath the bears' feet. They took to it immediately, and we almost ran over them. As we approached we might have shot them very easily; but the photographers were crazy for a chance at them, and, seeing that there was no possibility of their escape, we sacrificed our impatience in the interest of art.

The bears having swum a little while, crawled upon the ice. By this time we had wheeled round, and the photographers had a fine chance at them. The hunters were impatient, but they had not long to wait, for the delighted "colonel" soon thrust his head out of his photographic box and shouted, "I'm done with them, gentlemen." At this moment the bears took the water again.

We made short work of cutting through a tongue of ice which intervened; and, coming upon the animals as they swam, we ceased playing with them as a cat plays with a mouse before swallowing it, and at thirty yards gave them a volley, and three more bears were added to our trophies. The carcasses were soon hoisted on deck, and we then steered for Wilcox Point, without, however, seeing any bears by the way. Then we headed in for the Devil's Thumb, and, discovering a moderately firm floe, which seemed to be held in its position by some grounded icebergs, we steered for it, run the *Panther* a hundred yards into it, and proceeded to let our six prizes down on the ice, where we soon had the skins off, some for specimens, and some for robes and mats—each one who was the fortunate possessor of a skin following the bent of his fancy in the matter.

Pushing off from the floe, we steamed to within two miles of the Thumb, and anchored. Probably no vessel had ever been so near it as we were, and although our situation was one of some peril, we did not feel justified in losing the opportunity so auspiciously presented to us. We climbed the hills all round, and everywhere we went we discovered numerous traces of reindeer, but we did not succeed in finding any of the animals themselves. There can be no doubt that they exist there in considerable numbers, and had we followed them inland it is equally certain that we would have found any number of them. But for an enterprise of that description we had not sufficient time to stay—or, rather, the threatening nature of the ice, and the uncertainty of our situation, made it important that all hands should be at least within signalling distance, that we might steam out from underneath the Devil's Thumb upon the first threat of danger.

To climb the Thumb we found to be impossible, but we reached its base, and from there—an elevation of thirteen hundred feet, according to my barometer—we overlooked one of the most remarkable scenes that ever met the eye of man. Such a wilderness of ice, such a forest of icebergs, such boundless desolation, would be difficult to describe, or to be appreciated except by the actual observer. Let me, in a mechanical sort of way, make the attempt to convey to the reader's mind some idea of this remarkable scene.

The Devil's Thumb is an island—at least, without actually sailing round it in my boat (being prevented by the ice), there were such indications as to make it certain that, if not an island, it is connected with the main-land only by a very low and narrow isthmus. It lies at the head of a deep bay, and it is from five to eight miles long, by from three to five wide. The Thumb itself is on the farther side from the sea, and is about six hundred feet high above its base, rising like a church spire, and as abruptly. Down into the bay, to the north and east from the island, come two great glaciers, one about twelve miles wide, the other about three. These glaciers climbed up steadily, or descended, I should rather say, between the coast mountains in steady streams, which, joining together, and with others to the north and south of them, form a long level line against the sky; and this is the summit of the great icy sea—the *mer de glace*—which covers the whole length of the Greenland continent, and which, from its exhaustless bed, sends down through every valley opening to Baffin's Bay such streams as these. And these streams send off into the sea the icebergs, which are but trifling fragments of the glacier itself.

The icebergs coming from these two glaciers about the Devil's Thumb were altogether countless. They filled up the whole north side of the bay, and extended out to the sea for miles. The time of my visit was near midnight, and with a clear, bright sun illuminating the scene, scattering everywhere its splendors, I could but wish for something better than a simple note-book and the use of words to embody an idea of the view before me. An artist alone, with his pallette and his pencil, could convey any proper effect of it. My powers of sketching were quite inadequate. "Blob" might have done better, but no amount of persuasion could induce him to climb a hill marked in the devil's name. Of all the situations of the cruise, this view was the finest beyond comparison, and to see it was enough to repay one for all the trouble and vexation and hazard of a dozen such voyages. We missed a photograph of it for the same reason we missed "Blob's" sketch—a fearful superstition. Had it been called "The Pillar of the Church" instead of "The Devil's Thumb," the whole cabin mess would have climbed it willingly.

CHAPTER V.

AMONG THE ICE-FIELDS OF MELVILLE BAY.

I was much disappointed that we could not prolong our stay in the vicinity of the Devil's Thumb. But our situation there was indeed a hazardous one. The ice was crowding about us all the time, and, driven by a three-knot current that whirled it round in the wildest manner, it was not surprising that the captain should declare the Thumb to be no proper place for the *Panther*. Accordingly, after doing the best we could hydrographically, topographically, and artistically, we crawled out while the chance was good and steamed northward into the pack.

To describe our adventures of the next few days would be to repeat much of what I have said before about the pursuit of bears and encounters with ice-fields. Neither ice-navigation nor bear-hunting can present much of variety. Even to ourselves both became monotonous in the end; and we even received the cry of "bears" without excitement, and were knocked off our legs by the thumping of the *Panther* against the ice without emotion.

Besides the bears and an occasional seal (none of which were we lucky enough, however, to shoot), we saw no living thing except an occasional flock of little auks, or rotche, as they are called by the whalers. These are the cunningest little divers imaginable. They are family relations of the lumme already described; and, although only about one-third the size, are like them in color. The water is alive with shrimps about a quarter of an inch in length; and these little birds, whose flight is very rapid, come from the distant land to feed. Myriads of them whizzed over us, affording a fine opportunity for the sportsman. Sometimes large flocks of them would alight upon the water and, after satisfying their appetites, would crawl out upon the ice, and, sitting along the margin of it, dry themselves in the warm sun.

Our hunts after seals were most tantalizing. Great numbers of them came up out of the water, and stretching themselves on the ice in the blazing sunshine, went to sleep there. But they were all too shy for us. We approached them with steamer and with boat, but it was of no avail. If they did not sleep with one eye open, they certainly never slept with both ears shut; and long before they had come within effective range of our rifles, they were off the ice and into the water, and although they might bob up and down in the sea, looking at us within a distance of fifty yards or so, they were always careful not to expose themselves long enough to allow of our drawing a sight on them.

The weather was superb; for the most part the air was entirely calm, and in the perpetual sunshine our enjoyment was uninterrupted. Sometimes we were beset among the ice-fields, once or twice drifted upon an iceberg while we were helplessly involved among heavy floes, and there was therefore enough of danger to deprive the days of absolute stupidity. This ice-navigation, is never wholly free from hazard, and nothing can be more treacherous than the movements of the pack. Great skill and caution are always necessary on the part of the officers of the ship, and, since we were out of sight of land much of the time for several days, the mate had no temptation to indulge his favorite pastime of sounding with the *Panther's* keel. He would, indeed, be at all times a capital sailor but for his weakness for running the ship ashore.

I have, unhappily, none of those harrowing adventures to record which usually make up the accounts of Melville Bay voyagers. Once only did we encounter a real " nip." The *Panther* was then pretty badly squeezed, and we had a lively exhibition of the power of the closing ice-field. Strong though the *Panther* was, we could readily see that she would be as an egg-shell in the hand if caught where the ice was in rapid movement. Fortunately it was only a revolving floe which beset us, and not the moving pack that was passing down bodily.

At length, after winding and twisting about to our hearts' content, and having seen the Melville Bay pack and the Melville Bay icebergs in every aspect possessing interest for us, the *Panther* was brought up alongside a heavy floe many miles in extent, and there she was, for the last time, made fast. A consultation revealed the fact that no one cared particularly to go any farther. A meridian altitude fixed our position at latitude 75°, near the Sabine Islands—farther in the direction of the North Pole, certainly, than any pleasure-seekers had ever gone before in that quarter. We were at least a hundred miles within the "pack," and every one was abundantly satisfied with his performances, whether they had been sporting, artistic, scientific, or what not.

Our last day, tied up to the old floe, was a memorable one in our calendar. The temperature was quite warm, at one time reaching 60° in the shade, and, exposed as we had been so long, this seemed to us a sultry heat. And this was the more strange that we were in the midst of a perfect forest of icebergs. The floe to which we lay moored was, so far as the eye could perceive, limitless in extent—the thickness was about two and a half feet, and for the most part it was as level as the sea in a calm. The snows of winter had melted from its surface, and here

MOORED TO A FLOE IN MELVILLE BAY.

and there the water had gathered in shallow pools, giving something the appearance of a marsh. Through the field numerous icebergs protruded, like huge rocks rising above a plain; the universal whiteness, broken only by the deep blue of the water, produced a glare that was sometimes painful to the eye, and, when the sun was shining at its brightest, quite overpowering.

Our people amused themselves in various ways. Some carried out boards from the ship, and, dropping them upon the ice, went soundly to sleep upon them in the hot sun. Others played foot-ball; while some exercised their skill with pistol and rifle upon a target painted with ink upon the side of a berg. Others, again, ran foot-races, and all hands made the most of the strange and unusual situation. There were neither bears nor seals to attract to more serious pastime, and no living thing besides ourselves was seen in this brilliantly illuminated wilderness except a flock of rotche, which came from the northward, and dropped down in the sea only a little way from us. Afterward they climbed out of the water and stood in a row, bolt upright, on the edge of the ice, staring at us in a most cunning and saucy manner. No doubt they had come from the extensive rookeries on the north side of Melville Bay, where the shore is for miles and miles literally alive with them.

While the idlers were thus amusing themselves, the artists were busy enough; and, for myself, I found sufficient occupation in measuring and closely examining an iceberg which lay partly imbedded in the floe about two hundred yards from us. It was a very remarkable berg, both in form and dimensions, though, in the latter particular, many that I have seen exceeded it. Its greatest height, determined from a carefully measured base-line, was 230 feet, and its extreme length 1040 feet. We called it "the ruined castle," and, indeed, there was only required a very slight assistance from the imagination to complete the outlines of an ancient work of defense turned adrift upon the sea in some unaccountable manner, as if to make room for more modern inventions. I estimated its cubical contents at fifty millions of tons.

Our castled iceberg can hardly be appreciated even by a detailed description, for it is difficult to describe so grand an object even by contrasting it with familiar things. In the first place, there was an open portal and a lowered draw-bridge; but the latter did not look very secure, being but a portion of the ice-field on which we stood, that had been crowded into the opening. So we did not venture upon the passage, but rather gazed through the archway at the blue sky beyond, until the curiosity was satisfied, when we walked as far around the ruin as the nature of the ice would allow. The rear proved to be much lower than the front; and, in fact, the front and one side presented from both points of view a no bad imitation of a lofty wall (now partly crumbled down), which had once been the half of the wall inclosing the central space, or court-yard, to which the portal led. This space was about one-eighth of a mile in diameter, and was very rough and rugged, and it lay some fifty to eighty feet above the sea-level. When the sun came around to that side, and shone down upon that part of the wonderful ruin, and we stood upon the ice-field in front and in deep shadow, looking through the open portal, the effect was most enchanting; and it is, indeed, impossible to conceive of any thing more delightful in the way of light and shade and color than it presented. When the sun was shining on the ice, as seen through the portal, the surface had the appearance of delicate white satin. The shadows were the most tender and delicious azure, while in those places where the ice-field

THE ICEBERG CASTLE.

was removed from the berg, and an overhanging portion of it received the reflected light from the water below, the color was the most perfectly transparent green that can be imagined.

I have so many times described these icebergs in all their varying characters, that any thing more might seem like too much; but I can not pass from the description of this castle-like natural formation without alluding to the wonderful variety of shapes assumed by these floating ice-mountains. There is scarcely a conceivable form that I have not seen: birds and savage beasts and effigies of domes and towers, and other objects, animate and inanimate, are seen continually. Human faces stare at you on every side; huge busts of men and forms of women I have often observed; and once a giant statue stood against the sky, outrivalling the famous Colossus of Rhodes, which it imitated in form and size.

CHAPTER VI.

THE LAST WHITE MAN.

As this was to be our last tie-up in Melville Bay, and as every body was well satisfied that Melville Bay had been thoroughly "done," there was now some impatience to hear the order given to "cast off."

But the order did not come even with the close of the day, and there we were clearly to remain until the morrow. Meanwhile a light wind set in from the south-east, and, coming directly from the Greenland glaciers, it brought the temperature down below the freezing-point; and when at length "seven bells" aroused the ship's company from their slumbers, the *Panther* was a prisoner. In every direction, as far as the eye could reach, the sea, where it had been open the evening before, was now covered with ice. In many places this young ice would bear a man's weight. It was a very needless predicament to have been placed in, but these Newfoundland sailors must not for the world be robbed of their night's rest.

Luckily the *Panther* was strong, or we should have lain there beside the ruined castle all winter. It was at least a quarter of an hour after we had actually at length cast off from the floe before we budged an inch, and then it was a long while before we made much headway. By-and-by, however, we went ahead at the rate of one knot an hour, and then, after that, crunched through the transparent film that was on the sea. The crystals flew to left and right; and when the sun came out, shining upon the flying fragments, it seemed as if we were cutting through

WE STEAM AWAY FROM THE MIDNIGHT SUN.

a waste of jewelry. A few hours of this sort of running brought us into the clear water of an opening lead, and thence our flight from Melville Bay was made much after the same fashion as that of our going in—the same cutting through and breaking down of floes, and the same wild excitement as before.

Our good ship seemed to have a realizing sense of her situation, and to enjoy as much as we the prospect which had so suddenly overtaken us together of wintering in the dreaded "pack." Welch, the fireman, declared that the *Panther* was a ship " as knowed a thing or two."

When the day closed we had Wilcox Point and the Devil's Thumb abeam. The great ice-fields which on our way north had so much embarrassed us on entering Melville Bay had by this time either drifted or melted away; and now through an unobstructed sea we held our course for the Duck Islands, and steamed away from the midnight sun.

From the Duck Islands we groped our way down the coast through one of those provoking fogs which so often come to pester the life of the Arctic voyager, and which set upon us early in the night.

I do not remember to have ever seen any thing more gloomy than the scene before us when the fog lifted in the early morning. We had been lying to for some time, not really knowing where we were; but, as good-luck would have it, we found that we were pointed fairly between two remarkable islands, known from their conformation as Cone and Wedge. Beyond was a straight passage of twenty miles, between lofty, cavernous, brownish-red, rocky islets; and beyond these, again, was to be seen, in the far distance, the cold line of the *mer de glace*, from which come pouring down cold glaciers to the sea. Cold icebergs lay upon the leaden waters; a cold wind was moaning from the hills; and although the sun shone out after the fog had vanished, it failed to throw any glow of warmth over the general desolation, or to dissolve the oppressive chill.

Steering south-east, we passed presently around a large iceberg which had before obstructed the view, and then we opened a low point of land, rugged as any other land in sight, and as utterly without sign or trace of vegetation; and yet a little white house stood upon the naked rock, and the white and red emblem of Danish sovereignty fluttered from a little flag-staff on the roof. This was the house we had seen and photographed on our way north— the most northern house of all the world; and in this little house, in this fearful desert, dwells a Christian family, with no other human beings within fifty miles of them save a few ignorant savages.

The head of the family met us among the ice in a boat a mile or so away. He had a swarthy crew of skin-clad men, and as he hauled in alongside of us, and stood up in the stern of his boat, I recognized at once the sturdy figure, sandy hair, and striking features of Peter Jensen. I was heartily glad to see him, and had him on board and by the hand without a minute's loss of time. Then we steamed into a good anchorage and went ashore, and called upon his wife, and petted his children, and dined with him off venison and eider-ducks. The wife made us some capital cakes, and we had cigars and Danish pipes and excellent coffee; and we smoked and drank and chatted away the evening, and were very much surprised, when we came to think about it, that we had had a very pleasant time here in this remote and solitary place, within a thousand miles, measured as the crow flies, of the North Pole.

But there was something indescribably sad to me in the

THE MOST NORTHERN HOUSE ON THE GLOBE.

dreadful isolation of this family who had entertained us. It is worse than loneliness, for the savages around, with their filth and wretchedness, and their packs of howling, vicious dogs, can not give companionship to a woman bred in Copenhagen, nor to the three little children whom she nurtured with the carefulness of a Christian mother.

These children were two pretty flaxen-haired girls—Johana Maria and Jennie Caroline—of five and seven years. But the hope of the house was Julius Christian, aged three years and some odd months.

They had all been troubled with the scurvy, and I did not wonder at it. What could these poor children do to preserve their health by outdoor exercise and outdoor pastime in a climate where the snow is on the ground nine months out of the twelve, and where the sun is not seen in winter for more than a hundred days; where the house must be banked with snow, the windows double glazed, the stoves and lamps kept burning constantly, to ward off the piercing cold, which often sinks to 50° below zero, and even lower, and where howling gales, filling the air with snow-drift, are of almost daily occurrence?

The four rooms of the house were fitted up with a reasonable degree of comfort, and with great neatness. There were some ornaments upon the walls—photographs of relatives and friends, and cheap colored prints of Danish battle-scenes, in some of which Jensen had patriotically borne a musket in the ranks before he came to Greenland, and was deservedly proud of the share he had in the war of 1848 against the hated Prussian.

For warmth they had stoves and Danish coal; and then there were huge bags of eider-down, among which the children buried themselves through the dark cold nights, piled upon the beds, and one might think the cold could never reach them when they had crawled to rest. But even children can not sleep all the time, though it may be always dark; and the loneliness of that prison-house to those three little creatures, when the winter comes, was a painful thing to contemplate. But then the wife! The children were born there, and had no other associations; but through the desolate winter do the wife's thoughts not wander sometimes mournfully and regretfully back to the society and the changing delights and changing fashions of the world wherein she lived before she became a bride, and left it for this desert, simply that she might be with the man she loved? for surely there could be nothing else than love to tempt her there. She made no complaint; she appeared cheerful, and may have been happy. It was hard for me to think so. Hopeless, indeed, to her this life of toil, anxiety, and suffering, unless the blind god gives her some vast measure of bliss utterly beyond man's power of appreciation. Alas, how little men really know of the sacrifices women make for them continually! Was the man ever born who was capable of such an exhibition of unselfishness as this Betty Jensen? I doubt it.

And the life of her husband is a very hard and, as it seems to me, a very thankless one. Strange as it may seem, Jensen came here to seek his fortune. The little money that he had saved up from my expedition of 1860–'61, enabled him to return to Denmark, and there to marry, and come back to Greenland and set up for himself. He had been promised the charge of this remote settlement of Tessuisak, which is fifty miles above Upernavik, and on the very confines of the great ice-barrier. He was always a fine shot, an active man, and an expert hunter; and he thought by coming here he would in a few years accumulate a competency, which he would carry back to Denmark. But I fancy it must have been something of his restless nature besides that impelled him to this life.

JENSEN AND HIS FAMILY.

He had lived several years in Greenland before I knew him, and, like all other men who have returned to the primitive life of the hunter, he never again took kindly to other ways, but clung lovingly to independence. It is not, however, so with women, and hence to them the greater hardship and privation. Without the same motives to action, they can not find society in the animals of the chase.

Unhappily, Jensen had overestimated his skill and the resources of Tessuisak, and in spite of all he was disappointed. The whole productions of the place per annum do not exceed five thousand dollars, chiefly made up from seal-oil, eider-down, and bear and fox skins. On this Jensen receives but five per cent., a salary besides of five-and-twenty dollars, and one Government ration. There is no provision for his wife and children. Clearly the Royal Greenland Fishing Company never contemplated such a thing as a wife going to so distant and woe-begone a place.

But if the fact of Christian people selecting this remote, forlorn, and frigid corner of the world, voluntarily, for a residence is incomprehensible to the ordinary understanding, the pluck of the thing will be appreciated by all. I know of nothing that would require a greater degree of moral courage than to face life in such a situation. Yet Jensen gloried in the work he did, and grew very animated when he recited his bear and reindeer hunts, the skill and success he had in the seal and white-whale fisheries, and boasted of his good-luck in making the natives be to him, what no other Dane had succeeded in doing, "hewers of wood and drawers of water;" or rather, to speak practically, as we must of a region where there is no wood to hew, and where all the water used is made from snow, the butchers of his game, and the drawers of his blubber. In a small way he is a sort of feudal lord, with natural rights and privileges which I doubt if he would exchange for the benefits of an inferior station in some inferior latitude.

The population which he thus rules comprises sixty-two savage souls, scattered about in huts and tents upon the rocky hill-side. The dogs, which in the winter-time are used to drag the sledges, are beyond counting; and the stench that arose from the carcasses of decomposing fish and seals, and other offensive sources, exceeds belief. I pitied the wife, and mentioned it to Jensen. "Oh, she's got used to it, and don't mind!" One of the native families had, with peculiar impudence, pitched a tent close beside Jensen's door, and he told me that it could not be removed without giving offense to the whole village. Barren though the land, the Esquimaux, with laughable gravity, proclaim themselves the true proprietors of the soil, and they do not hesitate to tell the Danes—though not in hostile fashion, calling them foreigners—that they are intruders.

What made the presence of this tent the more obnoxious was that the wife was supposed to be a witch, and often made night hideous with her devilish incantations. Although nominally a Christian now, she can not yet refrain from her old practices. And surely if ill looks had ever any thing to do, as they always seem to have had, with the general make-up of a witch, she was entitled to be looked upon as the mother of them all, for a more frightful-looking being surely never walked in darkness and conspired with the evil one. Yet this monster had a child, and its innocent baby face did not exhibit any evidence that it was conscious of its dangerous parentage, but it sucked its fist as contentedly as any other baby that had been born all right and in the mortal fashion. Her

AN ARCTIC WITCH.

original name was Annorasuak, which is something equivalent to "Mother of the Winds." Her history, as I had it afterwards from Jensen, is not without romantic interest, and will be again referred to.

I could not part from this little family of Jensen without emotion. For seven long years the wife had seen no living soul from the great world from which her love had called her, and the children looked upon us with amazement. They had never seen a ship in all their little lives before, and the smoking, snorting *Panther* was a wonder in their eyes. We made them up a store of such good things as we had on board, including every thing of an antiscorbutic character that we could lay our hands upon, added a couple of tons or so of coals, and then, with Jensen on board to pilot us through the intricate passages between the islands, we bore away from this most northern house of all the world, and shaped our course for Upernavik.

CHAPTER VII.

THE FIORD OF AUKPADLARTOK.

On our way to Upernavik we wheeled into the fiord of Aukpadlartok, to which I have hitherto made allusion, and I verily believe there never was such another wilderness of desolation—such an interminable array of islands of ice and islands of rock; and when at last we saw another house like Jensen's, pitched like his upon just such another point of land, and reflected that these houses are dotted here and there in this dreary waste at intervals of forty and fifty miles, and that their inmates hold communication one with the other perhaps once in the winter with dog-sledge, and once in summer, and not more, with boat, it seemed as if proof was positive that life without social intercourse was really possible—a fact which I should never have believed for a moment otherwise.

The ice was so thick along the shore that we could not get within a mile of the little house and the miserable huts which surrounded it. So we had nothing to do but tie up to an iceberg, and take to a boat and pull in as best we could. The shore was reached at last, but only after we had passed through many very dangerous places, including a hole in an enormous iceberg, and then we were landed on the rocks, where we were met by the most renowned of all the Greenland hunters—a blue-eyed and fair-complexioned and most "mild-mannered man," named Philip, who was backed up by a staff of five sons—Christian, Wilhelm, Simon, Hans, and Lars; while still farther in the rear was the wife, Caroline, with her two daughters,

WE GO THROUGH AN ICEBERG TO CALL ON PHILIP.

Christina and Maria, and the various wives and sweethearts and children of all her five boys, the lover of Christina, and some forty other savages and half-savages, who constituted the promiscuous population of the village of Kresarsoak—"the village beside the mountain;" and the

PHILIP, THE HUNTER, AND HIS SONS.

mountain reared its great white crest five thousand feet above our heads, pushing itself away up among the clouds.

The family of Philip was a very different one from that of Jensen. His wife was a full-blown Esquimaux. His half-breed children were happy and well-contented, and rejoiced in the possession of every thing needful for the hunt or domestic comfort. Christian was married, and had a small hut and seven children all to himself. Simon ditto, but he lived with his wife and baby in a seal-skin tent. Wilhelm had recently been in trouble about his lady-love, who was a thorough-bred native, she at first preferring another fellow, who was a fine hunter, and evidently the superior of Wilhelm. But then Wilhelm was the son of the "governor," which made all the difference in the world; and so the marriage was settled upon, and was to take place as soon as the priest could come up from Upernavik to bless the nuptials. For the rest, they all lived in the paternal mansion, which had but one room, and was divided with seal-skins into a number of stalls like an oyster-cellar, and in these the different members of the family retired to rest among their bags of eider-down.

Having enjoyed the benefit of Philip's hospitality, which was displayed chiefly in the form of seal-steaks, smoked salmon, and coffee, I strolled out with Jensen, who had told me that near by once dwelt the witch Annorasuak, who now lived at Tessuisak, and had become a Christian—that is to say, after the Greenland fashion. I accepted with alacrity his offer to guide me thither.

Crossing the neck of a promontory, in half an hour we came down into a valley, or rather wide gorge, bounded on either side by lofty cliffs, that were broken by immense clefts, which had a most glaring and forbidding aspect as they frowned down upon us from underneath the great

O

white caps that untold winters had woven round their heads. Fitful gusts of wind came moaning down the gorge, chilling us to the very bone.

Our situation at the entrance to the gorge was very striking and remarkable. Looking up the fiord, we could faintly see the glacier of Aukpadlartok over the tops of innumerable icebergs, which crowded the fiord, and upon which the sun, breaking through the clouds that had obscured the sky for some hours previous, shone with great brilliancy, without, however, reaching us or giving any warmth. Looking up the valley, we saw the front of a small glacier, perhaps fifty feet high and two hundred yards over, which crossed the valley from cliff to cliff about a mile up from the sea, and from which was gathered a stream of limpid water that came rushing down over the rocks, breaking in falls and whirling in pools, and everywhere hurrying along as if it were glad to get its freedom again, and was making the first use of it by bounding away to the sea and the warm sunshine.

The ascent of the valley was difficult and laborious; but by dint of hard scrambling we succeeded finally in making about half a mile, when we had reached a point where the cliffs rose almost perpendicularly from the border of the stream, and were scarcely more than thirty yards apart. Between them the water rushed in a series of picturesque falls, the sound of which, added to the roar of the wind, that seemed as if it had accumulated beyond, and was being forced through the narrow passage, greatly heightened the gloomy aspect of the scene.

Continuing on our course, we finally reached the summit of the falls, and came then upon a level plain of considerable extent—a sort of natural amphitheatre. Here in this wild and desolate place, close to the fall and beneath the glacier, Annorasuak had, many years ago, chosen her residence. From here went forth her decrees, which stilled the winds or made them blow, and sent good-fortune to her friends, and disaster to those who disregarded her. The heathen natives held her in the greatest awe, and were glad to propitiate her with the offer of food, clothing, and every thing needful for her comfort; and even those who had professed to embrace the Christian religion held her in superstitious dread, and thought it no harm to add a contribution to the witch's wardrobe and larder. The ruins of her hut, which was entered through a long and intricate cleft in the rock, were still visible. I examined this ruin, and heard the story of this last trace of the heathen practices in Greenland, with intense interest, not alone on account of this circumstance, but because of the peculiar mystery which shrouded her history, and the romantic side of which culminated in a daughter — a girl with light complexion and black hair. The father of this girl was believed to be a criminal who had escaped from an English whale-ship, fled hither with this woman, and managed while he lived to avoid detection through her arts; for it was at the period of her flight there that she first assumed to be the "Mother of the Winds." From that time forth no native was ever known to enter the valley, except to a certain spot, where he left his offering; and even the Danes seemed to have a superstitious dread of it, associating it with the evil one. They called the glacier hanging above the witch's home "The Devil's Castle," and the valley itself borrowed its name from its wicked mistress. It was "The Valley of the Winds." The daughter's name was Annore—"Daughter of the Winds;" and she had been really taught to believe that she was born of the air.

Love, which is and always has been the disturber of so many human devices, finally broke up this nest of witchcraft and sorcery. A youthful Dane, named Elsen, saw the child, and had pity for her. His tenderness soon suggested means by which to approach without frightening her, and without her mother's knowledge. Then he fell in love with his wild favorite, and addressed the mission of Upernavik for help to save her. "Poor Annore," the lover wrote, in his despair at her condition; "she is a wild flower in the wilderness. Can the wild flower be transplanted? Will the lustre of the leaves come out in other soil, and will gentler airs bring brightness to the blossom? Poor misguided child!—her birth a mystery to her; her very name a falsehood to her mind perpetually. And yet she is taught to honor it, and taught to think with pride that she was born of the winds, and to the winds will go away again, to wander to and fro, doing good or ill, forever. Annore, poor Annore! Will the falsehood pass away? Will the daughter of the winds become a child of God?"

And the lover's question was answered favorably. The missionary became interested, and the two together managed, in the end, to entice the mother and daughter away; and through their efforts Annore became Nina, and the wife of Elsen; and Annorasuak, her mother, became Barbara, and the wife of a Christian native, and she is now the ugly hag that has pitched her tent at Tessuisak, right beneath the nose of Jensen, who hates her cordially.

We did not remain longer in the valley than was necessary for an inspection of the place. The wind shortly increased in violence, accompanied with occasional gusts of snow, and sometimes it fairly shrieked along the cliffs; and it seemed clear enough that if there ever was a place on earth fitted for the abode of evil spirits, this was it. As if to increase that impression, and leave no doubt at all about it, an ancient raven, with a ragged coat, flopped down near by, and set up a dismal croak. Then he walked off deliberately, muttering to himself the while in a sepulchral tone, and, mounting to the ruined wall of the witch's hut, he croaked again. Then he cocked his head to one side, and looked at us in a very sinister way out of one eye; after which he went to the edge of the fall and looked over into the foaming abyss. Then he croaked once more, flopped himself over to the other side of the stream, and, lighting on a rock, began sharpening his bill, as if preparing for a sacrifice, croaking all the while. He

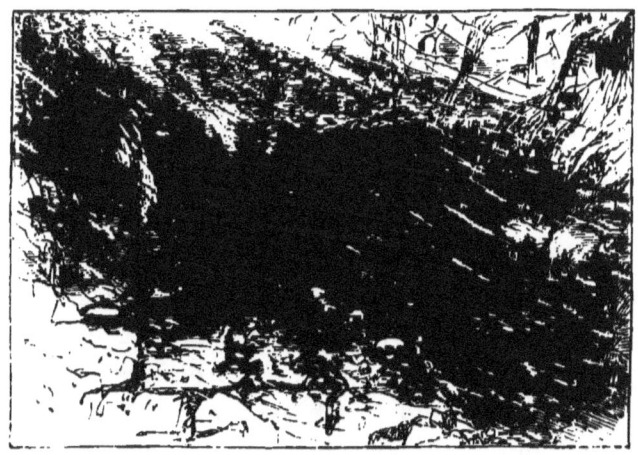

THE RAVEN.

seemed to know the spot, and to be at home there, for the moment he struck the rock I perceived there was a double echo, so that his voice resounded from cliff to cliff, until it seemed as if the air were peopled with spirits that were in league with him, and were answering to his call.

By the time we had reached Philip's hut it was snowing heavily, and it being clear from the first that we had come up the fiord for nothing, the icebergs being so thick above as to defy even the passage of a boat to the glacier, we got aboard with all haste, and steamed away.

CHAPTER VIII.

UPERNAVIK.

I HAD set my heart upon making a thorough survey of the fiord of Aukpadlartok. As recorded in a previous chapter, I had previously been there and penetrated to within five miles of the glacier. It was, therefore, with much regret that I found the water wholly impassable to a boat. Even the air was so thick that I could not see the front of the glacier, so that I failed to note any changes which might have taken place in the interval of eight years since I had visited it before. Philip told me, however, that during the past two or three years the discharge of icebergs had been much greater than formerly, and that if they continued to increase in the same proportion he would be obliged to quit the place, as he could hardly at any time get in and out from his hut. Indeed, his residence appeared to me even more dreary than Jensen's, for about the latter the icebergs were comparatively few, while Philip was thoroughly encircled by them. What measureless powers of endurance and hardihood such men as these must possess! I confess that I never look upon them except with astonishment.

Our voyage to Upernavik was without incident worthy of note, except that our mate was blessed with his usual fortune in discovering soundings. In a place where a rock was never before known to exist, he found one which by a miracle we grazed without damage to the *Panther's* keel or bottom.

To our arrival in Upernavik I had looked forward with

some real pleasure; and not the least among those which I actually found was a civilized bed, and other homelike luxuries which Dr. Rudolph was good enough to place at my disposal. And oh the luxury of that bed after eight weeks in the narrow quarters of a ship's bunk, always damp, and black with coal-dust, and daily rendered worse by the unsuccessful attempts of an idiotic cabin-boy to put it to rights and keep it clean!

The window of my room opened upon the sea, and was full of sweet flowers that had been nurtured tenderly by my good hostess, as if they were children. It was strange to look out through a little wilderness of roses, mignonnette, and heliotrope, upon a great wilderness of icebergs. The sea was, indeed, as cold as cold could be, and the waves broke fiercely right beneath me on the rocky shore; but about me all was peace and quiet—the pictures on the wall, the fire in the stove, the home comforts of the modest house which sheltered me—all spoke defiance of place or climate, and told a tale of tranquillity and contentment that was worth going thrice three thousand miles to see, even though the storms were never so threatening, and ice-barriers without number intervened.

We remained a week at Upernavik, and during that time I never saw the *Panther*. I never was so glad *not* to see any thing in all my life before. I was quite willing to believe that the artists were painting and photographing icebergs without limit, and were getting into their camera every thing from a native to a mountain, but I did not want to see it. My enjoyment of the little home into which I had fallen was too fresh to court disturbance. To forget for a time that there was ever such an enemy to man as a ship's cook, and to partake of some simple fare with which a woman's hand had had to do, was too great a luxury to be profaned, and I lived along through my week at Dr. Rudolph's in a state of bliss. I wrote, and read, and played with the children, Anne and Christian. I talked with Jensen about his life, and the Greenland legends which he had gathered in his long experience. I helped my host, the governor, to make up his annual accounts for the next ship home; and I bungled through my Danish with his amiable wife, making her laugh continually at my mistakes; and altogether, quite free from care, gave myself up wholly to enjoyment for the seven days.

Now the coming of the ship was a matter of serious concern to Govornor Rudolph. The store-rooms were very empty, and there was much danger of famine if the ship did not come at all. To the governor's family there would be a lack of every luxury. She was overdue almost a month, and great alarm was in the settlement already. But she did come at last, and I never saw people more rejoiced. The ship was the *Constancia*, and Captain Bang, her master, was as intelligent a man as he was good fellow. He spoke capital English, and helped us with our pipes and punch in the evening, and enjoyed the flowers as much as I did, and the delightful breakfast of smoked salmon, venison sausage, and pickled halibut, and the substantial lunch, and the late dinners, that were none the worse for the cigars and wine and Santa Cruz that he brought off one day to help out with; for the doctor was the most hospitable of all old-fashioned gentlemen; and having three times dined our whole huge cabin mess, and opened his house to every body every day, his supply of cigars and liquors, after a whole year's pulling at them on his own part, had run rather low. Our mess would gladly have replenished the doctor's fast-failing stock; but with true American energy we had gone to work at the start as if to get through with what supplies we had in the shortest possible space of time; and there was not now among us so much as a single " Havana," or even a bottle of ale, to bless ourselves with.

The doctor surprised me one day by coming into my room, and in his genial way calling out, " You know dis man; you know dis feller, eh?" producing from behind his coat a rascally face, which I never could forget in any length of time. It was the face of Hans Heindrich.

Now Hans is a man of some celebrity. In 1853 Dr. Kane took him from Fiskernaes, South Greenland, upon his famous voyage into Smith's Sound. His age then was about twenty years; and he lived well on board the brig *Advance*, and waxed fat, and tricked his master, from whom he finally ran away, and joined the Smith Sound savages, marrying one of their women, by name Merkut. Among these people I found him in 1860, and took him aboard with his wife, Merkut, and his baby, Pingasuk. I ought to have known better. He tricked me worse than he had tricked Dr. Kane. I am fully convinced that he was instrumental in causing the death of two of my command, though it was never possible to prove any thing against him positive enough to insure conviction. It is hard to collect evidence where there are no eyes to see nor ears to hear. Being unable to verify my suspicions, I brought him back in 1861, and delivered him over to the Danish authorities, from whom Dr. Kane had taken him eight years before. Even now he could not cease from mischief, breeding quarrels wherever he went; and his wife was in a state of chronic dissatisfaction because she could not live in her old-fashioned savage way, and her children (she had two now) were a burden on the poor-fund. I gave Merkut some money to buy clothes for the children, and within an hour it was all spent at the Government store-house for figs and sugar-candy.

The untutored savage is not a peculiarly delicious crea-

HANS AND HIS FAMILY.

ture under the best of circumstances. He is apt to have very crude notions about *meum* and *tuum*, and the truth is not in him. Truth, indeed, seems to be, like gallantry, a fine art, and men have to be cultivated to the understanding of it. But Hans was not altogether an untutored savage, for the missionaries had control of him before Dr. Kane took him in charge, and had taught him to read the Testament and Thomas à Kempis, and to sign his name. The story of his proficiency in these respects having got abroad, in connection with supposed services rendered to Dr. Kane's party in Christian charity, Hans has been made much of in a Sunday-school book that I have seen somewhere within a year or so, as a striking example of the power of Christian labor among the heathen—just as if he did not use what he had acquired for a cloak to hide his true character, something after the manner of Uriah Heep when playing a part before the pious Creakle and the zealous board of visitors.

I do not mean to be understood to give this as by any means a fair sample of the influence of Christian civilization upon the Greenlanders, for I have had frequent occasion to testify to the excellence of the native character in many conspicuous instances. Hans is nothing more than one of that very numerous class common to all peoples. Even the pastor of the little church at Upernavik can do nothing to help the mischief-making sinner; for the reader must know that Upernavik has a church. It was here that Mr. Anthon, now at Julianashaab, performed his first missionary labors. The pastor of this Upernavik flock surely fills Cowper's description of the Moravian brethren, going forth,

>"Fired with a zeal peculiar to defy
>The rage and rigor of a Polar sky;
>And plant successfully sweet Saviour's rose
>On icy plains, and in eternal snows."

A new pastor, accompanied by his wife, came out in the *Constancia* to take charge of the mission. They were a young couple. Certainly no one would charge them with undue regard to things earthly when they subject themselves to such banishment.

Yet one might, after all, be worse off than here in Greenland; and, for a certain length of time, I think the banishment might be bearable enough. One of the happiest, best contented, and most cultivated men that I have ever met, did not live much south of this, and he has declared to me that he would not exchange his Greenland lodge for the most comfortable quarters in his own fine city of Copenhagen. And it does seem strange that such a large number of superior men—superior in education and refinement—find their way to this inhospitable region, as governors, missionaries, and physicians. It is either because the home Government is particularly careful of its agents, or that the region possesses some peculiar attraction for thoughtful and reflective minds. "It is," said my friend before alluded to, "the best place in the world to read books in," and great readers most of these Danes in Greenland are.

Dr. Rudolph is a fine specimen of the best class of Danish gentlemen who accept appointments here, and who seem to take root and never desire to be transplanted elsewhere.

In early life he was an assistant surgeon in the Danish army. Later, he was largely engaged in private practice in the vicinity of Copenhagen. His health failing him, he went to Greenland as physician to the colony of Jacobshavn, and thereby saved his life; but his life once saved, he had no mind to renew the humdrum existence of powders and pills, and his old age now finds him both governor and physician of one of the most productive of the Greenland Districts, even although it is the most northern of all points of Christian occupation. His children are at school in Copenhagen, all except the two youngest, who are now with him; and there seems to be no end to his plans of doing for them out of his percentage of the Upernavik production, which furnishes him a moderate income.

Judging from the seeming shortness of the week I spent at Dr. Rudolph's house, I should say a winter would not be tedious; but then it must be borne in mind that my week was a continual sunshine. I was used to it then, as I had been before, and did not observe or think of it; but now to look back over the time, and remember a week, and weeks, and months even, passing away without once lighting a lamp; to take a walk at midnight as an appetizer for sleep, just before going to bed, and do it in the daylight; to watch through day and night the shadows going round and round, is to recall a now strange experience. I have, indeed, never seen a person with the least sentiment who has ever been beyond the Arctic Circle, whose fancy did not cling lovingly to that long, lingering day and the never-setting sun.

But all things must have an end, and so at length I found myself once more back in my damp and smoke-begrimed quarters in the *Panther's* cabin. On the same day the *Constancia* was ready to sail, and our captain offered Captain Bang a tow. He was going down the coast forty miles, to Proven, where he was to take in more cargo before returning home to Copenhagen. But, as ill luck would have it, a small iceberg had drifted into the middle of the harbor and grounded right in front of the two vessels, which lay almost side by side. It seemed at first as if we were both fast there, but the *Constancia's* cable slipped out and freed the ship, while ours stubbornly refused to budge; so that we had the mortification of seeing the vessel we were going to tow move off without us under oars. It was a most aggravating situation. Doctor Rudolph was on board the *Constancia*, on his way to Proven. He cried to us that he would be back in three days, and we were quite welcome to the harbor. The captain of the brig offered us a tow if we would only pass along a line. The order of things was quite reversed. The steamer was helpless, while the sailer was off.

Our captain, vexed by the detention (and these taunts did not in the least soothe him), was evidently coming to a desperate determination. "Pay out chain," he shouted from the bridge. Then he rang his bell to "back astern." The vessel moved away from the berg as far as the chain would let her go, and then he rang again, "Ahead full speed." Down the *Panther* came with a steady helm, and with her iron forefoot she took the iceberg fairly in the middle. The shock was terrific, and there was a great scattering of men on the deck and of plates in the pantry; but fortunately the iceberg at that point was sloping, and the *Panther* slid up about five feet out of the water, which partly broke the force of the blow. Then she slid back again, luckily with her masts all standing. The *Constancia's* people cheered us, and we backed off again and went at the iceberg once more, with the same result—we did not budge or damage it in any way further than to splinter off innumerable fragments, which covered the sea all around us. But the berg was thin at the centre where we had struck; and the captain, growing more and more determined, backed off and butted away at the berg again and again, until, finally, the sixth effort proved successful. The berg split with a fearful sound. The two masses, each pivoted on the bottom, rolled over with a great swash; the *Panther* sheered ahead between the fragments, and then, picking up our anchor, to the universal astonishment we steamed out of the harbor in triumph, and kept our promise to the *Constancia*.

Dropping the *Constancia* off Proven, we continued south through the night, and on the following morning sighted the lofty mountains of Disco Island. Passing the Waigat, and the great stream of icebergs which emerges from it, we kept close to the bold and picturesque shores of Disco, and on the following day dropped anchor in Godhavn, close beside the town which takes its name from the little landlocked bay.

CHAPTER IX.

DISCO ISLAND.

"A ROCKY islet in the sea,
 A lonely harbor on its lee,
  The roaring surf around!
Chill are the winds and cold the sky,
Dead in the dells the flowers lie,
  The snow is on the ground!

"A desert drear as e'er was seen;
It seems as if there has not been
  A trace of human life!
I write again. Upon the rock
I've found a home, a loving flock—
  A husband, child, and wife.

"And thus it is—here Greenland frowns,
The name to others harshly sounds;
  'Tis everywhere the same!
If we but taste the sweets of love,
It matters little—rock or grove—
  There's nothing in a name.

"God bless that home upon the rock!
God bless that happy, loving flock,
  And keep them from all harm!
My bark again bounds o'er the sea;
Away, away once more I flee
  To nothing half so warm!"
                        Our Sagaman.

Disco Island is one of the most notable localities in Greenland. There is a legend that a mighty sorcerer, or angeikut, dragged the island there from the south; and even to the present time they point out a remarkable hole in the rock, on its north side, through which the evil genius of the island rove his rope. The island is upwards of a hundred miles long, is everywhere very lofty, and presents the most superb lines of cliffs of trap rock that I have ever seen. On the south side of the island, in latitude 69°, there is a low and ragged spur of granite rock, near a mile in length, which incloses as perfect a little harbor as can anywhere be found, and this the Danes have expressed in the name Godhavn (Good-harbor), which they have given it. This rocky spur is a peninsula at low water; at high water an island. On the north side of it, facing the great tall trap cliffs which tower up two thousand feet above the harbor, stands the little town which takes its name from the harbor, though better known by the English whalers' name of Lievely, which is probably a corruption of lively, for the town is the metropolis of North Greenland; and, having been a general rendezvous for whale and discovery ships almost from the beginning of the present century, its metropolitan gayety has become widely celebrated.

It was on a cold, gray, misty morning that we arrived at Godhavn. There had been heavy frosts and a light spurt of snow; and the little town being hidden from view in the gloomy atmosphere, it is not surprising that it should have impressed our sagaman, as it did all of us, rather unfavorably. But this feeling speedily wore off after we had landed and called at the inspector's house—a house to me not new, for there I had in former years spent many pleasant days with the prior incumbent, Justitsraad Olrik, now director of the Greenland Company in Copenhagen.

The present inspector is Herr Krarup Smith, a young man of perhaps two-and-thirty, who possesses the same enthusiastic fondness for scientific discovery for which Mr.

Olrik was distinguished, and the same cultivated appreciation of its importance; and being obliged every year to visit each of the districts and subordinate stations within his inspectorate, he has made many valuable observations, and collected many rare and curious specimens; among which are some fossil remains of the limestone, coal, and slate deposits of Disco Island, and other localities of Disco Bay. This bay appears to have been a great carboniferous basin, coal being found to crop out on almost every side of it.

The inspector's wife seemed to be quite as well content with her Greenland home as the inspector was himself, and there never was a happier baby than the Greenland-born Elizabet, whose first birthday we were hospitably called upon to assist in celebrating immediately after our arrival.

The inspector's house is not, by any means, an imposing edifice, being of the usual pitchy hue; but it is comfortable, and sufficiently capacious. The suite of rooms —comprising billiard-room, dining-room, and parlor—into which we were ushered by the same Sophy who had presided there as housekeeper these many years past, and who wore the inevitable silver seal-skin pantaloons and dainty snow-white boots as of old, had nothing to indicate that we were three degrees north of the Arctic Circle. Some prints of fruits and flowers were hanging on the dining-room walls, and the parlor was literally strewn with books and family souvenirs, and also music. A piano stood in one corner, and bore evidence of being well used. Bright flowers were blooming in the windows, and the faces of two bright young ladies, one the sister of the inspector, the other of his wife, were there, as if on purpose to make the picture quite complete and leave nothing to be wished for.

These young ladies were on a visit, having come out from Denmark the previous summer; and now, at the end of the year, they were about to return in the *Hvalfisken*, a brig which came into the harbor soon after our arrival. I asked how they liked this Greenland life? They had no fault to find with it at all, except the ending of it. They would stay another year, only for the homes across the sea, where they were sadly missed, as I could well imagine they must be.

Godhavn is not so lacking in life as most of the other towns. Here all the Danish ships are obliged to come to receive their orders from the inspector, both upon their arrival and departure from the Greenland waters; and of late years, during the search for Sir John Franklin, here is where all the searchers came to taste the first sweets of home, after a long imprisonment in the inhospitable regions around Beechy Island and elsewhere. And none left without carrying away the most lively recollections of the place and of the genial Justitsraad Olrik; nor did any body ever forget the Justitsraad's housekeeper, the inimitable Sophy.

Godhavn is too far north for the production of such garden-luxuries as we found at Julianashaab on our first arrival in the country; yet little round red radishes were not wanting any more now than they had been when Mr. Olrik formerly invited me to his table. But they were grown beneath glass, and not in the open air, the earth being brought in barrels from Copenhagen. There was also a head of lettuce, reared in the same manner, for the perfection of the very excellent luncheon to which Mrs. Smith invited us upon our first appearance.

As Godhavn is the most pleasant and lively of all the Greenland towns, so Disco Island presents the most picturesque and attractive scenery. Looking from the town across the harbor, which is not over half a mile wide, you face the lofty cliffs of trap rock, which extend to right and left for miles. Above they are capped with snow; below, the waves break upon them fiercely, and the icebergs are ground to pieces on their sharp angles.

I walked out with the ladies of the inspector's family, and had a fine view of the cliffs from behind the town; thence we proceeded across the narrow neck of rocks around the head of the harbor, and, after strolling along a beautiful sandy beach which stretches in a grand curve for a mile, we entered a valley beside a broad and rapid stream, called Rothe River, which breaks through deep caverns of the most picturesque description, and over the tortured rocks dashes in falls of rare beauty. I can not imagine any thing more wild than the scene before us at the summit of the principal fall. Looking up the valley, I could trace the winding stream to an immense glacier that descended from the lofty hills. Directly abreast of these, to the left, was another glacier, which, having poured down over a very steep and rugged declivity, was twisted into the most fantastic shapes. Above towered the grand crest of Lyngmarkens Fjeld, over which snow-clouds were sweeping before a wind that did not reach us in our sheltered situation. The air in the valley was calm, and the day was unusually warm for the time of year. The light snow that had fallen three days before, and which gave such a gloomy aspect to the land upon our first arrival in Godhavn, had now disappeared, and there was still something of the summer green which had clothed the valley. Even bright flowers, though wilted by the frost, and drooping languidly, were there, yet they seemed to be pleading mournfully for life.

One must come to these Arctic wilds to perfect his love and reverence for these sweet gifts of nature. They seem to be clothed here with a new significance—an intelligence of their own, which warns them that their life must needs be short, and that they must quickly prepare for their end, and provide speedily for their posterity. From the time when "lingering winter chills the lap of spring" to that when the very slight warmth which the summer has given to the earth has been dissipated by the returning frosts—between the deep snows of those two periods—there occurs a remarkable series of transformations. The snow has scarcely disappeared before the seed swells into life; and in a few days green supplants the universal whiteness. Blossoms gay and smiling burst forth with corresponding rapidity; the new seeds are formed, and fall to be covered with their winter cloak; and from the beginning to the end there is scarcely an interval of six weeks. One can not look upon this astonishing growth —flowering, seeding, and decay—and witness this adaptation of life to the conditions of climate, without wonder. Alfieri has beautifully expressed the feeling in these lines:

> "Oh, 'tis the touch of fairy hand
> That wakes the spring of Northern land.
> It warms not there by slow degrees,
> With changeful pulse, the uncertain breeze;
> But sudden on the wondering sight
> Bursts forth the beam of living light,
> And instant verdure springs around,
> And magic flowers bedeck the ground."

The Governor of Godhavn, Mr. Frederick Hansen, whom I had before met at Proven and Upernavik in a similar capacity, was of our party; and, being himself a famous walker, it was proposed that we should attempt to scale the glacier to our left, and climb to the summit of the Lyngmarkens Fjeld—a feat which had never been performed. The great white rolling plain that stretched away so high above us was indeed tempting; and none of us were more eager to make the trial than the ladies themselves. Mr. Hansen, who had climbed every thing that it seemed possible to climb, was of opinion that the thing could not be done; and the first suggestion of the effort appeared, in fact, more like a jest than sober earnest. It came from one of the ladies, however, and gallantry alone was of itself sufficient to prompt a ready response. We would climb the glacier, certainly, if the ladies, who were "both young and fair," were so minded—of course we would; but it must be confessed that there were doubting eyes cast upon the Lyngmarkens Fjeld.

It being agreed that the effort was to be made, we returned to the village and had a game of billiards at the inspector's house. On the following day, in company with the "Professor," the "Prince," the "Colonel," the "Major," and our chief "Nimrod," I made a preliminary exploration. After ascending the valley to the falls, we pursued our course along the bank of a stream which tears down through a cleft in the solid rock about two hundred feet deep, and came finally to the glacier, by the side of which, sometimes on the ice and sometimes on the rocks, through the gorge formed by the ice-stream meeting the base of the cliffs, we climbed to an altitude of eighteen hundred feet above the sea. The ascent was very difficult. The ice was here broken up in the most wonderful manner. The lines of stratification showed a great variety of curves, especially in one place where it had poured over a cliff, as if it had been a tenacious, plastic, semifluid mass flowing down by force of gravity, and moulding itself in conformity with the changing bed over which it had descended.

The ridge of sand and rock that had been ploughed up in front measured one hundred and twenty feet in altitude. By watching it carefully we could see and hear it moving. A great boulder, losing its balance, rolled from the crest above, and, loosening a great quantity of stones, mud, and sand, came rolling down near where we stood, making a fearful uproar. At the same moment the tall cliff above us let loose some immense fragments, which, bursting in pieces like bomb-shells, bounded down the steep slope at its base; and the two avalanches, meeting in the gorge, changed their direction, and went crashing down to the valley at a fearful rate, directly over the track which we had pursued in coming up. Had this occurred a few minutes sooner we should have been overwhelmed; for not only were enormous rocks zigzaging their way along with increasing violence and velocity, but the air was filled with lesser fragments, which flew almost with the speed of lightning.

This catastrophe impelled us the more earnestly to continue the ascent, and to find, either along the base of, or over the Lyngmarkens Fjeld, a new way to Godhavn. But our efforts proved unavailing. The ice-cliffs could not be scaled, and there was nothing left for us but to take the back track, which we did with fear and trembling. Fortunately, there were no more avalanches to disturb us, and we arrived on board the *Panther* with nothing worse than great fatigue and a thorough drenching; for while we were upon the ice, to add still further to the discomfort of our situation, a heavy shower of rain, sleet, and snow set upon us.

The report of our failure to find a passage to the summit of the mountain did not at all discourage the courageous ladies; but, on the contrary, only inspired them with greater eagerness. Even the story of the fearful avalanche did not cool their adventurous ardor, nor the doleful account of the cold storm dampen their zeal. It was resolved to make the attempt by the great cliffs across the harbor.

The cliffs are there cut through by the most sublime gorges that eye ever looked upon. These gorges appeared, however, to be as inaccessible as the valleys of the moon.

Mr. Hansen laughed at the idea. "Impossible!" said he. "These brave ladies will climb with any body, as I know well enough, after a year's practice with them, but neither they nor you can go up that way."

But the matter of the trial could not be settled at once, as the next day promised a storm like that of the day before; so I gladly availed myself of Mr. Hansen's obliging offer to lead me to other fields of investigation, and for three days thereafter I was well employed.

Mr. Hansen communicated to me many interesting facts, and through his instrumentality and that of the inspector I was enabled to visit the coal-fields, which are here very extensive.

I found Mr. Hansen to be an enthusiastic naturalist. Among other valuable specimens which I owed to his kindness was a large collection of birds' eggs and skins, and some fossils. To the study of the birds of the region and their habits he has devoted much attention. The great auk, long since supposed to be entirely extinct, he told me had been recently seen on one of the Whale-fish islands. Two years before one had been actually captured by a native, who, being very hungry, and wholly ignorant of the great value of the prize he had secured, proceeded at once to eat it, much to the disgust of Mr. Hansen, who did not learn of it until too late to come to the rescue. How little the poor savage thought of the great fortune he had just missed by hastily indulging his appetite!

The great auk is not the only mysterious creature in

Greenland that seems likely soon to become entirely extinct, for there is, besides, the fierce and powerful amarok, which has been in latter times rarely seen, and is much dreaded. It is the national terror of the nursery; and children are frightened to sleep or kept at home with

THE GREAT AUK.

threats of calling the awful monster, whose rapacity is so great that he can take off any number of Esquimaux babies that you choose to name. This animal, which is an enormous wolf, is not, however, quite as fabulous as the old wives' stories would incline you to believe, one having actually appeared in the country within a few years, and, after committing the most fearful ravages among the dogs, and terrifying the people, was finally shot. His skin now adorns the Copenhagen Museum. The story has spread everywhere, and is related by every body with the same zest that a frontiersman would tell of an Indian raid.

Disco Bay, which separates the island from the mainland, is sixty miles wide, and is a splendid sheet of water. Several glaciers pour their frozen floods into it, and grand processions of icebergs stretch over it towards the outlets above and below the island. One of these glaciers is exceptionally fine. It is known as the Jacobshavn Glacier, or, as the Danes call it, Jacobshavn's Eis-strom; and this, since we could not at present climb the hills of Disco Island, we resolved to visit. Its name is derived from a little town near by, and for this little town we steamed away in the early morning, while the sun was silvering the mountain crests and melting away the chilly mists of the night.

CHAPTER X.

JACOBSHAVN.

THE view of the southern shore of Disco Island as we crossed the bay was truly magnificent. The gnarled shore, full of clefts and caverns, was white with the foam of the sea; the great tall cliffs were red with the glowing sun; the distant hills were bathed in purple, and long streaks of bright yellow sandstone, marking the coal-measures, broke in here and there to complete a picture which will be remembered long. The icebergs, too, were more than ordinarily beautiful. There are few places along the Greenland coast from which such large icebergs are discharged as Disco Bay. We stopped frequently to photograph them, and thus dawdled away the hours, so that we did not arrive at our destination until nightfall, for it must be borne in mind that there was a night now—the midnight sun having left us many days before, darkness coming on as soon as ten o'clock.

One of the icebergs that particularly attracted our attention had almost the perfect shape of a truncated cone. But its chief peculiarity was an immense arch running directly through the centre of it, which was apparently large enough for our ship to pass through, since it could not have been less than a hundred feet high and seventy feet wide. It would have been a very hazardous experiment to have undertaken to steam through the berg; but it would have been so novel a thing to have done, that I believe the consideration only of the berg's liability to fall to pieces about us restrained every body from asking the captain to do the thing. This remarkable hole had been once a portion of a great natural culvert through the glacier into which the waters from the surface found their way and drained off to the sea.

We carried along with us from Godhavn a native pilot; but owing to the lateness of the hour, and the great numbers of icebergs that lay about the mouth of the harbor, it was found to be impracticable for him to get us to the town before daylight, so he tied to some grounded ice. We managed, however, to penetrate to the harbor with a boat, and surprised the governor with an evening call.

Never had steamship been there before, and of course every body was given a new life by our arrival. Some of the governor's family had retired to bed; but our coming had quickly roused them, and every possible thing was done to give us welcome. The governor, or colonibestyrere, Herr Knud Fleicher, was personally known to me before, he having been at Upernavik in that capacity in 1853 and 1855. I was much surprised to find him there, and the surprise was not the less agreeable when he brought into the room a pretty, modest, and intelligent young lady of nineteen, whom he introduced as his daughter, saying to me, "Know you dis one? She comes to tank you." For what I could not at first understand; but when she brought in a mechanical contrivance which bore unmistakable evidence of having been devised impromptu, I recognized my own handiwork of sixteen years before, and in the young lady a deformed child, whom I had the great satisfaction of seeing now able to walk as well as any body upon legs apparently perfectly straight and sound—a circumstance which gave me not less surprise than pleasure; for when I had constructed the instrument for the helpless little girl of three years, there appeared to be but a small chance for her ever being any thing but a cripple for life.

She was followed into the room by her mother, who was a fine matronly-looking lady, and very neatly dressed in some dark stuff sprinkled with snow-white spots, and looking as fresh as ever. Three lusty sons came in also; so did the parson and the doctor, with their respective wives; and altogether the reception was a lively and agreeable one. The governor produced cigars, long Dutch pipes, and tobacco; a seal-skin betrowsered half-breed girl brought in a huge waiter with an urn of steaming coffee; and likewise hot water, sugar, rum, and sherry for the inevitable Danish punch.

The Prince was of course around, and was not long in getting the girls together; when he improvised a dance upon the green in front of the governor's house, which proved to be quite a picturesque affair, the more especially as the scene was lit up with lanterns stuck about on the rocks around; while above an aurora flashed across the heavens in the wildest manner, emitting tongues of flickering light of every hue, and throwing a weird brightness upon the sterile rocks, and ice, and snow, as well as on the gay and festive merry-makers. Nor were we inside the house without some lively entertainment. The governor's daughter treated us to some music on a piano, which, although not in the best of tune, was yet played with considerable skill; and, considering that music teachers do not abound in Greenland, the success of this young lady, who had never been south of the Arctic Circle, was quite remarkable. Then we had some songs of the *viva la vo* order, and the great Danish national air of 1848, *Den tapper Landsoldat* (The Bold Soldier-boy), with immense effect; after which we went on board to sleep, with the "*derfor vil jeg slaaes*" and the "hurrah!" and the rest of it ringing in our ears in a delightful manner.

On the following day we tried very hard to get to the

Jacobshavn glacier, first by the fiord, then overland, without, however, accomplishing our purpose. The fiord was so crowded with icebergs that no headway could be made even with the smallest boat, and it was, in fact, as much as one's life was worth even to make the attempt; and the overland journey was found to involve too much time and labor to be undertaken at so advanced a stage of the summer—at least thus thought the party generally, and that settled the matter. So it was resolved to go at once back to Godhavn. But, before doing this, we dined the entire white population of Jacobshavn on board the *Panther*, and I made two visits in the morning that gave me great satisfaction.

The first was to the missionary, whom I found to be one of those kind and gentle men with whom one would naturally associate the idea of the peculiar unselfishness needed in a missionary. Certainly, at least, if he had not a very unselfish nature he would not have been there. As it was, he seemed to be exactly the right man in the right place; and since he appeared to have plenty to do, and to do it with a will, I was glad that "his lines had fallen in such pleasant places." But not so his wife. What on earth was there for her to do in this land of desolation? nothing, as I could see, but grow sick as she had done, and shudder, as she must have done, when she looked out upon the dreary church-yard beneath her chamber window. Jacobshavn is one of the oldest of the missions in North Greenland, and contains, in connection with the church, a seminary for the education of the native youth who seek such instruction as may qualify them for teachers of their own people; for the missionaries have given to the natives a written language, which they never had before; and it is rare to find a man or woman who can not read and write. Until the Christian missions were established, the language of the people was only oral; and they did not possess, even in the crudest form, any means of conveying the most simple idea except by word of mouth. The "picture-writing" of our North American Indians was unknown to them. They have now at Godthaab a printing-press, established there by Dr. Rink; and not only have they printed many interesting historical accounts and native traditions, but have illustrated them with wood-cuts of native manufacture that are quite as creditable as specimens of art as those which illustrate the travels of Mandeville, and similar works of our own language published a few centuries ago.

In fact, these Esquimaux possess remarkable ingenuity. Even in their savage state their inventions are very creditable; a fact that was well proven during my second call in Jacobshavn, which was upon the surgeon of the district, Dr. C. G. F. Pfaff, in whom I had the good luck to discover an enthusiastic antiquarian. His opportunities have been great, and he has employed them well in gathering a very valuable collection of implements of ancient native manufacture, of which he had several hundred specimens—embracing knives, pots, lamps, axes, spear-heads, needles, drills, ice-hooks, etc.—all made of stone, and all of superior workmanship. The knives were very sharp; so also were the needles and drills; and, being made of chalcedony and other like minerals, it seemed very wonderful how they had managed to grind them down to sharp points and edges, and to polish them as if they had possessed all the appliances of the most skilled mechanics, with all the modern inventions. I have not seen anywhere so fine a private collection illustrative of the "Stone Age" of man's existence. This Stone Age of the Esquimaux, however, instead of having ended in a period of remote antiquity, comes down to the time when Fulton was inventing steamboats. The spear-heads were mostly of red cornelian, and these, as well as the other implements, were generally polished, and in every respect showed a skill superior to that of the North American Indians. The doctor was good enough to present me with a few samples of this native art; but the main collection he reserves for the Museum in Copenhagen, of which every Dane is so justly proud.

Jacobshavn, like all the other Greenland colonies, owes what prosperity it has mainly to the seal-fishery. Besides the seal there is the white whale, which arrives in its annual migration from the North about the middle of September. A great many halibut are likewise caught and preserved. This latter is of a variety peculiar to Jacobshavn, being caught there upon a bank of limestone, deposited from the water which comes from under the glacier.

It was a matter of much regret to me that that glacier could not be reached—the more so that it had, two years before, been visited by Mr. Whymper, who had conceived the idea of travelling over it to the interior of Greenland, a feat which I believe to be impracticable on at least any of the known glaciers of the South. My own journey of eighty miles inland at the remote North was the only successful effort of the kind that has ever been made; but this was in a region where the ice, owing to the conformation of the land, is exceptionally smooth. Greenland might perhaps be crossed in that quarter, though the undertaking would be an exceedingly hazardous one. No food could, in my opinion, be obtained by the way, as I entertain no doubt that the whole interior of the country is but one vast sea of ice. It is only on the outer land that the snow melts and flows to the sea. While upon this subject, it is not inappropriate to mention that to Dr. Rink we owe most that we have known hitherto of the Greenland glaciers, and I believe he was the first explorer who pointed out the origin of icebergs.

Jacobshavn needs no description further than to say that it is but a repetition of the other towns we had visited. It is, however, somewhat larger, and has a better climate than Godhavn, as was shown by the fact, if by nothing else, that we found upon our cabin table, when we were ready to sail, a small basketful of round red radishes, which the Fraulein Fleicher had raised in the open air, and obligingly sent off to us as a parting gift. In return we sent her some American table luxuries, considering ourselves greatly the gainers by the exchange; for not only were these Arctic radishes delicious in themselves, but they were a great surprise to us, grown as they had been in latitude 69°, and in the very shadow almost of a frowning and formidable glacier.

Of this glacier I had a fine view, just before leaving, in the afternoon. Climbing a lofty hill in company with the captain, I overlooked the fiord, and traced its winding course through thirty miles. The icebergs that had been detached and floated in the fiord must have numbered thousands; and as they moved along with the current, or touched the bottom, they were grinding against each other continually, and the air was filled with the ceaseless sounds of the avalanche tumbling from their sides. A grand scene of this description occurred near the mouth of the fiord. As we were about coming away, an iceberg of large dimensions went almost literally to pieces, first rolling nearly over, and then breaking up as it rocked from side to side. Others in the neighborhood became likewise disturbed; and as crash after crash followed each other in quick succession, the peals that rang along the cliffs from crag to crag were loud and piercing. Upon

ICEBERG IN JACOBSHAVN FIORD.

reaching the town, we found the people in a state of consternation. The disturbance of the ice which we had witnessed from the hill-top had been the cause of great waves setting out of the fiord; and, although the harbor of Jacobshavn was two or three miles distant, and is perfectly land-locked, yet the swell reached there, and the surf washed far up on the shore, greatly endangering the lives of some hunters who were in the act of landing from their kayaks. I was told that fearful catastrophes sometimes happen from this cause. Even when we reached there the water was still in motion; the ship was swaying to and fro, and the ice all over the harbor was snapping and crackling in a very spiteful and fiendish sort of way. When the disturbance had subsided so that a boat could come to land, we went aboard, and, after cautiously steaming among the icebergs at the mouth of the harbor, we headed for Disco Island, carrying with us pleasant recollections of Jacobshavn; and all feeling abundantly rewarded, save and except, perhaps, the trader, who found nothing to buy but a pin-cushion.

CHAPTER XI.

A WEEK IN GODHAVN.

We returned to Godhavn on the 10th of September, and for a week thereafter travelled about the Island of Disco as we found opportunity and inclination. To the geologist, as previously intimated, Disco presents a most interesting field of study, and the professor was accordingly busy all the while, pursuing his researches with characteristic enthusiasm. The artists were constantly at work with camera and pencil. In this, the metropolis of Greenland, it was not difficult for the pleasure-seekers to find opportunity to amuse themselves; and the captain whiled away the time by tearing to pieces the wreck of a whale-ship which had been run aground at the mouth of the harbor, as rumor had it, in order to secure insurance money. If such was the case, her people certainly took good care to insure their own lives, for the vessel was within sight of the town on a sandy beach, where the sea never breaks, and full a quarter of a mile out of the channel. The people were sent home in the Danish ships, and if they obtained their insurance they surely did not get their deserts.

To Governor Hansen I was again indebted for aid in such investigations as I desired to make—especially in relation to the coal-fields, which are chiefly interesting because of their being so far north. Vast quantities of vegetable matter were deposited here in a remote geological epoch, which goes to show that Greenland would once have deserved its name had human beings existed there to give it the one which is now as absurdly inappropriate as Achilles to an organ-grinder. I was enabled to obtain a good collection of specimens, many of which I owed to the politeness of Inspector Smith, and among others of particular interest, a fragment of a cone of an evergreen, that had ripened here in the era of the lower miocene of Europe. In relation to these coal deposits of Greenland, Professor Oswald Kerr has made many important discoveries, and from his able report I make the following extract:

"Among the most interesting specimens" [collected by himself] "were the flowers and fruit of a chestnut—the latter, however, in a very imperfect condition. The discovery of these proves that the deposits in which they are found were formed at different seasons—in spring as well as in summer. The known miocene plants of Greenland have now reached the number of 137 species; and those of the Arctic miocene flora altogether number 194 species. Of the Greenland species 46, or exactly one-third, agree with those of the miocene deposits of Europe. The determination of the age of the beds as lower miocene has been accordingly ascertained."

These coal-measures of Greenland are not confined to Disco Island. Extensive veins crop out as well on the main-land. On the north side of the Waigat coal is found in abundance, and also around the margin of the Great Omenak Fiord. This latter is, with the exception of Melville Bay, the most thickly studded with icebergs and glaciers of any part of the Greenland coast, and while viewing them it seems strange to behold in immediate proximity great black streaks of carboniferous deposits, suggestive of a former condition of life and heat instead of cold.

I had the more occasion to feel indebted to Mr. Hansen for his assistance, that he was busily engaged with preparations for returning to Copenhagen, with his wife and their little son Fred, a bright Greenland-born boy of four years. I found him well posted in the doings of naturalists. He even knew that there was a "Central Park Museum;" and at his request I took charge of a present he desired to make them—a commission which was duly executed, and politely acknowledged. I likewise did the same with the Smithsonian Institute, with a like result. Among those that went to the latter was a pair of gyrfalcon skins, which Mr. Hansen sent more than fifty miles to get for me. He was equally generous with his collection of native curiosities, and to a member of the party, who valued such things more than objects of natural history, he freely offered almost every thing he had; and I much fear there were a good many friends disappointed in Copenhagen that winter when the governor's empty boxes were exposed. This generosity was the greater that such articles have a commercial value at home.

The event of our week's stay in Godhavn, however, was the ascent of the cliffs facing the town, to the summit of Lyngmarkens Fjeld. Mr. Hansen could not accompany us on account of pressing business; and, in fact, he had no faith whatever in the success of the undertaking. Our party, when made up, consisted of the two young ladies mentioned in a previous chapter; the inspector and his secretary; and half a dozen adventurers from the *Panther*, including of course, the captain and the Prince. Armed each with a pocketful of lunch, we sallied forth at nine o'clock in the morning, and crossing the bay under as bright a sun as ever shone, in a most delicious autumnal atmosphere, we landed on a broad green slope, which we ascended to the base of the first crest or ridge of trap rock, where we paused to rest.

Up to this point we had followed the bank of a stream,

which was now seen to break through a cleft of immense depth, and tumbling then in a beautiful fall, came out from beneath a great cloud of spray in a rushing torrent of white foam. This ridge descends gradually towards the sea in a south-easterly direction, and then spreading out, presents a wide plain, which the action of the weather has left in a most singular condition. The softer rock has been worn away, while the more solid parts remain; and for a mile the aspect of the surface resembles a clearing dotted over with stumps. Some of the forms are quite remarkable: one about twenty feet high, bears the name of "Lot's wife."

After crossing this ridge the real labors of the day began, for we came then to the great slope of naked rocks which had fallen from the cliffs, that now towered above our heads until they seemed to touch the sky.

Of all the climbing ever done by "ladies fair," I think nothing ever could have excelled the performances of our very agreeable companions on that rocky slope. The stones were sharp, the footing was insecure, and the whole foundation on which we stood seemed liable to give way and send us all rolling down to the black gorges beneath, in the midst of a fearful avalanche. To look down made one fairly giddy; to look up made one tremble; and yet the ladies held firmly to their purpose, and were always the last to pause for breath, and the first to say, "Shall we go on again?" Their courage never flagged, as on and on, over the rugged stones and through the ugly gorges, we made our way, steadily nearing the Lyngmarkens Fjeld, which human foot had thus far never trod. It was not the height of it that made the climb such a serious matter—it was the great roughness of the track. Several times stones gave way, and feet and legs were jammed, skinned, and bruised; twice a general slide was threatened; but only once was there very serious alarm. Then two of the party had imprudently clambered on ahead, and loosened some rocks which went bounding past us, whirling away down into a cloud of vapor which rose out of a deep cleft from the foot of a water-fall. One rock seemed to be making directly for our fair comrades, who were then resting, quite unconscious of harm; but this the gallant captain, who was following up the two who were in advance, was quick and bold enough to intercept by throwing himself upon it bodily.

Over this rocky debris we climbed, how far I can not tell, though probably for about two miles; and then we stood at the base of the cliffs, and, by barometric measurement, 1500 feet above the sea. Here a cleft opened before us, which we entered, and between lofty walls of dark reddish-brown rocks, and beside the stream we had before followed to the falls, we ascended by a less difficult and dangerous route, until we reached the permanent snow, where the stream itself originated. This was 1700 feet above the sea. Here we rested, lunched, quenched our thirst, and then, upon the soft snow we mounted up to the glacier, 250 feet higher. The glacier only here and there showed its icy character, and, presenting but few crevasses, we found little difficulty in getting above the cliffs, and at length to the summit of the fjeld—a word which quite expresses its character, for nothing could be more desolate and barren than the great plain of whiteness on which we stood. We were then 3016 feet above the sea, and the view which burst upon us at that lofty height was extremely fine. The air being perfectly clear, except at one point away below us, where some light mist was trailing along the cliffs, we could see certainly at least eighty or ninety miles. Overlooking the village to the south, we saw the Crown Prince Islands, twenty miles away, sharply defined like dark specks upon a silvered surface. Beyond them, still with the silver setting all round, were the Hunde Islands; and the lofty coasts and hills of Bunkee Land, in the neighborhood of Egedesminde, rose farther in the distance, but still far within the bounds of vision. Looking east, over the top of the Great Skarve Fjeld, the mountains of Jacobshavn pierced the sky with their snowy crests, and all around in that quarter through an arc of seventy degrees the vast plain of the *mer de glace* appeared beyond the mightiest peaks, and melted against the sky in a pearly line of light. Behind us were the icy peaks and snowy plains of Disco. But the most novel exhibition was on the sea. Thousands of icebergs were scattered over the bay in all directions, presenting the most diverse shapes. Near by they were few in number, and widely distributed; but they multiplied rapidly, and their track became more concentrated towards Jacobshavn, until beneath the dark land they melted into each other and were lost to view between the walls of the great fiord. And yet in the scene before us this immense glacier of Jacobshavn was but a white streak, and the mammoth icebergs but pigmy specks.

We spent about an hour in this novel situation, wandering about over the white snow, which (the temperature being three degrees above freezing) was quite soft, though in places a firm crust had formed. We saw no true ice there, and, not being provided with any implements for digging, we could not ascertain at what depth the ice forms; nor were there any crevasses to embarrass us until we attempted to explore a way back by the Rothe River valley, where we were speedily interrupted. There was nothing left for us, therefore, but to return by the way we had come, after the fashion of that famous French army which marched up the hill and then marched down again. And the results of our labors were of quite as little importance to the world; but we had gratified a not unreasonable curiosity, and enjoyed an adventurous experience of a very unusual character.

Our opportunities for a demonstration were rather meagre. We did not have an American flag to float and salute; but, out of compliment to the ladies and to their country, which owns the mountain, we improvised a Danish one, using a red kandkerchief for a groundwork and two white ones for the cross. This being unfurled to the breeze and lustily cheered, we set out on our return journey, which, not having now the stimulus of ambition and curiosity to spur us on, was even more tedious, and seemed more wearisome than the ascent. At the gorge by the water-fall we were met by a messenger from the inspector's wife, with a hamper containing some refreshments, which were most eagerly devoured. They were, indeed, a timely gift. The thoughtful lady had watched the mountain-side with a telescope, and when we came in sight she graciously contrived this agreeable surprise for us.

It was eight o'clock when we reached the inspector's house, having been just eleven hours on the march. The sun had passed around behind the island, and the dark shadow of the cliffs was on the town; but above arose the great spotless crown of Lyngmarken, all radiant in the gold and purple light that burst up from the north.

The following day was a lively one in Godhavn. The *Constancia*, with Captain Bang, our friend of some days back, was there now; and both he and Captain Saxtorph of the *Hvalfisken* were eager, as were we also, to be on the way out of the region of icebergs before the nights grew any darker; but the *Constancia* had to remain for the last dispatches home from the inspector. We were, however, ready, and offered to tow the *Hvalfisken* out to sea, which offer being accepted, every preparation was made for leaving early the next morning. The passengers took up their quarters on board the brig; but, returning ashore in the evening, we had another pleasant entertainment at the inspector's hospitable house, the enjoyment of which was only broken by the knowledge that it was to be the last. I could but think, too, how lonely must be the inspector's wife on the morrow, with her two sisters gone away, and with not another white woman there to keep her company; for the new governor was a bachelor, and there was neither priest nor doctor in the place to bring wives there, even if they would.

There was even no one of her own sex with whom she could converse in the Danish language, except the half-breed Sophy, or Sophia Tabita, as she was universally known in all North Greenland—and even she was going away; for at last the little love-god had found his way through the hitherto impenetrable barriers of her heart, and in a month or so she was to marry the Colonibestyrere of Christianshavn, and, resigning the proud place of belle of Disco, would henceforth be buried in obscurity among the icebergs of Jacobshavn Fiord, where no ship ever comes by any chance, except the one ship of the year, and where none of the merry times of good old Lievely will ever return to enliven her new home.

The bright rays of the morning sun had just fallen upon the little town when we dipped our flag to the royal ensign which waved over the governor's house, cheered the inspector, and steamed away with the *Hvalfisken*. As we rounded the outer horn of the harbor I saw the inspector and his wife mount to the look-out station, where they stood watching the brig that followed us, and waving adieus to their sisters, from whom dangerous seas were sure to separate them for many a long year, and perhaps forever.

At length the island disappeared against the cliff, and we saw them no more; then the cliffs sank down—the Great Lyngmarken became a speck of brightness on the waste of waters; then it too was lost; and this "Land of Desolation," around which will always cling pleasant memories of hospitable people, unusual adventures, and a profitably spent summer, fades away, and an experience the like of which might be had by many at small cost and little risk, takes its place among the "departed joys."

We have still, however, one Greenland token left with us, and that we propose to leave behind us too, for dark clouds are rising in the sky, and a dirty night is coming on; besides, an ugly sea is getting up, and the *Hvalfisken's* hawser is in danger.

"Brig ahoy!" roars out the captain.

A head appears above the bulwarks, and an answering " Ay, ay," comes across the water.

"Stand by—we are going to cast you off."

"Stop, stop a bit," cries the sagaman.

"What for?" the captain asks.

"You shall see;" and sure enough we do, for he whips a scrap of paper from his pocket, on which something is written; he hands it round; we sign it, one and all; the captain puts it in a bottle, which he corks tightly, and, along with another bottle of more portly size, labelled "Reserve L. G. L.," he puts it in a tin box, which Mick ties to the hawser and lets fall into the sea. We hear a lively cry on board the brig as they haul in the line; we see a sailor find the box and take it aft; and we know, presently, that the paper is deciphered, and our pledges responded to, by the appearance of heads above the quarter-rail, the fluttering of handkerchiefs, and the unmistakable appearance of glasses raised at arm's length, all of which evidences of hilarity will be best understood by repeating the round robin our sagaman had written, and we had sent through the sea as our final adieu to "The Land of Desolation." Thus it ran:

> "We drop you a line, and we bid you adieu!
> Now fill up your glasses and pledges renew,
> In this wine of the South—this foaming Champagne!
> The Lady of Disco—that right queenly Dane,
> With whom we have left (let the wine freely flow),
> Our hearts and bright wishes and prayers also.
>
> "May the bleak Norland winter—that night of despair—
> Leave the bloom in her cheek and the gold in her hair,
> And the light in her eye, as bright as the blue
> Of the sky in the summer, the clouds breaking through.
> Those round her she loves, may the storms, sweeping wild,
> Pass over them gently—the father and child.
>
> "A bumper! The ladies in *Hvalfiskens* brig;
> Another! Her captain, that sailor so trig:
> To the governor too, his frau and his Fred;
> To *all* a good-night on their wave-rockéd bed;
> To the brig a good voyage. Hip! híp! and hurra!
> The last cup is drained, and—there's no more to say."

THE END.

www.ingramcontent.com/pod-product-compliance
Lightning Source LLC
Chambersburg PA
CBHW030301240426
43673CB00040B/1020